Teaching English From a Global Perspective

Edited by Anne Burns

Case Studies in TESOL Practice Series

Jill Burton, Series Editor

Teachers of English to Speakers of Other Languages, Inc.

Typeset in Berkeley and Belwe
by Capitol Communication Systems, Inc., Crofton, Maryland USA
Printed by Victor Graphics, Baltimore, Maryland USA
Indexed by Coughlin Indexing, Annapolis, Maryland USA

Teachers of English to Speakers of Other Languages, Inc.
700 South Washington Street, Suite 200
Alexandria, Virginia 22314 USA
Tel. 703-836-0774 • Fax 703-836-6447 • E-mail info@tesol.org • http://www.tesol.org/

Director of Publishing: Paul Gibbs
Managing Editor: Marilyn Kupetz
Copy Editor: Ellen Garshick
Cover Design: Capitol Communications Systems, Inc.

All names of teachers and students are pseudonyms or are used with permission. Teacher and
student samples are used with permission.

Chapter 2, Appendix B from R. G. Paulston, 1976, *Conflicting Theories of Social and
Educational Change: A Typological Review,* Pittsburgh, PA: University of Pittsburgh, Center for
International Studies (ERIC Document Reproduction Service No. ED130921). Adapted with
permission.

Chapter 12, Appendix C prepared by Judy Hunter. Used with permission.

ISBN 1931185182
Library of Congress Control Number: 2005901149

Table of Contents

Acknowledgments

My sincere thanks go to all the contributors to this volume. Working with them was a pleasure. Jill Burton, Marilyn Kupetz, and Ellen Garshick have been wonderful colleagues and a great support in the process of bringing this volume to fruition.

Series Editor's Preface

The Case Studies in TESOL Practice series offers innovative and effective examples of practice from the point of view of the practitioner. The series brings together from around the world communities of practitioners who have reflected and written on particular aspects of their teaching. Each volume in the series covers one specialized teaching focus.

❧ CASE STUDIES

Why a TESOL series focusing on case studies of teaching practice?

Much has been written about case studies and where they fit in a mainstream research tradition (e.g., Nunan, 1992; Stake, 1995; Yin, 1994). Perhaps more importantly, case studies also constitute a public recognition of the value of teachers' reflection on their practice and constitute a new form of teacher research—or teacher valuing. Case studies support teachers in valuing the uniqueness of their classes, learning from them, and showing how their experience and knowledge can be made accessible to other practitioners in simple, but disciplined ways. They are particularly suited to practitioners who want to understand and solve teaching problems in their own contexts.

These case studies are written by practitioners who are able to portray real experience by providing detailed descriptions of teaching practice. These qualities invest the cases with teacher credibility, and make them convincing and professionally interesting. The cases also represent multiple views and offer immediate solutions, thus providing perspective on the issues and examples of useful approaches. Informative by nature, they can provide an initial database for further, sustained research. Accessible to wider audiences than many traditional research reports, however, case studies have democratic appeal.

❧ HOW THIS SERIES CAN BE USED

The case studies lend themselves to pre- and in-service teacher education. Because the context of each case is described in detail, it is easy for readers to compare the cases with and evaluate them against their own circumstances. To respond to the wide range of language environments in which TESOL functions, cases have been selected from EFL, ESL, and bilingual education settings around the world.

The 12 or so case studies in each volume are easy to follow. Teacher writers describe their teaching context and analyze its distinctive features: the particular demands of their context, the issues they have encountered, how they have effectively addressed the issues, what they have learned. Each case study also offers readers practical suggestions—developed from teaching experience—to adapt and apply to their own teaching.

Already published or in preparation are volumes on

- academic writing programs
- action research
- assessment practices
- bilingual education
- community partnerships
- content-based language instruction
- distance learning
- English for specific purposes
- gender and TESOL
- grammar teaching in teacher education
- interaction and language learning
- international teaching assistants
- journal writing
- literature in language learning and learning
- mainstreaming
- teacher education
- teaching English as a foreign language in primary schools
- teaching English from a global perspective
- teaching literature
- technology in the classroom

◈ THIS VOLUME

The studies in this volume reveal the complexity and challenge for ESOL teachers in a world in which every teaching setting claims or contests a place for English. Teachers and teacher educators cannot afford to ignore the issues and challenges raised by this timely and important book.

Jill Burton
University of South Australia, Adelaide

CHAPTER 1

Interrogating New Worlds of English Language Teaching

Anne Burns

◈ INTRODUCTION

When I became a teacher back in the 1970s, the world of English language teaching (ELT) was a more comfortable and cozy place of people who followed neat and predictable methods—secure, especially for a native-English-speaking teacher, in the assumption that learning English meant learning to speak like me.

The rapidity of the global spread of English, long predicted but then still only imagined, has come as a surprise, the pace of change over 50 years or so more dramatic than anticipated: "In 1950, any notion of English as a true world language was but a dim, shadowy theoretical possibility, surrounded by the political uncertainties of the Cold War, and lacking any clear definition or sense of direction" (Crystal, 1997, p. vii).

Now, it is a truism that English is a lingua franca, a language used locally and internationally, not only among so-called native speakers but by anyone wishing to activate his or her role as a member of an international communicative network. And to be an English teacher today is to play an inevitable part in this globalizing enterprise, to recognize new areas for inquiry, now raised for the perhaps the first time in the long history of ELT.

My introduction to this volume canvasses some of the major themes and questions challenging the new worlds of ELT into which the emergence of English as a global language is taking the TESOL field. Each subsection raises an area for inquiry, encapsulated by a prefacing quotation, and then brushes broadly over some of the literature that has highlighted debates over the past 25 years. Inevitably, each question raises further questions. It is my hope that these continuing questions provide a point of departure but also a point of convergence for discussion, reflection, and interaction among teachers as they read the chapters in this volume. I invite you, the reader, to contemplate these questions and, wherever possible, to reflect on and critique them with your colleagues—or, perhaps even better, to use them as starting points for action research explorations (see Burns, 1999; Edge, 2001) of your local teaching context as a microcosm of a globalized teaching endeavor.

In numerous and interconnected ways, the chapters in this volume touch also on these questions and themes. The themes surface many times in an intricate and complex relationship across the various discussions and descriptions, so that they are not easily teased apart. As a way of organizing the contents and making some responses to the questions, however, at the end of each section I highlight which contributions in this collection take the central question as a major focus. My aim is to provide a way for readers to interrogate and compare their own responses with the pivotal issues highlighted by the contributors.

◈ WHOSE LANGUAGE?

> An international language is not the possession of a specific group. It is public property. It is not the vehicle of a single culture. It becomes the vehicle of any culture to which a user applies it. (Carrington, 1988, as cited in Bryan, 1994, p. 101)

By characterizing speakers of English through three concentric circles, Kachru (1986) foreshadowed the expansions and shifts increasingly associated with the intensity of the spread of English in the current world.

The *Inner Circle* comprises the "old-variety English using countries" (Kachru & Nelson, 2001, p. 13), like Britain and Australia, where English is the dominant language (L1) and the main vehicle for communication in public and other domains. These countries are also characterized by increasing language diversity through immigration. In *Outer Circle* countries, English may be relatively well established in institutional settings and popular culture but is paralleled by a repertoire of other languages, as, for example, in Denmark, India, Kenya, Malaysia, Mauritius, the Philippines, or Singapore. English is a second or additional language (L2) for the "English-knowing bilinguals" (Pakir, 1999a, p. 107) who live in Outer Circle countries. But it might even be an L1 for others. Both local and international varieties of English are used by speakers in a range of different contexts. Speakers in *Expanding Circle* countries, such as Japan, China, Korea, or Brazil, use English in more restricted ways, such as for scientific or business purposes. Although English may still be learned as a foreign language, its status as a language for international access and use is constantly being repositioned.

The three circles model is more than a convenient map of the spread of English. It is a dynamic portrayal of the fact that the ownership and use of English no longer reside with L1 speakers. Even in terms of sheer numbers of users, this cannot be the case. Graddol's (1997) estimates point to 375 million Inner Circle speakers, 375 million Outer Circle speakers, and 750 million Expanding Circle speakers—a total of 1.5 billion speakers worldwide (an inevitably conservative estimate 8 years after it was first proposed).

English, then, is an international commodity; speakers of English are more likely to be using the language with other multilingual speakers than with monolingual speakers, and for their own cultural, social, political, and economic purposes, removed from Inner Circle norms. Given this situation, the notion of the *native speaker* now calls up numerous queries. For example,

- Does being a native speaker automatically assume one has greater proficiency in the language than being a nonnative speaker?
- Are native speakers mainly people who are born and bred in Inner Circle countries?

- Are native speaker interactions intrinsically more communicative and of more worth than nonnative speaker interactions?
- Is native speakerness defined by ethnicity, associated mainly with Western/Caucasian backgrounds?
- Is a person brought up in a household speaking English and (an)other language(s) a native speaker?

Brown (chapter 2) outlines how the notion of internationalization that became an overarching institutional commitment at her university also underpinned the courses on World English that she taught. Guided by the university's International Vision Statement that students "will enter the 21st century as leaders in an emerging global community" (Office of the President, 2001, n.p.), the faculty in her department translated this philosophical stance into their teaching. She describes the courses, the content that underpinned faculty goals to create internationally aware professional language educators, and preservice teachers' various reactions to these ideals. Brown suggests that programs such as these are necessary if preservice teachers are to avoid being "ethnocentric instructors" with "inadequate or inaccurate understandings of various contexts of instruction" (p. 28).

Friedrich (chapter 3) looks at the issue of *Whose language?* from a rather different perspective. Hers is an educational situation where university instructors in non–Inner Circle countries are increasingly required to teach in English subjects that would previously have been taught in their mother tongue, Spanish. This requirement, illustrated in her context of Argentina, is not untypical of a growing universal trend. For her, it raised the question of how to design a program that would work to overcome the fears and shortcomings felt keenly by a group of business administration faculty. Working through and workshopping with these instructors on their concepts and myths related to World English, users of English, and native speakerness, she alerted them to the more comfortable possibilities of intranational and localized dimensions of practice, as "no universalizing initiative can account for all the possible uses or needs for English" (p. 44).

◈ WHICH SPEAKERS?

> An increasing number of scholars are . . . questioning the appropriateness of one native speaker norm in a time of large-scale migrations, cross-national and cross-cultural encounters, and increasingly linguistic . . . differences among speakers of the same language. (Kramsch, 1998, p. 16)

If English can no longer be said to be the property of an exclusive club of Inner Circle locations (Widdowson, 1994), then the notion of the native speaker as the norm for ELT must increasingly be called into question. Some (e.g., Holliday, 1994; Pennycook, 1995; Phillipson, 1992) argue that basing teaching on the norms of native speakerness is a sociopolitical issue. It fosters inequality, assimilation, and compliance with native speaker values (Tollefson, 1991); imposes the power and status of some on others (Holliday, 1994); impedes learners from adopting culturally preferred ways of interacting (Kramsch & Sullivan, 1996); constitutes a form of linguistic (Phillipson, 1992) and capitalist (Naysmith, 1987) imperialism; and reproduces and maintains global inequalities (Pennycook, 1995).

Others (e.g. Kramsch, 1998) argue that the maintenance of the native speaker model is unrealistic as it sets goals for learners that are unachievable. As it is essentially comparative, its dominance in the classroom inevitably becomes a deficit perspective on learner achievements and demotivates learning. The teacher's role becomes one of negatively judging the gaps between learner and native speaker production (and, in many cases, their own) rather than acknowledging learners' ongoing gains. Cook (1999) points out that the literature on L2 teaching and acquisition is rife with negative terms such as *deviance* and *failure*. Even where the difference of the L2 user is recognized, the native speaker implicitly dominates teaching and research.

Placing emphasis in the classroom on the idea of the L2 user rather than the native speaker shifts the emphasis toward the realities of the global uses of English. New ways of thinking can begin with changes in terminology, so that L2 speakers are referred to as *multicompetent* (Cook, 1999) or *expert users* (Rampton, 1990) or other terms chosen by learners themselves—thus defining people by what they are rather than by what they are not. Cook points out that *competence* is a neutral term used to refer to native speaker knowledge of the language and is free from evaluation against an outside standard. Multicompetence, therefore, recognizes without being judg-mental that people have knowledge of more than one language. Similarly, expertise is learned, relative, and partial rather than fixed or innate (Rampton, 1990).

Classroom goals can be redefined in terms of where learners are now in their approximation to the tasks and texts they need and want to use rather than in relation to externally imposed native speaker norms. The process of *approximation* can incorporate activities that begin with the teacher's and learners' L1s and build on language, ideas, and interests that can then be extended into the L2. Part of this process might include discussing what intercultural factors emerge for multicompetent users of English and what personal or social implications there are in the movement between languages. Approximation also means that learners and teachers can be more active and creative in selecting contexts, content, and roles that are of interest and relevance to them. They can make themselves and other L2 speakers the main goal and focus of classroom activities. Using L2 speaker models as a basis for classroom activities is still relatively rare in language teaching, but recent develop-ments in corpus-based learner data (e.g., Granger, 2003; Longman Corpus Network, 2004; Seidlhofer, 2002) hold promise as a way of providing learners with examples such as frequency of lexical items, syntactical patterns, and discourse features.

The notion of the native speaker is unlikely to fade away for some time to come, even if it is a pedagogical fiction. As Davies (1995) points out, "The native speaker is a fine myth; we need it as a model, a goal, almost an inspiration. But it is useless as a measure; it will not help us define our goals" (p. 157). Becoming aware of its persistence—"its ghostlike presence" (Cook, 1999, p. 190)—in the classroom can, however, be a valuable starting point for questioning assumptions that might underpin teaching practices:

- To what extent is your teaching motivated by native speaker norms and goals? Is the native speaker the model you have in mind, explicitly or implicitly, when teaching?

- What or who is considered to be an ideal English speaker by you and by the learners? Is this person an L1 or L2 speaker of English?

- Why is this person the model in your particular teaching context? What aspects of the person's use of English are valued?

- What activities could you develop that might draw on L2 speakers as the models for learning?

- How could competent L2 speakers be used more extensively in your teaching situation?

- What L2 resources are there in your teaching context that learners can use as a basis for learning English?

Meier (chapter 4) and Matsuda (chapter 5) call attention to the importance of finding ways to introduce teachers to the changing sociolinguistic and intercultural realities inherent in English as an international language. Meier, in describing an approach taken to teaching a seminar on interculture in a MATESOL program, suggests that teachers need to become intercultural "understanders" with "greater communicative flexibility that precludes a construal of language teaching as an attempt to produce native speaker clones" (p. 53). Matsuda examines the issues from the perspectives of the gaps between teaching perceptions and practices and the major goals of the national curriculum, which she perceived when researching in schools in Japan. Drawing on classroom observations and discussions with teachers and students, she notes the delimiting effects that preferences for native speaker norms and (U.S.) standards have on teaching and learning. These effects include misrepresenting the nature of English as an international language and the diversity of its speakers, reinforcing the primacy and superiority of the native speaker teacher, and setting unachievable goals of nativeness as the targets for proficiency and pronunciation.

◈ WHICH LANGUAGE?

The long-standing debate, even now not wholly laid to rest, over which language is better, that of Britain or of the United States, has had all sorts of effects over the decades, from establishment of the literary canon to what pronunciations and usages are correct and should, therefore, be taught. (Kachru & Nelson, 2001, p. 16)

From the 16th century, as English spread across the world through migration and colonization, it became "nativized" (Kachru, 1985, p. 11) in new locations by existing and new speakers, so that today it is possible to recognize different major varieties of Inner Circle English—Australian, British, American, Canadian, and New Zealand English. But it is also possible to speak of newer subvarieties of English, developing where English is extensively used because of historical, political, and social factors as a second or parallel language among L2 speakers in such places as Europe, Singapore, or India. These World Englishes have generally emerged in Outer Circle countries and have developed their own internally consistent phonological, grammatical, and lexical patterns that differ from other varieties but are used by English speakers on a daily basis.

In the field of ELT, British and American English have been widely regarded as the preferred targets. However, limiting learners' exposure to only one or two of the infinite variations of Ll and L2 varieties and representing them as universal norms denies the realities of the repertoires of World Englishes learners encounter when they go out into the real world. The relevant point is that English is an international language because it has not retained the narrow norms of one variety. It has had to be diverse and independent to become so widely used (Widdowson, 1994). In practice, therefore, learners may have considerably more exposure to regional varieties of English—for example, Australian, New Zealand, Indian, Singaporean, or Malaysian in the Southeast Asian region or Euro-English in the European Economic Community—than to the varieties that have been held up as the two normative models in most language classrooms.

Given this situation, language teachers in the 21st century will increasingly be challenged to assist learners to select the English variety they will see as the most appropriate in different circumstances. This selection will be made, not in terms of a single correct variety, but in relation to local usages, values, and requirements, and inevitably alongside or in combination with other languages. You may need to reflect on questions like the following:

- What variety of English do you present to learners? Why do you see this variety as essential or preferable?

- What variety of English is assumed in the textbooks and materials you use? Is it the main or only variety that learners are likely to encounter outside the classroom?

- Does the way you present your classroom activities assume the existence of a single variety? Do you introduce activities to raise learners' awareness of other varieties? If so, what kinds of activities?

- To what extent do you introduce local or Outer Circle varieties and discuss with the learners how, where, and why they are (or could be) used?

- Do learners have experiences of more than one variety of English? What are their attitudes and beliefs about these varieties?

Evans (chapter 6), writing from the viewpoint of a native-English-speaking teacher working in an Inner Circle country, Australia, notes the challenges that these kinds of questions pose for teachers, particularly when coupled with the expectations of learners who have come to the country and to the particular educational institution specifically to learn in a native-speaking environment. As she notes, this situation puts a teacher who is conscious of the sociolinguistic realities of global English "in a bind" (p. 75). Her contribution sets out an option that avoids both the Inner Circle norm and the anything-goes model. Her critical and comparative approach highlights for learners the intercultural and pragmatic choices they can make in a national context that is itself, after all, a locus of globalized English use.

❖ WHICH STANDARD?

> [Standard English] is a variety, a kind of superimposed dialect, which is socially sanctioned for institutional use and therefore particularly well suited to written communication. In its spoken form it can be manifested in any accent. (Widdowson, 1994, p. 380)

As English has spread and changed throughout the world, a constant concern has been that it will fragment into so many different varieties that English speakers will no longer be able to understand each other. Interestingly, this concern seems to be applied less to speakers within Inner Circle countries—Britain, Australia, the United States, Canada, New Zealand—than to those outside. As Brutt-Griffler (1998) comments,

> Most, if not all Inner Circle English speakers appear willing to meet on a common linguistic plane, accept the diversity of their Englishes and do not require of one another to prove competence in English, despite the considerable differences in the varieties of English they speak and the cross-communication problems entailed thereby . . . this situation must be extended to all English-using communities. (p. 389)

Although some commentators have argued for a single native speaker standard that should serve across all contexts (e.g., Honey, 1997; Quirk, 1985), others, taking a sociolinguistic point of view, contend that this argument is unrealistic. English is now so diffused across the world that it is more important for speakers of English to be able to communicate with each other. Therefore, if a stabilized variety does emerge, it will need to be one that is mutually intelligible to speakers across the world (Kachru, 1985; Strevens, 1983; Widdowson, 1994).

It is valuable for teachers of English to be aware of these arguments. The traditional fixation in many ELT contexts on the notion of working with one standard—at least in the case of spoken English—can easily lead to language misrepresentation. Where teachers and learners work with a basic premise that language is fixed and stable, this denies the adaptation, creativity, and hybridity that is essential if any language is to develop and thrive. It forces learners and teachers into a position where the main purpose for uttering the language becomes imitation rather than communication—especially communication that now takes place on a world scale. Given these arguments, Cook's (1999) recommendation that "language teaching would benefit from paying attention to the L2 user rather than concentrating primarily on the native speaker" (p. 185) becomes of interest.

An important aspect of shifting the focus to the L2 user is the notion of *intelligibility* (Kachru & Nelson, 2001, p. 21). Kachru and Nelson explain that this notion involves three components:

1. intelligibility (the speaker produces sound patterns that are recognizable as English)

2. comprehensibility (the listener is able to understand the meaning of what is said)

3. interpretability (the listener is able to understand the purpose or intent of what is said within the particular context)

S. McKay (2002) illustrates this concept as follows:

For example, if a listener recognizes that the word *salt* is an English word rather than a Spanish word, English is then intelligible to him or her. If the listener in addition knows the meaning of the word, it is comprehensible, and if he or she understands that the phrase "Do you have any salt?", is intended to be a request for salt, then he or she is said to be able to interpret the language. (p. 52)

Jenkins (2000) argues that a principal need in teaching English as an international language will be to find phonological norms and pronunciation models. Her research identifies key features that appear to have the greatest impact on intelligibility in interactions between two L2 users of English: articulatory settings (e.g., tongue shape, position of the lips), nuclear stress (e.g., how the stress in different parts of a sentence affects meaning in other parts), and particular segmental features (specific core sounds such as consonant sounds). She suggests that if teachers work on these features of pronunciation with learners, they can then focus on receptive rather than productive skills in order to help them achieve good communication. She also suggests that learners should be exposed to different L1 and L2 speaker accents to enhance their receptiveness to the range of English varieties. Using native speaker accents as models rather than norms, as Dalton and Seidlhofer (1994) suggest, also takes teachers and learners in a different direction from the notion of a single fixed standard.

Where learners' rather than teachers' English-language-using context becomes the main reference point for learning, the notion of the standard to be achieved can become the subject of interesting sociocultural exploration. You and the learners you work with can explore some interesting questions together:

- What notions of the standard for English are dominant in your teaching context? Are they different for spoken and written English?

- Why is this standard considered to be the most appropriate in your teaching context? To what extent do you discuss the concept of a standard with the learners? What are the learners' attitudes toward the idea of a language standard?

- What attitudes exist in your local context toward varieties that are considered to be nonstandard?

- Are these varieties introduced into the classroom in any way? What kinds of discussions take place in your context in relation to these varieties?

- What repertoires of standard and nonstandard English do you use yourself both inside and outside the classroom? What relative values and relevance do these repertoires have?

Tarnopolsky (chapter 7) describes a situation where, in the current absence of a codified international English, he introduced learners to two standard varieties of English, British and American, in response to their expressed needs and in the interests of providing learners with "a lingua franca that gives them the easiest and broadest access to the most diversified international contacts" (p. 91). He discusses the complexities he faced in designing such a curriculum and how his learners' responses led to ongoing modifications.

High school preservice and practicing teachers' attitudes are the focus of the chapter by Brock (chapter 8). He draws on his survey research in Macao to analyze the beliefs of the teachers about the role and importance of English, learning and teaching, the curriculum, and ELT as a profession. In particular he focuses on teachers' attitudes concerning which standards and norms they should adopt in their context. Although the teachers showed a preference for the Inner Circle varieties of British or American English, he notes that these options are still fluid, with considerable freedom on the part of teachers to make choices. He sees this as a positive situation but wonders whether in the future such decisions might be influenced by the more centralized policies of neighboring Hong Kong and China.

❖ WHICH TEACHERS?

> Monolingual teachers with little if any cross-cultural experience may have to stop and think about the situation in which English is acquired across the world. In most cases it is taught to nonnative speakers by nonnative speakers, neither teachers nor students (who themselves become the next generation of teachers) ever having any contact with a native user. (Kachru & Nelson, 2001, p. 18)

It is estimated that approximately 80% of the world's English teachers are bilingual speakers of English (Canagarajah, 1999b). Yet the reality in many ELT contexts is that native-English-speaking teachers are the preferred norm, even when these teachers may have no other qualifications than the ability to speak English. This state of affairs impacts negatively on the confidence and security of nonnative-English-speaking teachers, their sense of themselves as ELT professionals, and their evaluations of their proficiency and pronunciation of English (Seidlhofer, 1999; Tang, 1997; Thomas, 1999). However, recent debates have raised awareness of the fallacy of the native speaker teacher of English (Canagarajah, 1999b) and the importance of recognizing the role of the nonnative-English-speaking professional in TESOL (Braine, 1999; Liu, 1999; Medgyes, 1992).

The labels native and nonnative professional are themselves problematic; they suggest a simple dichotomy that does not allow for the range of language teaching and learning experiences, language aptitudes and proficiencies, training and professional development opportunities, and inter- and cross-cultural contacts that an individual teacher might have experienced. The stereotype that the nonnative professional learns English in an EFL context and is therefore unable to acquire native proficiency holds true no more than does the stereotype that the native speaker is one who has perfect command of the language and the knowledge, skills, and ability to teach it. As Canagarajah (1999b) notes, the assumptions embedded in this dichotomy are both linguistically inaccurate and politically damaging. Nevertheless, as several commentators have noted (Govardhan, Nayar, & Sheorey, 1999; Jenkins, 2000; Liu, 1999; S. McKay, 2002), discriminatory hiring practices based on no more than (so-called) native speakerness persist in numerous ELT contexts.

The argument that it is "critical to raise consciousness about the role of international teachers of English in the field and validate tools for their empowerment" (Brutt-Griffler & Samimy, 1999, p. 429) is now gaining ground. Among the strengths of nonnative teachers (Cook, 1999; Medgyes, 1994; Seidlhofer, 1999; Widdowson, 1994) are

- the experience of learning another language and, therefore, being role models for learners
- sound knowledge of the grammatical systems of English and the ability to anticipate the problems learners might encounter
- an understanding of how English will affect learners' linguistic repertoire in the country where they live
- knowledge of local culture(s) and language(s) and how English interacts with them
- an understanding of what methods and approaches learners will respond to and prefer, and what value these can add to the dominant Western methods used in ELT
- language, knowledge, and experience in common with learners

Patricia Williams, who lives in Denmark and describes herself as a "so-called" native teacher, highlights what native speakers lack:

> It is a tremendous disadvantage for students to have a native-speaker English teacher, especially at the lower levels, unless the teacher speaks quite good Danish. No knowledge of the students' mother tongue means that you cannot compare sentence (clause!) structures, nor anticipate, understand or sympathize with the difficulties the English grammar and pronunciation presents. This is frustrating for the student and makes the process very slow. Native-speaker teachers may tend to speak too fast and/or give too many examples that confuse rather than help students. (Burns & Coffin, 2001, p. 29)

Language teaching professionals should challenge their prevailing assumptions by answering questions such as these:

- In what ways and to what extent do you see yourself as a native or nonnative teacher? What advantages or disadvantages are implicated in these evaluations?
- Do you define yourself, or do others define you, as native or non-nonnative? Are there ways in which you define yourself that do not fit into either of these categories?
- What dimensions or attributes do you bring to either categorization as it applies to you?
- In what different ways do you believe native and nonnative teachers are effective in the classroom?
- What similarities in skills and approach to teaching have you observed for each?
- What skills and approaches do you bring that you believe teachers in the other category do not?
- What views do you hold about the relative advantages and disadvantages teachers in each category have in employment opportunities?

No single chapter in this volume takes this issue as its central theme. Matsuda (chapter 5) perhaps comes closest when she raises the issue of the unexamined preferences for native-English-speaking assistant English teachers in the high school situation she describes, as well as the implicit beliefs of the Japanese teachers she observed that they were less equipped to teach English because of perceived problems such as accent. Friedrich (chapter 3) and Vilches (chapter 9) also touch on the questions in this section.

Other writers have noted the lack of research on nonnative-English-speaking teachers. Commenting on Cook's (1999) article and referring to works also mentioned in this chapter (e.g., Braine, 1999; Kamhi-Stein, 1999; Medgyes, 1994; Tang, 1997), Milambiling (2000) notes that the issue of "the validity and even the necessity of nonnative models" for teaching and learning "has finally gained the notice of the TESOL field in the past few years" (p. 324). A positive sign of recognition that more research and attention to nonnative speaker teachers is needed in the field of ELT was the decision of the TESOL International Research Fund to make this area a research priority for 2003–2004.

◈ WHICH APPROACHES?

> The approach to English language teaching which is currently widespread is one which favours so-called authentic use, modelled on native-speaker norms, and which emphasises spoken language. Such an approach pre-supposes that the purpose for learning is to prepare learners for engagement in social interaction with primary communities in native speaking countries. (Widdowson, 1997, p. 145)

Communicative language teaching (CLT) has been a dominant approach to the teaching of English for the past two decades. Because of its emphasis on language as meaningful communication rather than language as form, it has come to be seen as the ideal methodological approach to language learning and the norm by which language teaching in general should be judged.

However, a number of commentators have raised questions about the appropriateness of CLT approaches, particularly in Asian countries. Pennycook (1995) sees the domination in the ELT industry of the major English-speaking countries— Britain, the United States, Australia, and others—as an essentially political activity that may be likened to a form of *linguistic imperialism* (Phillipson, 1992). These authors suggest that dominant, Western-based models of ELT pay little attention to local cultural and linguistic needs and are hegemonic in their impact. They argue that the ELT profession should be politically active in opposing this trend.

Others question the appropriateness of Western methods, materials, and teaching approaches on the grounds that CLT is not a culturally sensitive methodology (Canagarajah, 2002; S. McKay, 2002). Some argue that, with its strong emphasis on English-only in the classroom, it overlooks the value and relevance of the bilingual dimensions of language learning (e.g., Swan, 1985). Others (e.g., Ellis, 1996) argue that it assumes values and orientations not easily assumed in Eastern world views, such as the emphasis on individualism and self-expression, process rather than product, and meaning at the expense of form. More recent challenges have come from teachers located in non–Inner Circle countries (e.g., Li, 1998), who have identified issues such as

- the dissonance embedded in the cultural norms and philosophies underpinning curriculum and educational ideals (e.g., Confucian vs. Judeo-Christian)

- the widespread and fundamental disconnection between the syllabus approaches recommended and the public examination systems

- student resistance to the participatory approaches demanded by CLT methodologies

- teachers' feelings of insecurity and lack of fit with such methods

- the substantial redefinitions of teachers' and learners' traditional roles suggested by CLT approaches

- large classes and limited time to prepare interactive materials and activities

- lack of access to relevant local materials and authentic samples of language

Holliday's (1994) notion of *appropriate pedagogy* and Prabhu's (1990) concepts of *no best method* and the teacher's *sense of plausibility* in the teaching context potentially offer alternative way of thinking about language teaching approaches within the social and educational context of a particular country. Both native- and nonnative-English-speaking educators can consider what aspects of CLT, on the one hand, and more established local ways of teaching English, on the other, might offer students the most effective routes to learning within the local social and cultural environment. Teachers can consider what methods best meet learners' needs and expectations of learning and what particular roles adopted by teachers and learners best suit local styles and customs.

This is not to suggest that it is unimportant for teachers to be aware of the range of methods available to them. However, the methods and roles adopted may not necessarily conform only with the process-oriented, learner-centered philosophies central to Western methods of CLT (see Canagarajah, 2002; Kamhi-Stein, 1999; Shamim, 1996). Local teachers, as the implementers of curriculum change, should lobby through their professional associations and other avenues for a higher profile in curriculum decision making. In making such decisions, educators in their local contexts will need to be mindful of the global context of English and recognize the realities of English as an international language used in multiple contexts, for multiple purposes by multiple speakers. You can interrogate your teaching practices in such situations through questions like these:

- What are the main kinds of teaching approaches expected or mandated in your context?

- On what kinds of theoretical ideas and philosophies are they based?

- Are these theories and ideas consistent with the major social, cultural, and educational factors common in your environment? If not, how do they differ, and what changes would need to be made to adopt or adapt them?

- To what extent would such changes be valid, feasible, and workable in your teaching context?

- What aspects of alternative approaches to teaching would enhance those now most commonly used in your context?

- What are some of the most effective ways in which you have introduced new ideas into your teaching practice?

- What opportunities exist to work with other teachers to explore new approaches and practices for effective teaching? What role can you play in making this happen?

The issue of introducing teachers to more expanded and integrated classroom practices aimed at making learners more effective communicators is the central theme of Vilches' contribution (chapter 9). The project she was engaged in was informed by concepts of teachers as learners as well as the pedagogical notions of *foundation building* and *potential realizing*. What becomes clear in her description is that these concepts provided a way forward for the teachers being trained as well as for potential learners by augmenting existing teaching repertoires and exploring their feasibility through classroom implementation.

◈ WHICH TEXTS?

> Nearly every text that I look at uses two modes of communication: (a) language as writing and (b) image. Yet TESOL professionals continue to act as though language fully represents the meanings they wish to encode and communicate. (Kress, 2000, p. 337)

As English has been reshaped by contact with other settings, languages, and media, new forms of literacy and literature have flowed and merged with each other. The boundaries that once existed between written and spoken forms of communication have blurred (Crystal, 2001), as have the boundaries between texts and visual images. New forms of world literatures have also expanded and modified the shape of the language across the world and have reflected their own cultural settings and world view, in contrast with the expectations and standards of the Inner Circle. The teaching of English from a global perspective no longer implies teaching the canon of English literature but involves equipping students with knowledge of the diversity and nature of world literary texts, engendering new ways of responding to them, and comprehending the global *cultural flows* (Canagarajah, 2002) that mediate them.

The notions of *situated literacy* (Barton, Hamilton, & Ivanic, 2000), *multiliteracies* (Cope & Kalantzis, 1999) and *silicon literacies* (Snyder, 2002), which inform new literacies studies, give recognition to the multiple modes of communication that combine in complex ways to create meaning in contemporary texts. To teach from a global perspective, teachers will need to help students become intra- and intercultural explorers skilled in investigating and navigating hybrid and evolving forms of discourse, text, and visual image. As Kern (2000) comments, teaching from a new literacies emphasis highlights the importance of learners' agency in meaning making and means that teachers will need to focus on introducing learners to new roles of responding, revising, and reflecting on text. He notes that in order to deal with the texts that their learners will encounter, "teachers need a high level of competence in both spoken and written forms of the language, cultural knowledge, and a familiarity with literature" (p. 316). Questions such as the following will need to inform awarenesses of global textual practices:

- To what extent do you encourage learners to explore their own multiple interpretations of texts?

- What opportunities are there for learners to reflect on their own uses of different kinds of texts (including nonclassroom texts, the Internet, e-mail, mobile phone technology)?

- What opportunities do you provide for learners to bring these texts into the classroom and to explore and discuss them?

- Is literature from different writers in different world contexts a part of learners' classroom experiences? If not, why not?

- To what extent do your lessons draw on local literature and local writers?

- What concepts of literature does your current syllabus reflect? Does it reflect the traditional canon of mainly English literary works? Does it include literature from other Inner Circle countries? Does it include literature that reflects nonstandard Inner Circle varieties?

Samuel and Sithamparam (chapter 10), Bozzini (chapter 11), and Cooke (chapter 12) encourage teachers to grapple with these questions. Samuel and Sithamparam, working in a national context, Malaysia, that is itself characterized by strong post-colonial associations and multilingual linguistic interactions with English, ask readers to consider how four key tenets of multiliteracies theory play out in the real world. Having read the literature and actively reflected on its implications, the teacher learners in their MEd program researched their chosen learners' literacy interests and practices in print, cinematic, and electronic forms. These investigations led them far from the assumptions about individualistic, abstracted, neutral forms of literacy that had informed their previous notions of school-based literacy development toward awarenesses of "new text forms, such as Web pages on the Internet, computer games and digital messages on mobile phones" that now characterize "global-local texts" (p. 131).

Bozzini (chapter 11) makes the case for teaching literature in general, and the literature of global English in particular, as part of a rich repertoire of internationally oriented language learning. He lays out a broad and diversified range of contexts from which to draw literary resources and describes how he has integrated them into an undergraduate program in the United States. For those interested in incorporating his suggestions, he provides a set of criteria that can guide choices and activities as well as steps for incorporating a process-based methodological approach. Not only do his ideas offer a "focus on contemporary international literature in English at a time when the world as a whole has become interconnected by English" (p. 153), but they suggest ways for the productive expansion of learners' awareness of the range and creativity that global English has engendered.

Finally, Cooke (chapter 12) describes an ESOL credit-bearing course taught to undergraduates in Canada. The course draws on a range of multimedia texts that highlight contemporary international topics related to globalization and structural adjustment. The students are introduced to the texts through activities that develop their skills in critical thinking and writing through a sequence requiring interpretation, response, comparison of conflicting positions, critique of arguments, and the building of a case. At each step, the students are required to produce papers that extend their abilities to deal critically with contentious issues. Cooke argues that this approach deliberately leads students in a different direction from the prevailing tendency of ESOL practice to select topics that are neutral and nonpolitical.

◈ WHICH PRACTICES?

Teaching English as a global language might be a hot topic, but it proved surprisingly difficult to bring this collection together. My first assumptions—that there would be numerous TESOL practitioners out there bursting with ideas about teaching from a refreshingly new perspective—were not easily realized. Clearly, despite some of the theoretical debates of the past 10–15 years, classroom practitioners are still in a transitional and tentative phase of experimentation in coming to grips with the implications of teaching English as a global language.

As might be expected given these current experimental circumstances, the chapters in this collection draw on and reflect some of the major themes already outlined without necessarily being able to propose definitive practical approaches and solutions. Nevertheless, they explore the complex dimensions of the issues in interesting and enlightening ways and provide numerous practical suggestions for taking them forward and into the classroom.

Where might the contributions in this book lead the TESOL profession in taking up the new challenges that will be posed by the phenomenon of a global English? They suggest at least three possible immediate redirections of thinking for practitioners working in the worldwide field of ELT:

- Challenge entrenched notions of the native speaker and Inner Circle countries as the target models for ELT.

- Work toward identifying teaching and learning approaches for global English that will adapt most effectively to the educational environments of the local context.

- Acknowledge the reality that the majority of English teachers are not and will not be native speakers.

Pakir (1999a) points out that the internationalization of English is no longer optional but "inescapable" (p. 113). In the light of this reality, the TESOL profession urgently needs new sets of assumptions for ELT of the kinds suggested by the contributors to this volume.

◈ CONTRIBUTOR

Anne Burns is a chair professor in the Department of Linguistics and dean of the Division of Linguistics and Psychology at Macquarie University, in Australia. She has published and researched extensively in the areas of action research, curriculum development, the teaching of speaking, and literacy development. She is currently the reviews editor for *Reading in a Foreign Language*.

PART 1

Whose Language?

CHAPTER 2

World Englishes: Pedagogical Practices in the TESOL Preparatory Sequence

Kimberley Brown

❧ INTRODUCTION

Relationships among teachers, learners, and colleagues are based on their beliefs about who owns English and what dimensions of English need to be taught. The postbaccalaureate certificate and master's programs in TESOL at Portland State University (PSU), in the United States, aim to prepare professional language educators to understand the contexts in which they will teach. This preparation involves a formal commitment to introducing a World Englishes perspective in the program's core teacher education courses and to assessing the development of teachers' self-knowledge and intercultural competence.

This perspective, drawn from Kachru (1988), focuses on three dimensions of the use of English throughout the world. The first is a knowledge framework that accepts nonnative speaker in addition to native speaker varieties of English, the second sees local context as a positive force for language innovation, and the third suggests an identity dimension—English belongs to those who use it. One of the program's goals is for graduates to see their future classroom sites as zones of contact (Pratt, 1991/ 1996) in which dialogue consistently occurs about the use and users of English around the world.

This chapter describes how teacher education at PSU promotes a World Englishes perspective. I also describe how this commitment fits broadly into two presidential initiatives driving campus planning: comprehensive internationalization and assessment.

❧ CONTEXT

PSU is located in Oregon's largest city, Portland. The university serves more students and confers more graduate degrees annually than any other in Oregon. It offers more than 100 undergraduate, master's, and doctoral degrees as well as graduate certificates and continuing education programs. PSU currently operates on the quarter system, September–June, plus a summer session.

PSU's Department of Applied Linguistics offers an undergraduate degree in applied linguistics, undergraduate and postbaccalaureate certificates in TESL, and a master's degree in TESOL. Classes in the Department of Applied Linguistics are generally four credits each. This chapter focuses only on the TESL and TESOL degrees, most specifically the Methods I and World Englishes courses. It also briefly deals with some dimensions of the Understanding the International Experience and the Second Language Acquisition (SLA) courses.

For the undergraduate and postbaccalaureate certificate, 40 credits are required, and 46 are required for the master's degree. Among the required courses for both degrees are SLA, in which one lecture is devoted to a World Englishes perspective; two methods courses of four credits each, in which 4 hours are devoted to World Englishes in Methods I and roughly 3 hours in Methods II; and a course titled Understanding the International Experience that includes an intensive ethnographic interview project with a person from another culture and a pre- and postclass measure of intercultural competence, the Intercultural Development Inventory (Hammer & Bennett, 1994, 1999/2001). A four-credit elective, World Englishes, has been available since 1992 and is offered roughly every 2 years. Brown (1993, 1995, 1997) and Brown and Peterson (1997) provide full descriptions of the syllabus and assessments of how students' understanding of World Englishes has shifted after 30 hours of instruction.

As the following statement demonstrates, the university is committed to structural internationalization through policy and planning frameworks, programs, and staffing:

> Portland State University's future will be guided by the understanding, belief, and commitment that our students will enter the 21st century as leaders in an emerging global community. The University understands that international-ization must become integral to the fabric of everything that we do. (Office of the President, 2001, n.p.)

Because I served as vice provost for international affairs, I was familiar with classic literature on internationalization (Brown, 1999; Green, 2003; Green & Olson, 2003; Mestenhauser & Ellingboe, 1998). This familiarity enabled me to use institutional planning documents in a practical way to guide departmental activities that led to the curricular revisions detailed in this chapter.

Our program is committed to assessing the degree to which students achieve learning goals relating to internationalization. The institution's assessment goals have been paired with the internationalization goal through the World Englishes perspective within the core of TESOL classes in the Department of Applied Linguistics.

Based on this overall institutional perspective, faculty in the department have developed an understanding of what the university means by comprehensive internationalization. In terms of programs and approaches, it includes the following aspects:

- introducing theories or ideologies in applied linguistics courses that have been developed not only in Inner Circle but also in Outer and Expanding Circle countries

- using overt strategies developed by the department to draw international students and U.S. students in the three programs into closer working relationships with each other

- using a wide range of English language learning settings around the world as examples in the TESOL methods sequence and in SLA

- developing structures within the department that enable students to increase their contact with theories, methodologies, colleagues, and instructors from Inner, Outer, and Expanding Circle settings

❖ DESCRIPTION

What follows is a detailed description of the World Englishes material taught in the Methods I course and the assessment criteria and results from the 2003 assessment. In presenting this description, I also refer to assignments in the Understanding the International Experience and World Englishes courses.

SLA and Understanding the International Experience

The SLA course introduces students in a 1-hour lecture to dimensions of the World Englishes paradigm, specifically the idea of monolingual bias in SLA research (Kachru, 1994; Sridhar, 1994). Understanding the International Experience puts little emphasis on a World Englishes paradigm but focuses strongly on student self-awareness and assessment of intercultural competence as well as an extensive ethnographic interview project. In this course, students are formally introduced to the notion of the classroom as a contact zone. Pratt (1991/1996) defines a *contact zone* as one in which ongoing relations occur "not in terms of separateness or apartheid, but in terms of co-presence, interaction . . . and interlocking understandings and practices" (p. 528).

In Understanding the International Experience, students come to understand more about their own perspectives on culture and language through an intensive ethnographic interview project that requires a minimum of 5 hours of interviews with a person from another culture. By interacting with this person, students come to better understand the ideologies they hold about English and about U.S. culture.

Methods I

The work presented to students in Methods I coincides with readings and lectures they undertake, which aim to help them identify epistemological frameworks in the English language teaching field. During the first week of class, students are asked to identify their underlying assumptions and ideological presuppositions about teaching English. In preparation for beginning the 4-hour unit on international dimensions of teaching described below, the students respond to six discussion questions (see Appendix A).

Following this preparation, students spend approximately 2 hours of course time exploring what Paulston (2000) terms the *social cartography* of language teacher education (see Appendix B, which draws from Paulston, 1976). Students learn about competing ideologies in language education and begin to identify where the information they have been taught fits on a continuum of ideologies and epistemologies. For example, they learn that much of the most popular work on curriculum design falls under systems theory (Nunan, 1998) whereas critical work in adult refugee education falls under neo-Marxist theory (Tollefson, 1991).

This initial work enables students to begin to address a primary course goal, stated in the syllabus for Methods I: "By the end of the course it is expected that you will be able to place your decision to become a professional language educator in the context of where and how English is used throughout the world."

To become more familiar with a variety of contexts, graduate students also read Kenny and Savage's (1997) *Language and Development: Teachers in a Changing World.* The readings in this volume provide the basis for 6 hours of discussion, each student leading a discussion on one chapter and taking notes on the discussion of another.

International dimensions of language teaching are further considered through 4 hours of selected readings (Baxter, 1980; Brown, 1997; Canagarajah, 1999a; Pennycook, 1989) and discussion. These readings introduce the students to the concepts of teacher identity and language proficiency among Japanese teachers of English (Baxter, 1980), international dimensions of the power of English (Pennycook, 1989), a world languages (i.e., World Englishes, or Kachruvian) perspective (Brown, 1997), and the power dimensions associated with the notion of *native speaker* (Canagarajah, 1999a). Students are also introduced via Graddol's (1997) work to demographic predictions about the state of English language use around the world.

Students explore materials for teaching speaking and other language skills through a short project that involves brainstorming ideas about three international products: tea, coffee, and potatoes. This activity gives rise to discussion about how an ESL/EFL class can focus on international topics and respect students' various cultural perspectives while teaching specific English skills.

Drawing on resources obtained from the Internet, students prepare a poster project dealing with some dimension of language teaching. For example, in winter 2003, 8 of the 35 course participants presented topics dealing with the relationship of English to the maintenance of indigenous languages, comparisons of U.S. and German English language education systems, and teaching U.S. pronunciation. The three students preparing the poster on U.S. pronunciation first investigated some formal dimension of World Englishes. The choice to look up how English is used in the world demonstrates that these students were exploring teaching toward global intelligibility rather than native speaker pronunciation (i.e., varieties of British and American English). It seems unlikely that the students would have chosen these topics if they had not had a comprehensive introduction to internationalization, critical thinking, and World Englishes as part of the course.

As part of the course evaluation, students were asked to respond in four ways:

A. Comment on the degree to which the discussion groups and the Kenny and Savage (1997) text helped you meet the course goal of international-ization.

B. Comment on the degree to which our preliminary course discussions and readings about users of English and ideology of instruction have helped or not helped you meet the course goal of internationalization.

C. In our examples of materials design for speaking and pronunciation, we have used some general materials such as maps and topics that lend themselves to the use of international information. Please comment on the degree to which this materials design exercise helped or did not help you meet the coarse goal of internationalization.

D. Comment on the degree to which you have gotten to know fellow students from other countries and how in-class activities have helped or hindered this process.

International students had one additional, optional question:

E. Comment on the degree to which this class has been cognizant of differing needs and expectations you may have compared to the noninternational students.

For the Methods I course, a majority of the class's 35 students indicated that, through the introduction to internationalization, critical thinking, and World Englishes, the course had met the goal of placing the teaching of English in an appropriate context (see Table 1; because so few students responded to Question E, responses only to Questions A–D are shown).

Question A

The text was, at times, interesting. However, its focus was extremely limited— only business training in a solely capitalist framework was explored. This does not represent a range of use of English worldwide. Additional readings would have been helpful.

While the text seemed marginally useful at times, the activity itself did create (for me) a feeling of being part of a cohort, and without fail the activity spurred conversation about teaching, international contexts, politics (and our place within that framework). I think it was useful and met the above goal. This was actually one of my favorite parts of this class.

I thought is was an excellent assignment, but some changes might be useful. 1) A different text, one more global in scope—but I know that this is the only text of its kind. 2) To that end, I think it would be useful to select certain chapters for the book more relevant to ESL—some chapters glossed over this and weighed too heavily on abstraction, vagueness, and business; in addition to this our time would have been well served researching and presenting on one city/country/area per person in terms of development and language issues, such as literacy in Brazil, ESL in East Bloc Europe, etc., Bilingual Education and Development in Guatemala.

TABLE 1. AGGREGATE RESPONSES TO INTERNATIONALIZATION QUESTIONS

Question and topic	Responses			
	Helped	Minimally helped	Neutral	Did not help
A (graduate groups)	10	4	—	1
B (readings and discussion on ideology)	25	3	—	2
C (materials design exercise)	17	4	—	5
D (student contact)	20	7	—	1
E (recognition of international students' needs)	a	a	a	a

[a]Insufficient responses to tabulate.

Question B

I think that the methods curriculum at PSU is commendably geared toward the inclusion of as many perspectives on English education as possible. The early focus on ideologies and different uses/needs for English established an international framework that lasted throughout the class.

My horizons were definitely broadened with regards to number of English language speakers, Inner Circle, Outer Circle, etc. It also made me think more about the politics of language teaching and the involvement needed as far as students, teacher, and community.

I'm not trying to be cynical, but I didn't see the applicability. In fact, I'm fairly weary of listening to references to "colonialism," "linguicism," etc. World history, foreign demand for English and ideological differences explain these situations best (to me anyway).

Question C

I think the exercises were helpful in that we had to place them in context. We had to look at something from another culture's perspective.

I enjoyed designing activities/tasks with using world maps. When I think about English, I feel as if we can communicate with others who are from different countries. That make me excited since English is almost a universal language. I believe that this materials helped me meet the goal of internationalization.

This was so briefly touched on and I felt that it came from kind of one angle, "Make sure to expose language learners to different accents." The Web discussion was good as well, but I felt it needed to be addressed more.

Question D

The class activities have been helpful in many ways. Getting individual perspectives from students from other countries expanded my view of internationalization.

I would say that the class has offered plenty of opportunity for me to interact with international students, and within class time. I have enjoyed doing so, but because of an extremely tight schedule I haven't really expanded that beyond class. I appreciate their presence in the TESOL Methods classes and I think the class benefits from the perspective they provide.

I am also an international student, and this class has been a good chance to know many things from different cultures.

These comments show that whereas students felt the course had met the goal of comprehensive internationalization, they also believed many things could have been done differently to achieve the goal. To me, the fact that the students suggested improvements means that they not only understood what the future context of English language teaching is likely to be but also moved beyond this knowledge to reflect on how to link it with their future choices as professional language educators.

Interestingly, one student also commented on how unusual it was to see a link between an administrative goal of the institution and course activities:

Preliminary course discussion re English and ideology of instruction were a useful "eye opener" that did, I feel help to meet the course goal of internationalization. However, it can be frustrating to be in a class in which a separate administrative agenda ("internationalization") is part of the curriculum. I cannot recall if that aspect was included in the course description.

World Englishes

World Englishes is a four-credit, 30-hour optional course (see Brown, 1995, for a full course syllabus and materials, although the references are now a bit dated). The primary course goals are to

- familiarize students with the current debate in linguistics regarding the future of English as an international language
- help students recognize that a variety of models for English exist
- show that localized varieties have emerged from local needs
- demonstrate that English does not belong simply to those in the Inner Circle (see Kachru, 1988)

The 10-week course begins with a historical overview of how the World Englishes field has developed and then moves to current research controversies. The next portion of the course introduces students to six Outer and Expanding Circle varieties using online resources for speech and writing samples and concludes with a 2-week section on material design for the ESOL classroom.

In an attempt to discover whether students' attitudes toward English around the word shifted after participating in this course, I worked with a colleague to compare students' thoughts on teaching internationally after 4 hours of World Englishes material in the TESOL Methods I course and after 30 hours of exposure in the World Englishes class (Brown & Peterson, 1997). We found that students who had taken the World Englishes course showed vastly different knowledge structures about "the sociolinguistic realities of the spread of English as an international language" (p. 44) than did those who had taken only the TESOL Methods I course.

The prospective teachers' extended exposure to the notion of World Englishes in the dedicated course allows them to become more responsive to teaching to the context they are in. One student in the TESOL MA program described this change in the following way:

> I strongly support . . . [the] call for the integration of a WE [World Englishes] perspective into MATESOL programs. . . . I have always taken my position as a gatekeeper and cultural politics within the classroom very seriously, but only through ongoing exposure to the WE perspective have I begun to develop the deeper understanding necessary to teach responsibly. When I think about the degree to which I had already been exposed to/developed an understanding of intercultural communication, and the degree to which the additional exposure to a WE perspective has benefited me, I can only hope that . . . more teachers in training like me (who would be entirely in support of a polymodel perspective, but are unaware it is an issue) can walk away from the MATESOL program with the tools to effectively use their position to work against ethnocentrism and linguicism.

A World Englishes class can also explore various ideological perspectives. I have suggested (Brown, 2002) that Canagarajah (1999b, pp. 40–47) and Krishnaswamy and Burde (1998, pp. 30–37) outline two such perspectives. Neither follows ideas proposed by Kachru (1988); rather, they present views about the use and users of English that draw students into expanding investigation of competing epistemologies. For example, Canagarajah argues that focusing on macrolevel variables related to language planning and policy is a necessary but insufficient way to analyze the spread and function of English. He also suggests that more researchers should look at what educators in Outer Circle countries are writing about English language teaching methods. He accepts much of Kachru's work but moves beyond it. Even more to the left of Canagarajah on the political spectrum, Krishnaswamy and Burde argue that Kachru has developed theories about Indian English using "models of linguistic perceptions developed in the monolingual West" (p. 35). Becoming familiar with a wide range of beliefs about the future of English and its users permits teacher learners to reflect deeply on how they will teach English.

◈ DISTINGUISHING FEATURES

The expanded focus possible in a course completely devoted to World Englishes can change how teacher learners conceptualize their profession, as shown by the data gathered from classroom research data and from formal and informal evaluations of classroom tasks and student attitudes. This section focuses on how this TESOL preparatory program has integrated required and optional World Englishes content into the curriculum.

Program Goals Tied to Institutional Policies

The Department of Applied Linguistics has consistently set out to measure its success in implementing a World Englishes perspective within its core TESOL preparatory courses. In doing so, it has tied this goal directly to a broad institutional commitment to comprehensive internationalization and evaluation. Thus, in its programs, the department has deliberately connected World Englishes theory to the comprehensive internationalization policies of the university.

Learning Goals Measured in Relation to Institutional Policies

Student learning goals within particular courses have been directly measured in relation to the university's policies. Through a key core course, students are introduced to the notion of critical thinking and examine competing ideologies about the teaching of English. Those who are interested can go further and immediately build on their introduction to World Englishes theory by taking a full course on this topic.

Emphasis on Adapting Course Materials and Design to Local Needs

Both TESOL methods courses look at various teaching ideologies reflected in readings and actively acquaint students with ethical and ideological dimensions implicit in their decisions about what to teach to whom and where. The emphasis is on adapting materials and course design to reflect local needs.

◈ PRACTICAL IDEAS

A set of practical ideas has emerged from the program's theory base and experience.

In the Methods Sequence, Prepare Students for World Englishes Material

- Introduce dimensions of ideology and social cartography within a methods sequence as a precursor to World Englishes material.
- In the TESOL methods sequence, provide a base of at least 4 hours of material related to World Englishes, but do not assume attitude change will occur for course participants.

Focus on Outcomes

- Craft learning outcomes and assess them. Conduct classroom-based research to measure what students are learning.
- Use standardized measures of intercultural competence such as the Intercultural Development Inventory (Hammer & Bennett, 1999/2001) to compare pre- and postclass or pre- and postprogram results.

Broaden Students' Horizons Beyond Their Own Program

- Link higher education internationalization commitments in universities around the world to the World Englishes paradigm.
- Design, develop, and share ideas about teacher education and English language teaching projects that come from around the world. Use technology to introduce students in methods courses to varieties of English (see Baik & Shim, 2002b).

◈ CONCLUSION

Comprehensive internationalization as a campus governance principle can provide the institutional scaffolding to support the introduction of a World Englishes perspective into the TESOL methodology sequence. The design and assessment of learning objectives for the TESOL methodology course sequence in conjunction with the notion of comprehensive internationalization supports this perspective.

Such a perspective, associated with critical thinking exercises, can help teacher learners identify how particular ideologies are associated with particular theories and activities in the language classroom. Teacher learners who can identify these ideologies are better able to construct rich understandings of the role of English throughout the world. They can visualize their future classrooms as contact zones, spaces where their beliefs about teaching and learning as well as the basic demographics of the spread of English meet the beliefs of their learners. Both teachers and learners can be more reflective about this contact when they are prepared to see their classroom as a space to explore how English is used around the world, by whom, and for what purposes.

Eminent scholars in World Englishes, such as Yamuna Kachru (personal communication, March 1999), have suggested that a World Englishes course should be an elective in a TESOL program, not a requirement. It is my belief that the power of change that can occur after lengthy exposure to World Englishes materials is critical to the pedagogic competence of teacher learners. At PSU, the Department of Applied Linguistics will continue to assess the degree to which it is meeting stated institutional, program, and classroom goals. To this end, the department hopes to offer the World Englishes class annually in the future or to offer students a language varieties course that would alternate with World Englishes.

The global spread of English itself does not pose a threat to professional language educators. However, if teacher learners have inadequate or inaccurate understandings of various contexts of instruction, this will cause them to design inappropriate curriculum and materials. They will be ethnocentric instructors who cannot make adequate use of contact zones and will be unable to teach their learners to do so. Teachers of English must teach about different varieties of the language within the context of critical thinking and comprehensive internationalization if the profession is to move smoothly through the new millennium of language instruction.

❖ CONTRIBUTOR

Kimberley Brown is associate professor of applied linguistics and international studies at Portland State University, in the United States. Her primary research interests are in World Englishes, culture learning in the language classroom, and internationalization across the curriculum. She has held a variety of administrative positions at her institution and leadership positions in TESOL and NAFSA: Association of International Educators.

❖ APPENDIX A: METHODS ASSIGNMENT WITH DISCUSSION QUESTIONS ABOUT IDEOLOGY

In groups of three or four, examine each of the following statements. Respond to the questions posed, react to the statements, and provide examples from your own experience to support or refute notions that are introduced below.

1. All TESOL preparatory programs must first expose pre-service teachers to the notion that there are competing epistemological frameworks surrounding them. They need to be able to read critically and identify these frameworks. (Brown, 2002, p. 446)

What are some types of underlying assumptions and ideological presuppositions you hold about teaching English?

2. Repeated demonstrations of the close interdependence between Western social research and capitalist political economy attest to the close ideological dialectic between research (including the concepts, theories, methods, and practices) and the context of its production. (Hamnett et al., 1984, p. 50)

If you have been teaching prior to coming into this class, pause for a moment to think about connections you may have seen between concepts and practices you engaged in. Can you think of any economic connections between them? If you have not been teaching, think about your prior experience learning a foreign language. Does the statement by Hamnett et al. reflect your experience or not? Why?

3. There are three axes that define development: forms of knowledge that refer to it; the system of power that regulates its practice; and the forms of subjectivity fostered by this discourse, e.g. those through which people come to recognize themselves as developed or underdeveloped. (Escobar, 1995, p. 10)

Many authors have argued that knowledge of English can help people attain better jobs and better futures for their children around the world. What do you believe about these ideas? How does Escobar's comment support or refute the idea that English language proficiency serves as a way out of difficult economic circumstances?

4. The issues surrounding internal versus external evaluations of project 'success' or 'failure' . . . the pervasive controls or organizational ideologies and personal agendas in many settings, are not geographically con-strained. They belong to all educational discourse communities and as such they influence profoundly their orders of discourse and the discur-sive practices of their members, irrespective of location and site. (Candlin in Kenny & Savage, 1997, p. xv)

Can you think of some examples of discursive practices? What about examples of controls or ideologies or personal agendas that have affected you as a language teacher or language learner?

5. After all, people are not only authors of their own identities, they are as much animators of the identities that are authored for them by others. They are subject to the exercise of power. (Candlin in Kenny & Savage, p. xvi)

6. So it is that through discourse, individuals' sense of professional identity is both constructed and maintained. (Candlin in Kenny & Savage, 1997, p. xvi)

Think about teaching and learning situations you have been in. What are some phrases or expressions your instructors have used to help you think about your sense of professional identity?

We have used the phrase *professional language educator*. How do this and other phrases help construct or maintain your sense of professional identity?

◈ APPENDIX B: BACKGROUND NOTES: THEORIES IN ESL AND BILINGUAL EDUCATION (PAULSTON, 1976)

Definition of reform (from Simmons): "Those changes in educational policy which cause major changes in either educational budget, the slope of the pyramid of school enrollment, or the effect of educational investment on individual and social development."

Consider Paulston's comments:

1. All planned change efforts imply a commitment to a certain view of reality, and acceptance of certain modes of realizing those ends. Those assumptions constitute the conscious or unconscious bases for selecting specific courses of action and thus they precede all tactical decisions. To the extent that change agents cannot identify those basic assumptions and their implications, they cannot explore the full range of effective strategies of change.

2. Three things influence planning and the implementation of reforms: ideology, power, and perceived group interest.

The Equilibrium Paradigm

Evolutionary and Neo-Evolutionary Theory

1. Characterized by notions of progress, by stages of development from lower to higher order forms.

2. Education functions to maintain stability and changes from simple or primitive forms to more complex modern forms in response to change in other structures.

3. Places an emphasis on linked stages of socioeconomic and cultural development

4. Cohen's neo-evolutionary model: Schools are essentially conservative institutions that indicate a uniform and standard system of symbols to which all can be trained to respond uniformly.

5. Butts: Western educational models will help to provide underprivileged people with a greater share than they now have of the promise of human dignity and welfare.

6. Educational-system reforms in developing countries should be patterned on experiences and models from the advanced technological societies.

Structural-Functionalism

1. Structural/functional (S/F) theorists focus on the homeostatic or balancing mechanisms by which societies maintain a "uniform state."

2. Adaptive change is fine but sudden change is not. A system imbalance should require no more than small incremental adjustments.

3. Intrasystem conflict is viewed as pathological, as an indicator of systematic breakdown.

4. S/F theorists accept inequality in society and see it as a necessary condition to maintain the existing normative order

5. When change or reform occurs in the educational subsystem, it is the result of interaction between society and the schools and follows in some five steps: (a) a need arises in society; (b) the school is assigned the task of meeting the need; (c) change in the educational structure takes place to accommodate the new function; (d) the new role is assumed by schools; and (e) latent and manifest changes take place in society as a

consequence of the new educational functions. Thus schools may introduce significant changes into society, but because schools are only passively related to social change, they serve essentially conservative functions and tend to reinforce the status quo.

Systems Theory (after Bushnell, 1971)

Diagram

Inputs ← Traditional System → Outputs

↓

Diagnose problem

Formulate objectives

Identify constraints

Research and development efforts ← Select potential solutions → Systematic change strategies

↓

Inputs ← Improved system → Outputs

Distressed Liberal Genre

1. A largely atheoretical genre which, while essentially S/F in world view, calls for basic educational reform as a strategy for ameliorative social reform.

2. Research in this genre is clearly within the equilibrium paradigm and largely avoids discussion of the role that power and conflict must play in structural change efforts. . . . It rarely views inequities as the consequence of social-class self-interest leading to structured inequality.

Conflict Paradigm

Marxist and Neo-Marxist Theories

1. Formal education is viewed as a part of the ideological structure that a ruling class controls to maintain its dominance over the masses, and because formal education is dependent on the dominant economic and political institutions, it cannot be a primary agent of social transformation; it can only follow changes in the imperatives of the economic and political social order.

2. From the Marxist dialectical perspective, national reforms will only take place when they are viewed by dominant political and economic elites as defending or advancing their interest vis-à-vis nonprivileged groups in their society.

3. Only with a socialist revolution and the ensuing ideological and structural changes toward equality in the larger socioeconomic and political context of education will it be possible to eliminate the inequitable exploitative character of schools

4. Neo-Marxist theory rejects metaphysical and deterministic notions as historical inevitability and class struggle and largely settles for study of interest-group conflict.

Cultural Revival and Social Movement Theory

1. Cultural-revitalization theory focuses not on social classes but on deliberate organized conscious efforts by members of a society to construct a more satisfying culture (Wallace, 1956).

2. Revitalization movements occur under two conditions: high stress for individual members of society and disillusionment with a distorted cultural Gestalt. Where such processes take place as in mass movements, ethnic movements, or revolutionary movements, they all require members to profess adherence to the movement's ideology or evaluative principles about the ends and means of human action, and emphasize the need to reduce stress through collective efforts for change.

3. Horton contends that significant structural change in educational systems will always be a function of the emergence of mass underdog movements seeking to put a radically different cultural system into practice.

Anarchistic and Utopian Theory

Anarchistic and utopian theories of social change share the Marxian goal of radical social transformation, and the concern of cultural revival and revitalization movements for individual renewal. In marked contrast to all the previously noted theories seeking to explain and predict educational reform processes, they rarely bother to validate their call to reform with the findings and methods of social science, or to put their theory into practice. The utopians' often insightful critiques of existing inequalities and evils in education may serve to provide impassioned discussions, but utopian analysis rarely takes into account how existing oppressive power relationships and lack of tolerance for deviance or change in any given social setting will influence reform efforts of whatever scope or magnitude. Typically, the utopians begin with a critical analysis of socioeducational reality and rather quickly wind up in a dream world.

Examples of Reading You Have Done That Fits in Certain Categories

Equilibrium

- notional-functional syllabus design (S/F)
- needs analysis (systems theory)
- contrastive analysis diagnostic theories (systems theory)
- communicative competence models (systems theory)

Conflict

- theories about linguicism (neo-Marxist)
- Iran's rebuilding of its English language program after the revolution (cultural revival)
- Nicaragua's literacy campaign (combination of neo-Marxist, cultural revival and utopian)
- Jim Cummins' work on needs of ethnic minority schoolchildren in Canada (cultural revival)

- Jim Tollefson's description of what is happening with U.S. refugee policy (neo-Marxist)
- Freire's approaches to educational reform (utopian) (includes work by Wallerstein & Auerbach)

Summary Points to Remember

1. "Acceptance of an intellectual paradigm by scholars in a research field enables them to cope with uncertainty and information overload, through the simplification of reality that the paradigm represents. It also imposes and standardizes a set of assumptions and conceptual biases that, once begun, are difficult to recognize and overcome. This is the challenge for the next generation of scholars" (E. M. Rogers, *A History of Diffusion Research*, 1971, p. 85).

2. As you read, try to put things into some kind of intellectual paradigm— What does the author say? What do you say?

3. The bulk of English language teaching information which we read falls within the Equilibrium Paradigm.

CHAPTER 3

When Teaching in English Is One's Business: Helping Business Faculty Use English as an International Language of Education

Patricia Friedrich

◈ INTRODUCTION

The growing importance of English in the international arena and its role in higher education are undeniably topics of interest for educators and linguists. The internationalization of university programs, the diversity of student populations, and the demands of research even in non-English-speaking countries mean that faculty members all over the world face the challenge of teaching and lecturing in English.

Due to the growing enrollment of international, non-Spanish-speaking learners, business administration faculty at my university in Argentina must regularly teach and lecture in English. In this chapter, I describe their anxieties and the solutions proposed to them—how they can cope with their own shortcomings and fears, and how a focus on overall communication strategies can help university faculty better handle the demands of a general internationalization. This internationalization, in turn, means a growing adoption of English as a language of international education.

◈ CONTEXT

The School of Business offering the program is an internationally recognized center of executive education, ranked among the top 30 schools worldwide (Financial Times, 2001). Located in the greater Buenos Aires area, this prestigious private business school takes pride in having instructed over 5,000 students from 19 countries in its 25 years of service. A variety of business education programs are offered by the institution, which is known for its master of business administration (MBA), considered a required credential by many employers in the business world, as well as for programs that are custom designed for specific firms.

The MBA Program

The MBA program offers two different class arrangements: full-time and executive. Like most MBA programs, this one teaches students how to maximize value from a pool of limited resources (e.g., how to manage human resources successfully or coordinate efforts to produce goods or services). To achieve the goals proposed by their graduate programs, faculty at the Business School play multiple roles, lecturing and exposing students to a variety of learning experiences (e.g., case discussions, debates, and oral presentations)—in English as well as in their native language, Spanish. For this program, the growing internationalization of business programs has meant the enrollment of international students and the need for faculty to travel abroad to teach custom-made programs in other countries. A good command of oral English is thus more than a desirable skill.

Although most Latin Americans speak Spanish (Brazilians being the most notable exception), as far as education is concerned, going global on many an occasion means adopting English as a lingua franca. In joint programs with Brazilian attendees, for example, the use of English prevents the possibility that Brazilians will have to work harder than their Spanish-speaking counterparts to understand what is being presented. Obviously, the adoption of English is even more critical if the course is taught in the United States or if a large number of international students with multiple language backgrounds enroll. Additionally, there is a growing awareness that if faculty are to reach international scientific channels beyond the Spanish-speaking world, they must publish in English.

The acknowledgment of the current status of English in education led the school to request that I design a program to ease the faculty into the increasingly bilingual requirements of their posts. I designed the program in two stages. The first focused on oral communication and the immediate need to lecture and conduct discussions in English. The second, ongoing at the time of writing, targets written English and the need to publish in that language. This chapter deals mostly with the first stage of the program; I discuss the second in terms of future directions for the program.

Participants

The program was designed for up to eight senior- and intermediate-level faculty members, all between 30 and 50 years of age. Given that all participants were experienced teachers, I assumed that they had good classroom teaching and management skills. I also assumed that their English proficiency was at least at the upper intermediate level (determined on the basis of being able to carry out fluent conversations in English despite occasional problems with suprasegmentals, vocabulary, hesitancy in speech, and grammar). Primary concerns expressed by the faculty during the design stage included

- a feeling that they were not themselves when teaching in English: that they could not maintain their teaching persona when teaching in a foreign language (e.g., make jokes, tell anecdotes, or be relaxed)

- lack of vocabulary: that although they could handle the grammatical demands of teaching in English, they did not have enough vocabulary at their disposal to teach efficiently

- listening comprehension problems when two native speakers interacted: that the common background and assumptions of their native-Spanish-speaking students as well as their speed of delivery during discussion sections would be a barrier to comprehension

- anxiety over students' attitudes toward their variety of English: that people attending their classes would belittle their English and that other

Spanish speakers would find it pointless to listen to "bad" English when they could be taught in "good" Spanish

As these concerns indicate, a central element of the program would have to involve dissipating myths and helping faculty members cope with their preconceptions about language and foreign language use. A second element would have to address language awareness among business students, using the faculty as the awareness-raising element.

◈ DESCRIPTION

To assist faculty members in lecturing and leading discussions in English, I designed a seminar course that met once a week for a 100-minute session (see the syllabus in Appendix A). During these sessions, I conducted activities that targeted the overall topic of oral communication in English.

One of the most important scheduling issues to overcome was the overbooked calendar of participants, a recurring theme for language instructors who teach professionals and academics. These time constraints caused me to consider the format of brown-bag lunches, which in the end I adopted. An immediate advantage of this setup was the informal atmosphere, which tended to have a positive impact on performance.

Another decision made in the face of schedule restrictions was the almost complete elimination of homework. Because the initial stage of the program focused on oral communication, I decided that the class would encourage full participation during the meetings and keep assignments to the bare minimum, that is, preparing for presentations.

Theoretical Assumptions

The theoretical assumptions of the course revolved around a World Englishes perspective (e.g., Kachru, 1992b; L. E. Smith, 1992) on English use, the overarching concept of communicative competence (as understood by Berns, 1990; Canale, 1983; Canale & Swain, 1980; Savignon, 1983), and the concentric circles of English model proposed by Kachru (1992b). What these elements have in common is an appreciation for the "pluralistic nature of a language" (Berns, 1990, p. 32) and the need to take specific contextual characteristics into account when teaching language (see Appendix A for details).

That is, the learners I worked with in Argentina and their needs differed in many ways from the needs of Hispanic immigrants to the United States or Chinese business executives conducting business primarily in Asia. The course design would have to take such differences into consideration. In addition, the participants would have to make a significant shift in their understanding of language and language relations, especially given the parameters of traditional language learning in Argentina.

Appreciation for Nonnative Varieties of English

The first significant change I wanted to introduce was an appreciation for nonnative varieties of English; hence my choice of the concentric circles of English model as a framework. The participants were surprised and actually a little relieved when they discovered the multitude of contexts in which English is used natively (Inner Circle), as an official or additional language (Outer Circle), and as a foreign language (Expanding Circle). They were also relieved to learn that in their professional careers, they would be likely to use English with other nonnative speakers to the same (if not a greater) extent than they would with native speakers. The learners were also attracted by the idea that different levels of intelligibility naturally existed between and within the circles and that negotiating meaning was a possible way out of miscommunication. Negotiation of meaning was an appropriate way into issues of intelligibility because of the participants' business background, where the concept of negotiation is common.

Another important discovery for the participants was the effect of the cultural component of communication on intelligibility Their surprise at this discovery evidenced the lack of sociolinguistic discussions during their previous English learning experience. We often discussed how different cultural standpoints affected comprehension and how culture was an umbrella term for many different groupings (e.g., national, field specific, age based). With that realization came enthusiastic discussions of the generation gap, miscommunications with fellow South Americans, and clashes at the workplace.

Focus on Communicative Competence

Traditional foreign language teaching in South America has relied heavily on the concept of proficiency (understood as the level at which one can use grammar, vocabulary, and other linguistic elements in combination) and on native models of English (British and American) not only as a hypothetical goal but primarily as a prerequisite for being considered a user of English. Moreover, South Americans tend to make a direct association between the quality of one's English and one's pronunciation patterns; hence the faculty members' worry that students might not approve of their English unless they could become accent free (a contradiction in terms, given that it is impossible to speak without an accent). Although more practitioners in countries like Brazil and Argentina are now incorporating sociolinguistic elements into the language classroom, the seminar participants had studied English at a time when language courses revolved primarily around grammar and, as a consequence, tended to validate the myths that were then considered the norm.

Because an overemphasis on perfecting linguistic features alone tends to perpetuate the myths described above, the decision to anchor the course in the notion of communicative competence seemed all the more appropriate. I did not completely deemphasize pronunciation and other linguistic features, but I shifted the criterion for deciding to work on a linguistic feature from perfecting it for the sake of being more nativelike to making the overall element more intelligible to the largest audience possible. Hence, a focus on intelligibility, that is, "the degree to which we are saying what we want to be saying, think we are saying, or ought to be saying . . . and how we interpret what is being said to us, or what we are reading" (Nelson, 1995, as cited in Berns, 1990, p. 34) was a pillar of the seminar design. The working definition of intelligibility I adopted allows for an examination of three levels of understanding: narrow intelligibility (recognition of words and utterances), comprehensibility (at the word and utterance level), and interpretability (the meaning behind the word or utterance).

This audience's appreciation of academic and theoretical discussions made me feel comfortable exploring topics related to linguistic theory. Moreover, I assumed that if I was responsible for turning the participants into agents of change within their own classrooms, then I needed to make them aware of some theoretical aspects of language learning and use (e.g., terms such as *varieties, phonology,* and *linguistic and extralinguistic features*). On the other hand, I could not assume that they had any previous theoretical knowledge of linguistics. In fact, a participant came to me after our second meeting and explained that he had no idea the study of language could be that scientific. Therefore, any theoretical and background information presented would have to strike a balance between the participants' appreciation for academic matters and their lack of familiarity with linguistic issues. During our weeks together, we browsed through academic texts, and I shared some of my research interests so as to legitimate the systematic study of language in the minds of the learners.

The course, however, was not designed to be a theoretical debate around linguistic concerns; it had a very concrete short- and midterm goal: to make participants better able to deal with the demands of teaching in English. A good deal of our efforts would have to concentrate on practice. For that reason, many activities were designed to address the often-neglected level of strategic competence.

According to the model of communicative competence used for this study (see Figure 1), strategic competence helps a person cope with shortcomings in grammatical, sociolinguistic, and discourse competence. As explained above, traditional foreign language teaching usually focuses heavily on grammatical competence while neglecting strategic competence. For the course I intended to design, it seemed appropriate to reverse the tactic and focus more heavily on strategic competence than on any of the other levels.

The rationale for this decision was that working on the strategic level has a visible, short-term impact and, as a consequence, boosts learners' confidence in their ability to use language, which tends to improve performance. Additionally, a focus on strategic competence would allow me to build on the participants' repertoire of strategies for teaching in Spanish, as explained in the Practical Ideas section. Finally, I could focus on making participants see oral language as a means of communication (among other means, e.g., body language, use of visuals, facial expression) rather than as the goal of communication.

Grammatical competence:	Knowledge of the sentence structure of a language
Sociolinguistic competence:	Ability to use language appropriately in a given context
Discourse competence:	Ability to connect sentences in an overall theme or topic
Strategic competence:	Ability to compensate for imperfect knowledge of the above

FIGURE 1. Communicative Competence (Canale, 1983; Canale & Swain, 1980; Savignon, 1983)

Presentations

At this point, my course had theoretical and practical components. To put them together, I incorporated small classroom presentations by participants.

The 10- to 15-minute presentations (or classroom simulations) were designed to allow learners to experiment with techniques and strategies in alignment with the linguistic topics we discussed. In these microteaching sessions, the participants could explore the material by presenting topics they were likely to have to teach in English. They were free to incorporate visuals and materials to achieve their teaching goals. The participants and I assessed the presentations and provided feedback, keeping the goals and objectives of the course in mind, using assessment sheets (see Appendix B) to remind us of the relevant criteria (i.e., overall intelligibility and ability to establish successful communication).

Pronunciation and Suprasegmentals

Pronunciation and suprasegmentals (stress, intonation, volume, pace, rhythm, and pausing) are often the focus of many hours of attention and work in oral language programs. But because they affect only word or utterance recognition, I chose to work on them only when they became an issue. Researchers (e.g., L. E. Smith, 1992) have demonstrated that comprehensibility and interpretability have a larger impact on overall intelligibility than word recognition does. Thus, because the program's central goal was to make participants more intelligible in the broader sense (and not necessarily nativelike), and because successful communication does not require the mastery of all patterns of pronunciation, stress, and intonation, I selected only certain features for close scrutiny.

Examples of features not covered in the course are the Spanish final /l/, which differs from the final /l/ in standard American and British English, and the Spanish retroflex, as in *perro,* which frequently makes its way into English but does not seem to interfere with intelligibility for most listeners. They were therefore unnecessary targets in a short course. On the other hand, I targeted the difficulty many Spanish speakers have in differentiating between voiced and voiceless consonants, such as /z/ and /s/, because the difference is phonemic in English (and allophonic in Spanish) and can thus lead to confusion. An example is the words *sip* and *zip* when they are both pronounced with an initial /s/. Suprasegmentals were treated the same way: I diagnosed problems during discussions or presentations and addressed them if they impeded communication.

◈ DISTINGUISHING FEATURES

Shift From Linguistic Features to Oral Communication Strategies

The most salient difference between this program and regular language programs was the focus on oral communication strategies in English rather than on linguistic features of English. Inspired by the Oral English Proficiency Program in Purdue University's English Department (which aims to increase the intelligibility of international teaching assistants in the English-speaking classroom), I designed the program around the basic assumption that the faculty members were specialists within their areas of expertise and that English was a means (not an end) for others who want to partake of the faculty's knowledge to establish contact with them.

Although framing the language program this way may seem to have no serious repercussions, the fact that it eliminated the need to be English language specialists or aim for the usually elusive native speaker command of English had a positive psychological impact on the attendees. Referring to language as a means rather than an end lowered their expectations for their own performance to a more realistic level and raised the level of the performance. Additionally, this framing of the program allowed participants to appreciate other (extralinguistic) means available for communication, which tend to be neglected if too much emphasis is put on language form. For example, South Americans, like most Romance language speakers, tend to rely heavily on body movement, gestures, and facial expressions, which contribute very efficiently to intelligibility. All of these features were already a part of the faculty's repertoire when they taught in their native language. An overemphasis on linguistic features alone tends to cause learners to forget that they already have these tools. If learners of language are free to explore whatever means they have available to establish communication, they will come up with creative solutions, and their performance will improve greatly, which is the ultimate goal of the program.

Valid Models for Teaching

My goal in this course can be expressed in one word: intelligibility. Related to this goal is the matter of valid models for teaching. Contexts where English is primarily used as a foreign language, such as the one described here, have generally adopted Inner Circle (native) varieties as models. Having such a variety as a model is, however, no guarantee that learners will easily achieve intelligibility. If English does not serve as an intranational language, ignoring models beyond the Inner Circle achieves little. I believe that familiarity with other varieties, aligned to the development of good communication strategies, is a first step toward successful communication in English in a world where English use has as many facets as it has users. Thus, exposing students to different varieties and legitimizing variation are necessary components of language programs that explore English in a global context.

In the program described in this chapter, follow-up sessions and assessment of participants once they are teaching in English will ensure that the process that started with the seminar does not end there. The teaching situations faced by each faculty member will certainly call for further reflection, both on my part and on the part of the faculty. Such situations will also serve as a drawing board for subsequent programs for other faculty.

Expansion to Written Communication in English

At the time of writing, the program is being expanded to include written communication in English and the demands of publishing in English. In the same spirit of the oral communication component, this stage aims to ease the faculty into publishing in English as well as Spanish so as to reach more readers.

Preparing the faculty to write in English presents challenges that differ from those relating to oral communication. First, localized solutions have to be considered differently because the central purpose of writing is to reach out to a broader audience. Additionally, written communication relies almost exclusively on linguistic and rhetorical skills, unlike face-to-face oral interaction, which involves many other means. The possibility of reaching out to a larger audience also complicates the matter of cultural assumptions. It is one thing to become familiar with the needs and cultural orientation of 30 students in a classroom and another to communicate successfully with the readership of a professional journal, which may number from a few to several thousand. Finally, because the Business School itself, as opposed to the Linguistics or English Department, is behind the initiative, the rest of the school and faculty must be involved.

These issues caused me to consider exploring writing-across-the-curriculum (WAC) programs as a source of inspiration for a Written Communication in English program. The most obvious contextual difference between traditional WAC programs and my situation are that

- faculty rather than students are being taught (so writing cannot be expected to be literally practiced across the curriculum)

- no language or rhetoric and composition program exists to back up the project

In spite of the differences, some basic features of WAC programs apply (Maimon, 2000, pp. xii–x):

- a belief in the need to involve teachers and learners beyond language programs in the process of developing writing skills

- the assumption that writing is a complex process, akin to thinking, and should be treated as such

- the need to create a nonhierarchical environment for writing development

- a belief in writing as a mode of learning

The program, in the design stage at the time of writing, will have a seminar component; topics will include approaches to writing and writing techniques, the development of a paper for publication (from the outline to the draft and its subsequent submission), process writing, and peer review. Additionally, I hope to have participants form writing groups that meet independently to discuss one another's materials. Finally, I plan to arrange conferences to discuss individual problems or challenges participants face in their writing.

The writing program for the faculty is closely aligned to what researchers have called a rhetorical approach to writing, in which the instructor's job is "to help introduce students to the conventions of academic discourse in general and to the discourse conventions of particular disciplines—much as we would try to introduce newcomers into an ongoing conversation" (McLeod, 2000, p. 3). Because the faculty members are, in a way, newcomers to the challenges of bilingual scientific production, this analogy seems all the more appropriate.

The two stages of the program described in this chapter are bound to undergo significant changes each time it is offered. I hope to incorporate new ideas, and others will be refined or altogether abandoned. By sharing my experience, I hope to motivate other individuals faced with designing and teaching new language programs to discover in their own environments the necessary inspiration to tackle specific challenges and problems. Although the demands for English use are global, the solutions and opportunities in language teaching are local and need to reflect the needs of the community in question. Teaching English in an increasingly global environment presents many challenges but makes program and course design an exciting and rewarding task.

◈ PRACTICAL IDEAS

The 10-week program was a mixture of lectures followed by discussions, awareness-raising and communication achievement exercises, and presentations by the participants. These teaching suggestions are based on my experience in this course.

Link Concepts and Use

Make explicit links between the concepts taught and their usefulness for classroom teaching. During the class sessions, some common questions were "How is the idea of negotiating meaning with your audience relevant in the context of your classroom?" and "What changes in your classroom practice have you made now that you understand that intelligibility depends on the context?"

Use a Workshop Approach

Conduct some class meetings as workshops. In my program, this approach served as a kind of laboratory of classroom techniques. A typical example was the meeting about questioning and answering skills, in which learners could experiment with different techniques for asking questions, clarifying answers, and checking their own understanding of questions. These techniques were later incorporated into their presentations.

Assign Oral Presentations

Use oral presentations as a culminating activity. In my course, presentations provided an opportunity for participants to use the techniques and concepts presented in a more structured way. The presentations were videotaped for later viewing and teacher and peer evaluation (see Appendix B).

Make Your Rationale Explicit

Discuss your rationale with the learners. Emphasize the fact that leading discussions is as important as giving lectures because discussion connects the theoretical material to the participants' sociolinguistic reality. Some of the topics the class explored were intelligibility and communication, English and its users, myths about English and its users, nonverbal communication, and optimization of the use of questioning and answering skills.

Show Learners What They Can Do

Raise learners' awareness of the skills they already have at their disposal but do not often remember to use. Awareness-raising exercises make learners conscious of and excited about what they can already do. Some practical ideas in this respect follow.

Teach Circumlocution Instead of Focusing on Lack of Vocabulary

Ask learners to write a noun on a card and, below the noun, to write two words they would most likely use in trying to explain that noun without using it. For example, for the word *farm,* the two related words could be *animals* and *countryside.* Learners swap cards and make the others guess the noun by describing the term without mentioning it or the two related words. Follow up by discussing circumlocution as a possible strategy in situations where participants lack one or more vocabulary items but still have to get their meaning across.

Work on Extralinguistic Communication

Sit learners back to back, and ask them to simulate a telephone conversation. Discuss why it is more difficult to understand without seeing the person who is talking. Discuss the importance of body language as a complement to oral communication. To follow up, play charades.

Work on Asking for Clarification

Have all individuals but two leave. Have one of them read a short tale or anecdote to the other, who cannot ask for clarification. Then have the listener tell the story to an incoming participant. The story will obviously change with each retelling. Discuss what would have been different if asking for clarification had been allowed.

Encourage Learners to Keep a Journal

When no homework is required, you can still encourage learners to keep a journal in which they document any aspect of the course that surprised them, drew their attention, disappointed them, or struck them as particularly useful. Encourage them to share their views at the end of the course or to submit a summary of their ideas to you as feedback.

◈ CONCLUSION

The global (macrolevel) spread of English calls for communal initiatives at the local, microlevel. In domains such as education, no universalizing initiative can account for all the possible uses or needs for English. The requirements of my course have led me to focus on aspects of language use that may be more or less relevant in another context. With this chapter, I hope to call attention to the need to consider the sociolinguistic dimensions of English as a central concern for ESL/EFL practitioners worldwide and to the fact that the goals of English language teaching must be corroborated with this consideration.

◈ CONTRIBUTOR

Patricia Friedrich is an assistant professor of rhetoric and composition at Arizona State University West, in the United States. Her research interests involve the global spread of English, cultural forces impacting communication, and World Englishes. She has published in journals such as *International Journal of Applied Linguistics* and *World Englishes* and was guest coeditor of a special issue of the latter about English in South America.

❖ APPENDIX A: ANNOTATED COURSE SYLLABUS

COMMUNICATION IN ENGLISH SEMINAR

Week 1: Scope of the Course, Communicative Competence, and Models for Nonnative Englishes

Issues facing learners of English are discussed. Although the subject is not treated with the same depth as would be the case with linguistics students or preservice English teachers, I refer to terms such as *model, variety, native and nonnative speakers, standard, intelligibility,* and *communicative competence.* The relevance of such terms to the sociolinguistic reality of participants is then discussed.

Week 2: Attitudes of Students Toward English in the Classroom/Delivery

First block: Studies about students' attitudes toward English, its users, and its uses are presented. Misconceptions about English and its use are addressed. Participants then discuss ways to address the issue of attitudes in their own classrooms.

Second block: Practical ideas that have a positive impact on the audience at the time of delivery are offered. Aspects discussed include holding the attention of the audience, cultivating welcoming gestures and facial expression, and avoiding self-absorption.

Week 3: Questions and Answers/Achieving Better Communication Through Strategies

This workshop session allows learners to experiment with different levels and types of questions, using a model such as Bloom's (1956) taxonomy of questions. After different types of questions (e.g., knowledge, analysis, and evaluation) are discussed, learners formulate different kinds of questions about material they usually teach. Learners then discuss how and when to ask such questions and how to address, praise, or critique learners' answers. Learners also practice answering questions and checking for comprehension.

Week 4: Visual Aids and Nonverbal Communication/ Presentation Guidelines

First block: Learners explore different ways to incorporate visual aids into their presentations. Aspects discussed include the overloading of slides with information, the use of text in handouts as opposed to slides, and the selection of the most viable visual aids. Learners then create a visual and critique each other's material. Other forms of nonverbal communication are explored. A game of charades demonstrates how communication is achieved nonverbally.

Second block: Participants discuss the guidelines and the assessment sheet for the 10-minute class simulations to take place during the next two meetings.

Weeks 5 and 6: Simulations

Depending on number of participants, 1–2 days are devoted to presentations. Ideally, they are recorded for later viewing and critiquing. The instructor and other participants fill out an assessment sheet. If well tolerated by the group, oral commentaries can also be used.

Week 7: Cultural Issues of the English Classroom/ Being Culturally Appropriate in a Multicultural English-Using Class

This discussion-based meeting revolves around the overarching topic of cultural implications of speaking to an audience in English. Examples of topics that can be appropriate within one culture but inappropriate within another are presented. A discussion on how to remain relatively neutral and avoid offensive topics and language while speaking in English follows. Because this course is taught in a business school, the example used is the cultural differences represented while people close deals within different cultures. Learners discuss how small talk, frequent smiles, use of humor, direct and indirect refusals, periods of silence, and unsolicited praise are generally interpreted by American, Japanese, Brazilian, British, and Argentine individuals.

Week 8: Topic to Be Announced

The topic of one meeting is left open for a subject of particular interest for a given group. Sometimes, learners find it reassuring to devote one whole session to pronunciation problems that make them difficult to understand. Paraphrasing and using circumlocution, as well as developing vocabulary, are other common requests.

Week 9: Final Simulation (All Participants, With Open Audience)

This session is conducted similarly to the previous presentation sessions. One idea would be to invite a general audience to be present so that participants can demonstrate what they have learned to the community or their peers.

Week 10: Feedback Session—Journal Entry

The last meeting can be used as a feedback session. If learners have kept a journal, this is the right time to ask them to share their thoughts with their peers.

◈ APPENDIX B: ORAL PRESENTATION ASSESSMENT SHEETS

Instructor

	Lowest			Highest	Comments
1. Overall intelligibility	1	2	3		
2. Use of visual aids	1	2	3		
3. Use of nonverbal communication	1	2	3		
4. Questioning skills	1	2	3		
5. Ability to address questions	1	2	3		
6. Rapport with audience	1	2	3		
7. Interaction	1	2	3		

8. Pronunciation/intelligibility	1	2	3
9. Suprasegmentals/intelligibility	1	2	3
10. Grammar-vocabulary-fluency	1	2	3
11. Delivery (organization, detail)	1	2	3
12. Overall impression	1	2	3

Peers

1. I could understand my colleague most of the time.	1	2	3
2. I learned from the visuals used.	1	2	3
3. My colleague made good use of gestures and expressions.	1	2	3
4. My colleague asked relevant questions.	1	2	3
5. My colleague was friendly and nice to the audience.	1	2	3
6. Overall, I was pleased with the presentation.	1	2	3

Comments:

PART 2

Which Speakers?

CHAPTER 4

How to Spell *Culture* in Language Teacher Education Programs

A. J. Meier

◈ INTRODUCTION

The global spread of English is accompanied by an increase in face-to-face communication involving many varieties of English, including those with evolving identities and functions (e.g., English as an international language, nativized Englishes). In turn, contact and negotiation of meaning among a large number of cultures have grown. Because culture informs speakers' linguistic choices, expectations, and interpretations, the development of cultural understanding becomes of paramount importance for effective global communication.

Culture accordingly needs to assume a more prominent role in the goals of English language pedagogy. This culture, I submit, should be spelled with a small *c* rather than a big *C*. Small-*c*, or *subjective*, culture, as it is often termed, encompasses underlying values and beliefs whereas big *C* culture involves artifacts (e.g., the arts, institutions, cuisine; see, e.g., Bennett, 1998a). It is culture with a small *c* that offers the basis for developing the cultural awareness and communicative abilities required by the expanding contexts of English use and their variety of interlocutors.

Today's English language teachers—whether they teach EFL, ESL, English as an international language, or English for any other function—must thus be prepared to deal effectively with small-*c* culture in their language classrooms. This preparation, I believe, requires teachers to understand the relationship between language and culture and develop their own intercultural sensitivity. This belief underlies the approach and content of the one-semester seminar on intercultural communication described in this chapter. (Seminar, as used in this chapter, refers to an upper-level MA class that focuses on a specific topic and typically involves more teacher-learner involvement and fewer participants than other classes do.) The seminar, offered in an MA TESOL/applied linguistics program at a state university in the United States, focuses on culture with a small *c*. In other words, the focus is on understanding and appreciating different cultural value orientations and their potential influence on communicative behavior. This forms a necessary basis for exploring how teacher learners can best address culture in their future teaching contexts. Also included are teacher learners' perspectives on the seminar as expressed in audiotaped interviews, written surveys, and written reflective essays.

◈ CONTEXT

The MA TESOL/applied linguistics program that offers the intercultural seminar is housed in the English Department of a midwestern U.S. university that has an enrollment of approximately 13,000 students. The program typically admits 20 teacher learners each academic year, approximately 47% of which represent a variety of non-U.S. nationalities (e.g., Chilean, Colombian, Costa Rican, Indonesian, Japanese, Korean, Omanese, Russian, Taiwanese, Tibetan, Vietnamese). The TESOL faculty comprises six full-time professors, all from the United States.

Teacher learners are required to complete 11 classes, each meeting 3 hours a week for 16 weeks, to earn either an MA in TESOL or a combined degree in TESOL and another language (i.e., French, German, or Spanish). Combined majors complete 15 of the 33 required hours in their chosen language in the Modern Language Department. The classes offered in the MA TESOL program cover general and applied linguistics, including two methodology classes. A final research paper of approximately 30 pages is also required for the MA degree, as is the successful completion of a 6-hour written comprehensive exam.

The teacher learners in the MA TESOL program take one seminar, which typically varies in topic each semester according to the current focus of research and interest of the professor teaching it. For the combined majors, the seminar is one of three classes from which they can choose (the other two classes are Computer-Assisted Language Learning and Testing). Because the teacher learners take the graduate seminar in the final year of their MA program, they know one another quite well. Rarely have any of them had prior class work in intercultural communication.

On completion of their MA degree, most international teacher learners return to their countries to teach English in public schools or at universities; approximately two teacher learners a year pursue a PhD in the United States. A large majority of the U.S. graduates of the MA program remain in the United States to teach in university intensive English programs or, increasingly, in bilingual or ESL programs in public schools, while a small number leave the United States to teach in different types of settings. A varying number of the teacher learners have had prior language teaching experience or are engaged in language teaching while enrolled in the MA TESOL program.

◈ DESCRIPTION

For three consecutive fall semesters from 2000 to 2002, the topic of the seminar was intercultural communication. Ranging in size from 9 to 12 teacher learners, the seminar met once a week for 3 hours throughout a 16-week semester. Almost all of the teacher learners had had experience living in another culture, and I (the instructor) had lived, worked, and studied in another culture for approximately 15 years.

Goals

The goals of the intercultural communication seminar were based on the belief that a culture-general approach, which provides tools for dealing with new situations, is the most relevant, effective, and inclusive for the broad variety of language learning contexts in today's world (see Meier, 2003). This approach stands in contrast to culture-free or culture-specific approaches, focusing on developing learners' awareness of the role culture plays in perceptions of contextual variables and consequent linguistic choices, and on strategies for negotiation of meaning in intercultural communication (Meier, 2003). Within the variety of today's language learning contexts, English may function, for example, as a second language (ESL), a foreign language (EFL), an additional language (EAL), or an international language (EIL). Indeed, the distinctions between the evolving functions of English in global contexts are deemed to be increasingly blurred (e.g., Bamgbose, 1998; Widdowson, 1998). This indicates a demand for greater communicative flexibility that precludes a construal of language teaching as an attempt to produce native speaker clones. Accordingly, the aim of the seminar was to lead the teacher learners not to become knowers of a specific culture who are to transfer this knowledge to their learners, but rather to become understanders of the role that culture plays in communication. Therefore, the goals of the seminar, described below, tended to be more affective than cognitive.

One goal of the seminar was to develop a language-culture awareness, part of which is the recognition that the same symbol or linguistic behavior can embody different meanings in different cultures and that different perceptions of reality can differentially inform expectations for what verbal or nonverbal behavior is appropriate for a particular context. Language-culture awareness thus entails an understanding of how cultural factors affect one's thoughts, feelings, values, and perceptions.

A second goal was to develop an intercultural imagination in thinking about cultural groups and their communication, thereby developing an appreciation of the validity of various viewpoints and discourses different from one's own. This goal was construed in at least two ways: developing an emic, as opposed to etic, point of view (i.e., an insider vs. an outsider view) and recognizing the distinction between description (an actual report), interpretation (attribution of social meaning), and evaluation (positive or negative judgments regarding the interpretation) (see Gudykunst, 1998).

A third goal involved learning to anticipate potential areas of misunderstanding and develop skills to deal with miscommunication. This goal leads to the development of strategic competence (see, e.g., Bachman, 1990; Canale, 1983). Subsumed under this goal was the development of a certain degree of context sensitivity in terms of awareness of contextual variables and their possible meanings. This third goal was an extension of the previous two goals, which formed a prerequisite for it.

Fourth, teacher learners were expected to become familiar with contemporary theories, concepts, issues, and perspectives as well as with research studies on intercultural communication and on the role of culture in the language classroom.

Fifth, teacher learners were expected to develop a familiarity with teaching approaches, techniques, and activities; their goals; and the principles guiding them. This included an awareness of resources (e.g., books, Web sites) that provide ideas for a variety of cultural activities. A final goal was for the teacher learners to learn the processes of scholarly dialogue and writing on culture and communication.

The achievement of these six goals especially addressed the use of English involving interlocutors with diverse linguistic and cultural backgrounds, a situation becoming more prevalent as English expands its international or lingua franca roles.

The teacher learners in the seminar gained a perspective on language and culture that was essential if they were to prepare their own students for the communication demands placed on them.

Attaining the Goals

To attain the goals cited above, I employed techniques that can be broadly described as either didactic (e.g., introduction of concepts, readings) or experiential (e.g., role play, simulation) as they were applied to the following summary of the seminar topics. Many of these topics were addressed through both didactic and experiential techniques. For example, Topic 3 involved a simulation that led to an introduction of concepts through instructor presentation, readings, and a follow-up exercise.

1. culture (definitions, cocultures)

2. stereotype versus generalization

3. perceptions (emic vs. etic, description vs. interpretation vs. evaluation)

4. nonverbal communication, communication styles, value orientations

5. education and learning styles

6. the culture-discourse relationship in the workplace, the justice system, health care, and education

7. TESOL and culture

8. culture-specific critique

9. communication skills and conflict negotiation across cultures

10. the Developmental Model of Intercultural Sensitivity (Bennett, 1993)

Didactic

The readings for the class fell under the didactic rubric. The required textbook, Samovar and Porter's (2001) *Communication Between Cultures,* provided a basic overview of the field of intercultural communication and acted as a springboard for further readings and activities. A recommended resource book for teaching activities was Fantini's (1997) *New Ways in Teaching Culture.* Readings for the seminar that supplemented and complemented the textbook encompassed a spectrum of areas within intercultural communication and can be roughly grouped as follows:

- views of culture and intercultural communication (Bennett, 1998b; Bhawuk & Triandis, 1996)

- cultural influences on communication in varied interactions and settings (Caulk, 1998; Corson, 1995; Dobler, 1998; Farrell, 1998; F. L. Johnson, 2000; Precht, 1998; Skow & Stephan, 2000; Ting-Toomey, 2000)

- specific cultures (Gannon, 2000; Gao, 1998; Ramsey, 1998; Stephan & Abalakina-Papp, 1996), cocultures (Braithwaite & Braithwaite, 2000; V. McKay, 2000; Siple, 2000)

- ethical considerations in training (Paige & Martin, 1996)

- TESOL (Cortazzi & Jin, 1999; Damen, 1987, textbook evaluation selections; Hyde, 1994; Meier, 2003; Paige, Jorstad, Siaya, Klein, & Colby, n.d.; Picken, 1999; Sercu, 1989)

The readings were discussed in class in pairs or small groups and as an entire class. In one discussion procedure, I asked the teacher learners to present an actual example or scenario to illustrate a point made in a reading or to comment on an idea they found particularly interesting. To ensure the engagement of everyone in the class and encourage a more collaborative discussion with less instructor-focused direction, I sometimes asked seminar participants to nominate the next individual to contribute, especially at the beginning of the semester.

An instructor-designed course packet provided a collection of additional exercises, notes, and extensive bibliographies for relevant areas (e.g., intercultural studies, cross-cultural speech act studies, culture in the language classroom, cognitive and learning styles). Other handouts included examples and excerpts from ESL/EFL books (e.g., Ford, Silverman, & Haines, 1983; Levine, Baxter, & McNulty, 1987; Shulman, 2001). I modeled their use in class with the teacher learners as participants, followed by a critical evaluation of a particular exercise and its appropriateness for varied teaching settings. The selected textbook excerpts and exercises were congruent with a culture-general approach or could be adapted to be so.

Activity sheets or questionnaires were also designed to raise the teacher learners' awareness of their own values, beliefs, and language behavior. For example, one activity sheet contained five symbols for which the teacher learners gave their spontaneous interpretations, which were then shared, compared, and discussed (see Singer, 1998). The teacher learners in the seminar also identified culture-specific references in a newspaper article. Blommaert (1991, p. 23) provides an authentic intercultural dialogue, gone awry and repaired, for which the teacher learners analyzed the differing interpretations leading to the misunderstanding and subsequent clarification. A further dialogue task came from Storti's (1994) book, which offers numerous brief dialogues containing subtle differences in underlying cultural assumptions between the interlocutors. It was the teacher learners' task to identify these differences.

In another exercise, the teacher learners ranked themselves along a Likert-like scale for a list of selected value orientations. They also analyzed and discussed foreigners' observations of a particular culture (adapted from Kohls & Knight, 1994, or collected or designed by me) in terms of the underlying values and beliefs informing them. Critical incidents, which present a brief scenario involving a cross-cultural misunderstanding due to different assumptions and expectations, provided an opportunity to consider contextual variables and alternative interpretations of the characters' behavior, and to discuss strategies for avoiding or dealing with the misunderstandings. I either designed these critical incidents to suit the particular group of teacher learners or adapted them from those in Brislin, Cushner, Cherrie, and Yong's (1986) book. Although some critical incidents provide a list of possible explanations to choose from, I preferred to omit these, allowing teacher learners to propose their own. At times, the teacher learners created their own critical incidents.

Experiential

In the experiential realm, I employed numerous activities requiring active involvement. Role plays, for example, focused on turn-taking behavior, nonverbal behavior, and conversational style. If at least two pairs of teacher learners in the class represented two different cultures, they performed contrastive role plays (e.g., enacting a doctor's visit, returning merchandise, seeking lost luggage at an airport) with the rest of the class observing and identifying differences and similarities, and proposing possible explanations for the latter.

The class also engaged in simulations such as Albatross (Batchelder & Warner, 1977), the card game Barnga (Thiagarajan & Steinwachs, 1990), and the Tag Game (see Fowler & Mumford, 1999). Albatross involves a mimed minidrama depicting a scene from an imaginary culture. After the enactment, the observers described and interpreted the drama's events. Albatross was especially effective in leading teacher learners to recognize their tendency to interpret and evaluate others' behavior on the basis of their own cultural assumptions. This activity effectively set the stage for introducing the differences among description, interpretation, and evaluation, which occurred early in the semester to enable the teacher learners to apply these distinctions in subsequent activities. Barnga simulates a situation in which rules regulating behavior are slightly different in a context where communication is limited. The card game stimulated a great deal of follow-up discussion about communication barriers, differing cultural norms, and ways to deal with conflict. The Tag Game addressed differences in perception as participants, each with a similar but somewhat different tag attached to them, grouped and then regrouped themselves based on their tags.

In another experiential activity, the teacher learners conducted interviews outside the classroom in conjunction with a related textbook reading. One such assignment, for example, focused on family traditions, another on religious traditions, and another on educational issues. For the latter, teacher learners interviewed professors and teaching assistants.

The class also made use of closed role plays or discourse completion tasks from published speech act investigations, whereby the teacher learners responded to such elicitation devices, compared their responses with each other and with those elicited in the relevant published study, and discussed the reasons for differences and similarities as contextual variables were considered.

Videos

Eleven videos, commercially produced films as well as those specifically designed for intercultural communication purposes (and thus more directly didactic), were used to further investigate aspects of intercultural communication. They were shown in the following order: *Rainbow War* (Rogers, 1985; a silent film), *A World of Gestures* (Archer & Silver, 1991; didactic), *Crosstalk* (Twitchin, 2003; didactic), *Better Off Together Than A-P-A-R-T* (Bennett, 2002; didactic), *A Different Place: The Intercultural Classroom* (Sohier, 1993; didactic), *The Shower* (Zhang, 2001; clip only), *Awakenings* (Kramer, 1991; clip only), Japanese commercials (a home-taped selection), *Guess Who's Coming to Dinner* (Kramer, 1967/1995) and *The Joy Luck Club* (Wang, 1994) (clips of the latter two were viewed together and contrasted), and *Postville: When Cultures Collide* (Tundel, 2000; didactic). Films, being at one remove from the viewers' personal experiences, typically offer a low-threat way to elicit cultural insights.

Teacher-Learner Roles

At the beginning of the semester, I articulated the teacher learners' dual roles in the class, namely, that they would be functioning as observers and participants as they engaged in an activity, and subsequently described and analyzed their responses (in what I termed *metamoments*), evaluating an activity's strengths, weaknesses, adaptability, and suitability to various contexts. The teacher learners thus gained exposure to activities and materials they might themselves use while gaining firsthand experience as a participant. Another stated philosophy of the seminar was that the exploration and learning in the class was a journey of sorts that the students and I were embarking on, each bringing our background experiences and beliefs to be learned from and shared.

Class Requirements

Work receiving a mark or grade in the class included the teacher learners' critical discussion of the readings, their oral presentations, and their participation in and evaluation of activities. They also completed two written essays of three to four pages, responding to two of eight questions based on topics in their required textbook; they were asked to consult two additional outside sources for this essay. A further writing assignment was to summarize five published articles addressing the role of teaching culture in English language classrooms. In a more creative and experiential requirement, the teacher learners designed and facilitated an intercultural communication activity (either one designed for an English language classroom or a more general one) involving the entire class.

The seminar culminated in a 20-page paper and a reflective essay of about 8 pages. Topics for the final paper included an analysis of the role of culture in the following areas: health care, humor, silence, conflict, time, emotions, nonverbal communication, speech acts, culture shock, advertising, rhetorical patterns, English language pedagogy, children's films or literature, and language teacher education. The teacher learners selected their topic from a list or proposed their own. Most of the papers were critical literature overviews, but some entailed data gathering via questionnaires or interviews. The teacher learners also wrote a 400-word summary of their paper, which was distributed to all members of the class. The reflective essay, which averaged about 4 pages, involved a self-analysis of the teacher learner's development throughout the semester and an evaluation of the varied readings and activities.

◈ DISTINGUISHING FEATURES

Teacher Learner Perspectives

One of the most important aspects of any class is the participants' perspectives: What did the teacher learners feel they gained from the seminar described above? I elicited their general comments and their reactions to specific activities and readings as a part of the seminar.

An activity that found universal acclaim was Albatross, a simulation used in the first class. The teacher learners found it to be eye-opening, and effectively placed at the beginning of the seminar. They also commented positively on its use to introduce description, interpretation, and evaluation, and on the usefulness of this three-way distinction.

Bennett's (2002) video, *Better Off Together Than A-P-A-R-T,* was also popular, and was viewed as an engaging summary of concepts previously addressed in the seminar. One teacher learner expressed the desire for the video to be shown twice, the second time at the end of the semester. Bennett's (1998b) "Golden Rule" article likewise received overwhelming endorsement, with the teacher learners finding it "thought provoking" and "a good basis for stimulating discussion."

The required textbook used in the course was found to be "readable, insightful, and practical"; "informative without being overly complex"; "well-written, easily read, and prompt[ing] much discussion." The teacher learners' presentations were noted as "useful," "enjoyable," "interesting," and "a good way of practicing ideas for my own teaching." A consistent comment at the end of the semesters indicated a desire for more than one teacher learner presentation. The use of videos was also deemed to pique interest and be useful in illustrating cultural points with a different medium. A couple of teacher learners commented that the two written essays were positive for them in allowing them to express their own thoughts and to be encouraged to do reading outside the textbook. Barnga was also repeatedly mentioned as a beneficial and enjoyable experience, as it underscored the tendency to make judgments in terms of one's own norms and raised awareness of the way in which even small differences in norms can cause conflict.

Based on comments from the first time the seminar was offered, I introduced Bennett's (1993) developmental model of intercultural sensitivity earlier in the two subsequent seminars. This proved to be a good decision as the model could be referred to throughout the semester in considering the appropriateness of various activities for learners at different stages of cultural sensitivity.

Many comments expressly indicated personal growth. One teacher learner, for example, found that "it has been insightful for me to analyze my own thinking and world views." A comment representative of others is the following: "I began to understand how rich my own cultural identity is." Yet another teacher learner found that the seminar had provided her with "a type of peace in dealing with my own identity in cross-cultural communication." Another comment reflects a change in perspective that will likely be conveyed in the teacher learners' own language teaching:

> This semester helped me realize that one cannot simply develop a neat set of rules and use them to explain how different cultures and languages operate because this name-and-categorize approach does not account for the complex nature of language and culture, leading the students to overgeneralizations or cultural and language stereotyping.

One teacher learner described the seminar as "one of the best class experiences I've had in the TESOL Department." Another said, "This class was one of the most valuable university classes I have ever had; 'different' has now become more palatable and less frightening to me." Others expressed the belief that such a class should be required of all teachers and future teachers.

The comments above are positive ones; indeed, despite my encouragement to be critical about the activities and readings, the teacher learners' only negative comments were the typical complaints of too much work, but even these were not common. The seminar was far from perfect, but the teacher learners' comments from three different seminars indicate that such a seminar or class can have positive effects on its participants that will inform their classroom teaching in significant ways, regardless of setting.

Deep-Structure Interculturalist Approach

The existence of an intercultural class seems to be a less-than-standard feature of MA TESOL programs. Nelson (1998), for example, found that only 40% of the programs listed in the *Directory of Professional Preparation Programs in TESOL in the United States, 1992–1994* (Kornblum, 1992) offered an intercultural communication or culture class. Of the 75% that responded, the predominant topic was specific cultural groups, which is precisely what the above-described seminar sought to deemphasize. The latter thus derived its greatest distinctiveness from its deep-structure interculturalist approach, which is based on a belief in the importance of subjective culture in communication and the desirability of a culture-general approach in the language classroom.

This approach resulted in the seminar's goals (see the Description section), which eschewed transmitting a prescriptive set of rules or facts of language-and-behavior to either teachers or learners. The seminar represented a more anthropological approach that aimed to develop cultural understanding rather than teach cultural rules or simply describe surface behavior. Such an approach well serves the varied global uses of English and reduces misplaced pressure on nonnative teachers.

Diverse Readings and Activities

The readings for the course were drawn from a broad range of sources (e.g., intercultural studies, applied linguistics, language pedagogy) and were complemented by activities such as simulations, critical incidents, and videos that engaged teacher learners in ways not usually experienced in a graduate seminar. In this way, future and practicing teachers gained an understanding of the language-culture connection, an intercultural sensitivity, which provided a basis for making principled decisions regarding goals and activities within the varied teaching contexts in which they would find themselves.

Dual Role of Students

The role of the teacher learner as participant and observer was a central and clearly articulated feature of this seminar and, according to the teacher learners, was a very much appreciated one. This dual role was especially important because the great majority of the activities in the seminar were the products of Western scholars and educators. As participants and observers, the teacher learners directly confronted the cultural bias of the activities and made suggestions for adapting or discarding them for particular contexts.

Broad View of Culture

The broad view of culture adopted in the seminar, which also addressed communication across cocultures of what is generally viewed as one culture, was another distinctive feature of the seminar. The cultures of the deaf, the elderly (as well as other generational groups), and those who are other-abled were explored (both intra- and interculturally), and the constructs and strategies for intercultural communication were applied.

In sum, the seminar resulted in significant personal development as the teacher learners developed their own teaching philosophies as well as an awareness of their own language-culture behavior and attitudes. The seminar thus, crucially, also recognized and addressed the human being embodied by the teacher as she or he acquired a global perspective in English language teaching.

◈ PRACTICAL IDEAS

Offer the Seminar and Its Contents in Different Ways

Intercultural communication need not be offered as a seminar. I did so because it was the most efficacious way to offer such a class without embarking on the lengthy procedure of proposing and enacting curricular changes. Such a class might also be offered, for example, in a block style, that is, meeting for larger blocks of time over a shorter period. If a separate class is not feasible, materials and activities as described above could be incorporated into existing classes. In fact, any methodology class should address the issue of culture. The inclusion of culture in language teacher education is a necessity, not a luxury.

Be Mindful of Classroom Climate

In a class that explores the values and beliefs of subjective culture, a nonjudgmental atmosphere that engenders trust and cooperation in learning must be established. Should the teacher learners not know each other well at the outset, time must be spent on icebreaker activities. Also, getting to know each other initially in pairs or smaller groups poses less of a threat than speaking in front of the entire group. This issue is especially pertinent for participants whose primary language is not English.

Likewise, begin the class with less threatening topics (e.g., body language instead of religion or gender issues) and activities (e.g., minilectures and nonprovocative films rather than activities eliciting self-examination or self-disclosure, or simulations such as Barnga). In a seminar such as this, it is important to be sensitive to the ongoing interactive dynamic as well as to the teacher learners' comfort levels with various activities.

Select Readings and Films in Accordance With the Student Population

Select class readings according to the teacher learners who make up the class. For example, the readings for contrastive cross-cultural communication might be based on the cultures represented in the class, which provides an added impetus for a critical treatment of the readings. Another textbook, similar to Samovar and Porter's (2001) *Communication Between Cultures,* that might be considered for an intercultural communication class is *Experiencing Intercultural Communication* (Martin & Nakayama, 2001). Descriptions of more than seventy films, suggestions for their classroom use, and ways to procure them are provided by Summerfield (1993).

Adapt Assignments to the Educational Setting

The extent to which you assign short essays and longer research papers and administer quizzes or exams will clearly depend on the teacher learners (e.g., the number in the class, their motivation, and their past academic experience), their instructors, and the time allocated to the class as well as institutional requirements and accepted procedures.

Quizzes

You might give a short content quiz (e.g., true-false, matching, and short-answer items) on the assigned readings for each class. I did so in only one semester due to time constraints, and although the teacher learners predictably complained several noted, at the end of the semester, that the quizzes caused them to read more carefully than they might have, and they thus advocated a continuation of such quizzes.

Journals

You might ask the teacher learners to keep a journal in which they record their responses to class activities and discussions and relate these to their own experiences. Although I encouraged teacher learners to do this as a reference for their final reflective essay, I did not formally read or monitor journals. The time available and size of the class play a significant role in such decisions.

Textbook Review, Film and Media Analysis

Another option for a formal project or assignment is a review of the cultural content of a textbook or textbooks. The readings by Sercu (1989), Cortazzi and Jin (1999), and Damen (1987) could provide a framework for this activity. Another possibility is an analysis of a film or films using constructs introduced in the seminar. In fact, you might consider initiating a weekend film-and-discussion series if interest warrants. You might also explore advertisements, television commercials, or situation comedies as sources of data for language-culture analysis.

Encounters Outside the Class

Encounters that involve teacher learners in intercultural experiences they would not normally seek out are another possible requirement for an intercultural communication class. Depending on the setting, these encounters could be found within the university community or within the local community. They might, for example, consist of attending relevant lectures, forums, or performances (e.g., theater); visiting a religious observance; becoming a conversation partner of someone from a different culture (face-to-face or via e-mail); or attending and observing mixed-culture classes (e.g., intensive English classes), to name just a few. Both a written and an oral report could serve as follow-ups to the encounter.

Rich cultural resources exist in any group of teachers or teacher learners and in the varied settings of teacher education, regardless of particular institutional constraints. The seminar presented in this chapter is a model for adaptation rather than adoption.

◈ CONCLUSION

Focusing on the language learner should not result in giving short shrift to the important role of teachers and their education. Teachers will transfer their attitudes toward and understanding of intercultural communication to their classrooms and the interactions therein. The seminar depicted above provided teacher learners not only with a solid basis for their future pedagogical decisions as regards language and culture but also with constructs for becoming better observers and analyzers of their further involvement in intercultural communication. An awareness of the role of culture in global issues of communication is essential if teachers are to make informed pedagogical decisions.

It is to be hoped that the future brings a regular appearance of such seminars in MA TESOL program offerings. A further goal would be to require a class with the described approach, content, and activities, a goal repeatedly expressed as desirable by many teacher learners enrolled in the seminar described here. The reflective essays written by the teacher learners clearly show that they felt the seminar had a positive, transformative effect on them, one that would carry over into their classrooms and their personal intercultural encounters. It is time that culture spelled with a little *c* finds widespread dissemination in language teacher education. Without such education, language classrooms will experience little change; change is critical for the effective use of English in its varied functions and settings around the globe.

◈ CONTRIBUTOR

A. J. Meier is a professor in the MA TESOL/Applied Linguistics Program at the University of Northern Iowa, in the United States. She has published in the areas of pragmatics and culture, language and gender, cross-cultural apologies, politeness theory, and language teacher education. She has taught theoretical and applied linguistics and presented intercultural communication workshops in continuing education programs in the United States and Austria.

CHAPTER 5

Preparing Future Users of English as an International Language

Aya Matsuda

◈ INTRODUCTION

As a sociolinguist, I find the current landscape of the English language fascinating. No other language today is used as widely as English, in terms of the number of users and the variety of functions, and it provides endless opportunities for various sorts of language research.

As an ESL teacher, however, I find the current situation challenging. It questions the most basic, taken-for-granted assumptions English teachers hold about the way they teach ESOL. Which variety do they teach? Whose norm or standard do they try to conform to? Who should be presented as English speakers? Whose culture? What type of uses? Acknowledging the (socio)linguistic complexity of the English language is like opening a can of worms; one question after another challenges traditional assumptions about English language teaching (ELT)—that nonnative speakers learn the language to communicate only with native speakers (usually Britons or Americans).

Such a complication, however confusing and overwhelming it may be, is inevitable if English language curricula are to better reflect reality and teachers are to be more effective in preparing learners for future use of English. It is especially so in a curriculum where the goal is for learners to learn English as an international language (EIL), the context of this chapter. My aim is to analyze current ELT curriculum practice in a particular national context, as illustrated by a typical high school setting. I consider what features distinguish such practice and suggest ways that it could be modified to reflect what is currently known about the changing sociolinguistic profile of the English language, especially its status as an international language.

In a traditional perspective on curriculum, the Inner Circle countries are considered the owners of the language, and teaching and learning are expected to conform to Inner Circle norms. The curriculum changes I propose are based on a belief that using English for international communication requires awareness of the current spread of English and of variety in forms, functions, and users of the language, and that simply conforming to Inner Circle norms is not only inappropriate but also inadequate. This approach goes beyond the traditional linguistic and cultural focus of most ELT curricula.

◈ CONTEXT

My suggestions are made in the context of a hypothetical but typical senior high school in Japan. Japan is often cited as an example of an Expanding Circle country, where English is used not for daily communication but for international communication, for example, between Japanese and non-Japanese speakers. English can also be found in advertisements and pop culture (e.g., magazine titles, song lyrics in Japanese pop music), but the uses in those cases are mostly symbolic.

The major use of English on a regular basis is among those who have direct contact with foreigners, such as immigration officers, government officers in areas where a large international population resides, and international business negotiators. Scientists also use English for publications and conference presentations (see Matsuda, 2000, for a more detailed description of the use of English in Japan).

Chuo High School (a pseudonym) is the kind of school with which I became very familiar through my research into Japanese high school students' attitudes toward English and is an example of a context where an EIL approach could be implemented. Chuo High School is a private senior high school (Grades 10–12) in Tokyo, with approximately 1,200 students and more than 60 full-time and 20 part-time teachers. Its academically oriented curriculum is moderately competitive, and all students, at least initially, plan to continue their education after high school at 2-year or 4-year colleges, universities, or vocational schools. Although private schools typically do not follow the national curriculum in the same way public schools do, this school follows it closely in core academic subjects (Japanese, English, mathematics, natural and social sciences), and most courses use textbooks approved by the Ministry of Education.

The English department is the largest in the school and offers a variety of English courses specified by the national curriculum (general English courses, oral communication, reading, and writing) as well as its own course that prepares students for university entrance exams. Although the national curriculum recommends that classes be held 2–4 hours a week, some English courses at Chuo High School meet 5 hours a week.

As in any required foreign language classes, students in English classes at Chuo High School demonstrate varying degrees of motivation and linguistic competencies. Except for a few students who have lived abroad or participated in exchange programs, they have never used the language for actual communication. The primary reasons for taking English classes are that they are compulsory and that university entrance exams include English. However, students generally agree that it is important for them to learn English because it is an international language. They perceive English to be essential for international understanding and access to other countries, and are fascinated by the increased international opportunities they believe knowledge of English would bring (Matsuda, 2000, 2003a).

The national curriculum followed at Chuo High School emphasizes the importance of EIL. Reflecting a belief that the future of the country depends at least partially on its people's English ability, the most recent national curriculum puts great emphasis on foreign language education. Specifically, in the new curriculum for secondary schools (Grades 7–12), foreign language is a required course, and the foreign language is specified as English at the middle school level (Grades 7–9)

(Curriculum Council, 1998; Monbusho, 1999a). In Grades 10–12, theoretically any foreign language could be taught, but English is almost always the first choice.

◈ DESCRIPTION

Three goals in the national curriculum for foreign language are (a) to deepen the understanding of cultures and languages, (b) to foster a positive attitude toward communicating in the target language, and (c) to develop practical communication ability. The curriculum includes general English courses as well as those focusing on specific skills (writing, reading, oral communication). These courses all aim to achieve the three goals above, which all relate to facilitating communication skills in the target language as well as international perspectives and the spirit of international cooperation and collaboration (Monbusho, 1999b, p. 11). Despite the international emphasis of the national curriculum, however, current practices in high school English courses in Japan typically do not have international coverage; rather, they focus almost exclusively on Inner Circle models for teaching. Some examples drawn from my research at Chuo High School illustrate this point.

Preference for Inner Circle English

Teachers at the school had a clear preference for American English. When asked about this preference, one teacher said that, as the United States was the most influential country both economically and culturally, it would not make sense to consider other varieties as the target for teaching. In class, he and his colleagues often made references to U.S. society and culture. Occasionally, they referred to the pronunciation and vocabulary differences found among American, British, and Australian English. However, they made no references to English varieties elsewhere, including postcolonial countries such as Hong Kong and Singapore, which are closer to Japan geographically and where English plays a significant role in society (Matsuda, 2000).

In 1987, the Japanese government initiated the Japan Exchange and Teaching (JET) Program to bring to Japan young people who could support foreign language instruction and promote international understanding locally. For at least a decade, Chuo High School had had foreign teachers in the English department, all of whom were from Inner Circle countries. The three I observed all taught oral communication courses in which they referred extensively to their home cultures, U.S. or Canadian. Although this in itself provided students with an opportunity to learn about and be in contact with English speaking cultures, the exclusive focus on teachers from Inner Circle countries led the learners to perceive these as the only English-speaking cultures.

Unsurprisingly therefore, learners at Chuo High School knew very little about varieties of English other than American and British. When I surveyed them about their knowledge of English varieties outside the Inner Circle, the most frequent responses were *don't know* and *not sure*. During interviews, they stated that they did not know English was spoken in countries such as Singapore, India, or the Philippines and that they were not interested in learning such varieties. They perceived American and British English as the standard varieties to acquire in preference to any Outer Circle varieties such as Singapore English, although they also admitted that they had no knowledge of these varieties (Matsuda, 2003b).

In the textbooks used, English speakers and uses of English outside the Inner Circle were also underrepresented. The overwhelming majority of the main characters in these textbooks were from either Japan or the Inner Circle. In the few instances where characters from Outer Circle or Expanding Circle countries appeared, they had lesser roles than Japanese and Inner Circle characters did (Matsuda, 2002). Consequently, the majority of the dialogues were either between Japanese characters and native English speakers or exclusively among native English speakers. Exchanges exclusively between nonnative speakers, which are increasingly the case (Graddol, 1997; Jenkins, 2000; L. E. Smith, 1983; Widdowson, 1994), were found much less often.

Negative Perceptions of Japanese-Accented English

One implication of the features of teaching and learning outlined was that learners and teachers had negative perceptions of Japanese-accented English. As the major varieties taught were American and occasionally British English, the learners believed these were the only acceptable forms and therefore that their own English was unacceptable. At Chuo High School, although a few students recognized an accent as inevitable, the majority believed that English pronounced with a Japanese accent would be unintelligible, even though most of them had never had opportunities to communicate in English. As one student put it, a Japanese accent was "not cool" and was disappointing (Matsuda, 2003b, p. 492). In class, some Japanese teachers of English regularly apologized for their bad pronunciation, and both teachers and students equated accented speech with an inability to communicate orally with native English speakers.

No Discussion of EIL

I indicated earlier that one of the national curriculum goals is to deepen international understanding of cultures and languages, in this case through the use of English. However, discussion of how the English language has spread and is used internationally is rare. The newest edition of a reading textbook used at Chuo High School, *Unicorn English Reading* (Ichikawa et al., 2003) includes 16 readings that address a wide variety of topics, including environmental issues, history, education, intercultural exchange and understanding, world peace, sports, and economics. However, none addresses the influence of English internationally or its colonial past (or present).

In addition, teachers do not seem to believe this topic is either interesting or important. During the 3 months I spent at the school, only one teacher touched on the issue of the *linguistic imperialism* (Phillipson, 1992) of English. In class, he described e-mail exchanges with an English-speaking colleague in Boston. Although he struggled to compose a short message, his colleague would send back a long reply immediately. He told his students how unfair he thought it was that his colleague always got to use his native language simply because he happened to speak English. When asked, the teacher stated that he did not believe this anecdote interested students much. However, several students approached me after class and also complained how unfair it was to have to learn another language while English speakers used their first language in most places internationally.

◈ DISTINGUISHING FEATURES

Neglect of Varieties of English

The literature on World Englishes suggests that when English is transplanted to a new sociocultural and sociolinguistic environment, it deviates from its original form in order to become more appropriate in the new context. Each *nativized* (Kachru, 1992b) variety becomes legitimate in its context, even when it differs from more widely used varieties. Consequently, there are multiple varieties that could serve as instructional models in EIL classrooms.

In the ELT situation described above and in the majority of high schools in Japan, Inner Circle Englishes, in most cases American English, are usually presented as the only legitimate varieties. This assumption about which variety is legitimate is reinforced by Japanese EFL teachers' preferences for Inner Circle Englishes (Chiba, Matsuura, & Yamamoto, 1995; Matsuda, 2000, 2003a; Matsuura, Chiba, & Yamamoto, 1994). The textbooks used in Japanese classrooms also reinforce the Inner Circle notion of English. For instance, in an analysis of seventh-grade introductory EFL textbooks approved by the Ministry of Education (Matsuda, 2002), I found that all were based on American English.

Even if American (or British) English is selected as the target instructional model, it is important for students to understand that this English is one of many varieties they may come across in the future. The neglect of English varieties outside the Inner Circle in the prevailing curriculum may lead to confusion or resistance when students are confronted with an unfamiliar variety. Unfamiliarity may even lead to negative attitudes and lack of respect for such Englishes and their speakers if students see them as deficient rather than different from the American and British English that they are more familiar with. To become more aware of and familiar with varieties other than American or British English, students need increased exposure to multiple varieties of English. This does not mean, of course, that students must acquire multiple varieties; however, increased exposure to different varieties would facilitate better understanding of the multiplicity of forms of the target language.

Contact Mainly With Inner Circle Users of English

The native-English-speaking teachers students had contact with were from Inner Circle countries. This dominance of Inner Circle speakers is a prevailing feature of the demographics of assistant English teachers (AETs) recruited through the JET Program. During the first year of the program, all 848 AETs came from Inner Circle countries, specifically the United States, the United Kingdom, Australia, and New Zealand. The program began recruiting in two other Inner Circle countries, Canada and Ireland, in 1988 and later in three Outer Circle countries: South Africa, Singapore, and Jamaica. But participants from the Inner Circle have consistently and significantly outnumbered those from the three Outer Circle countries; in 2000, 98% of the 5,444 AETs came from the Inner Circle (Monbukagakusho, 2001).

Such factors in the school environment reinforce students' views that only speakers in the Inner Circle count (Matsuda, 2003b), thus overlooking the rapid increase in the use of English among so-called nonnative speakers of English. With such a picture of English users constantly presented to them, students will not understand the significant use of English among nonnative speakers and may therefore not envisage that they can take advantage of the opportunities that accompany the use of EIL.

Negative Attitudes Toward Their Accent

Although nativelike pronunciation may be desirable for certain purposes, it is not the most crucial aspect of communicative effectiveness. Placing too much emphasis on nativelike pronunciation could be counterproductive when learners feel embarrassed about their accent and hesitate to use the language for that reason. Through increased exposure to other nonnative English speakers as well as opportunities to interact in English, a curriculum can encourage learners to understand that their accented English can be effective in international communication and can facilitate more positive attitudes toward their accent.

Need for Discussion of the Past, Present, and Future of the Spread of English

The classroom example above of e-mail exchanges between a Japanese teacher of English and a native speaker of English in Boston suggests that discussion of the spread of English and the complexities of the power inequalities reinforced by the use of English internationally could be an engaging topic for high school students. To become responsible users of EIL, students need to understand the history, current status, and future implications of the spread of English. Such knowledge would allow students to contextualize better the language and their perceptions of it and to critically examine their role in shaping the future of English in Japan and internationally.

❖ PRACTICAL IDEAS

There are many ways to facilitate a better sociolinguistic understanding of the English language in the instructional situation discussed above. Below are some examples of strategies for preparing learners more effectively for the use of EIL within the current curriculum. One important aspect of these strategies is that they can draw on existing, but possibly underutilized, resources in the school.

Introduce Students to English Speakers From Various Backgrounds

One way to increase learners' awareness of different varieties of English is to enable them to interact as much as possible with speakers of such Englishes. Students can be exposed to different varieties of English while interacting with people from parts of the world they are not very familiar with. Such interactions also provide opportunities for authentic communication, which is often difficult to achieve in an EFL context. Positive engagement in these interactions would also enable learners to perceive that their English, while accented, can be effective in communicating with other English speakers. They can also increase their awareness of English varieties by focusing on different language features and comparing them.

The English speakers with whom students have contact may also be English teachers. As noted in the Distinguishing Features section, nonlocal teachers in EFL countries are overwhelmingly from Inner Circle countries. However, qualified teachers of English from Outer and Expanding Circle countries can be just as effective in complementing native-English-speaking teachers and nonnative-English-speaking, local teachers of English (Matsuda & Matsuda, 2001). Chuo High School, for example, regularly hires two or three non-Japanese teachers of English to teach oral communication and assist with other courses. A few years ago, one teacher was from Eastern Europe and had a master's degree from the United States, while at another school, one of several non-Japanese teachers was Indian. In both cases, students responded to them as positively as they did to English teachers from the Inner Circle because these teachers provided them with an opportunity to practice using English for actual communication, just as other non-Japanese teachers did.

Another way to introduce students to speakers of various Englishes is to invite international visitors or residents in the community to class. Chuo High School has short-term exchange programs with schools in the United States, Europe, and Asia, and thus regularly has international visitors on campus. Exchange students usually have their own curriculum and have little direct contact with Japanese students, but they occasionally visit English classes or participate in extracurricular activities. Visiting and hosting students are curious about each other's lives and use whatever linguistic resources they have to learn from each other, English being the most common mutual language. These interactions could be built more consistently into classroom activities. In addition to providing opportunities for using EIL, such personal contacts can broaden students' interests and encourage them to learn more about the countries their international friends come from.

Focus on Communicative Effectiveness

One limitation of the exclusive representation of an Inner Circle variety of English, as I discuss in the Description section, is that students may think that it is the only acceptable variety and that communication is not possible unless they acquire nativelike proficiency. Local and standardized language exams that are based solely on Inner Circle norms serve to reinforce such assumptions. Students do not consider themselves English users, even when they can conduct conversations with international visitors, because their pronunciation is not nativelike and their vocabulary is limited (Matsuda, 2000, 2003b). The idea that only native speakers qualify as English users prevents students from making any claims to ownership of English and exploring ways to use the language for their own benefits.

One way to address this problem is to redefine the goals of language instruction in terms of communicative effectiveness rather than grammatical correctness based on U.S. or British norms and to evaluate students accordingly. This, of course, does not mean that grammatical accuracy is unimportant. However, the required level of grammatical competence should be defined in context, and arguably the native standard is not what most EIL learners need.

Through such instruction, combined with opportunities to use the language for communication, students are more likely to realize that nativelike pronunciation and perfect grammar are not prerequisites for successful communication. Getting feedback on aspects of language learning other than how closely they approximate the language of native speakers not only facilitates the development of communicative competence but also encourages learners to use English in spite of their accents and fosters a more positive attitude toward their own utterances in English.

Supplement Teaching Materials

In the EFL classroom, textbooks tend to play a dominant role in the curriculum (Bardovi-Harlig, 1996). Especially in a country like Japan, where public schools are required to use textbooks approved by the government, the books gain great authority and may become the de facto curriculum. However, such EFL textbooks, as discussed earlier, tend to be Inner Circle oriented (Iwata et al., 2002; Kiryu, Shibata, Tagaya, & Wada, 1999; Matsuda, 2002). English uses and users from the Outer and Expanding Circles, although not completely absent, receive only peripheral attention. In order to raise students' awareness of the increasing role English users from the Outer and Expanding Circles have in shaping the English language, teachers need to compensate for this imbalance in textbook representations.

One way to do so is to extend current limited references by highlighting non-Inner-Circle populations as well as the plurality of English. Classroom discussions can, for instance, address explicit statements made in textbooks about the forms and functions of English. Such statements as "Pronunciation of English varies in different countries and regions" (Shimaoka, Aoki, Matsuhata, & Wada, 1997, p. 40) and "English is a world common language. It is an important means of communication when speaking with people from other Asian countries, too" (Sasaki, 1997, p. 95) can become the basis of oral or written tasks and be addressed in more depth.

Another strategy is to bring in supplemental materials that introduce students to different varieties of English. Movies, videos, and audio clips, which are already found quite often in oral communication classes, can be used to introduce varieties of English and to facilitate discussion about the place of English in parts of the world that may not be covered by the textbooks. Databases of World Englishes that contain examples of different varieties from different genres are also available (e.g., Baik & Shim, 2002a).

Relate English to Other Subject Courses

Cross-references to other courses that address similar issues can facilitate an awareness of the world and the spread of English. For instance, in World History, students learn about the rise of the British Empire, which has direct relevance to the spread of English. A geography class may focus on areas of the world where English has some distinctive function (e.g., a lingua franca in India). Courses in world studies or contemporary politics cannot avoid such topics as power; peace and international policies; and political, economic, and educational divides, which have also been the subject of debate in the study of World Englishes.

Team teaching a lesson or unit would be ideal, but when that is not plausible, making reference to what students learn in other courses would help them anchor the language in its historical and present context. Many EFL teachers already talk in class about their experiences in an English-speaking country or the use of loan words in a local language because they feel such metalinguistic awareness is useful in motivating students to learn English (Matsuda, 2000); there is no reason such discussion cannot be expanded beyond the Inner Circle English-speaking countries and no reason other courses students are taking should not be used as a resource.

Expand Foreign Language Offerings

Although it may sound paradoxical, the international dominance of English is a reminder of the significance of other languages. Although English may be an important language to learn for international communication today, that fact does not make English better or more important than other languages in the world. It would be naive and arrogant to think that English is and always will be the most appropriate choice of the language for intercultural communication (Graddol, 2001). Responsible users of EIL need to be aware of the potential threat that English may pose to other, especially minority, languages and be sensitive to other languages in the world, including their own.

Also, from a more practical point of view, English may not be the language of choice in all cases of intercultural communication. Though English is more widely used and learned than any other language, not everyone in the world speaks it. Even those who speak English may prefer to use other languages for personal, social, or political reasons. In such situations, knowledge of languages other than English may become more valuable.

One way to sensitize students to the power relationship between English and other languages and to better equip them linguistically for intercultural communica-tion is to offer other foreign languages. This choice is especially relevant in communities with a substantial number of immigrants; offering instruction in the major languages immigrants speak helps students get to know members of their community better. The languages of neighboring countries, for example, Chinese and Korean in the case of Japan, would also be good candidates for such offerings.

◈ CONCLUSION

This chapter has focused on one aspect of ELT: the sociolinguistic representation of the target language vis-à-vis the needs of EIL learners. Of course, other issues need to be closely examined when designing or revising a curriculum, such as the quality of exercises and activities or the appropriateness of vocabulary selection, and a description of the sociolinguistic representation alone is not a complete curriculum. However, by focusing on a component that, from my research findings, seems to be completely absent in existing curricula in Japan, I aimed to illustrate that programs that prepare learners for the use of EIL must provide a comprehensive landscape of English uses today. I have also attempted to show that it is possible to adapt an existing program without giving up everything that is already in place.

Inevitably, the suggestions made in this chapter complicate EFL teaching, which is often based on a traditional, monolithic view of English in which learners are given the impression that there exists one correct, standard way of using English that speakers of all other varieties should strive for. However, even though it might be complicated and challenging, a curriculum based on a more inclusive and pluralistic view of English has strengths that traditional ones do not have. Such a curriculum better prepares learners for their future uses of English and better reflects the complex reality of EIL.

◈ CONTRIBUTOR

Aya Matsuda is an assistant professor of applied linguistics at the University of New Hampshire, in the United States, where she teaches undergraduate and graduate courses in TESL and linguistics. Her research interests include sociolinguistics and language teaching, World Englishes, and intercultural communication.

PART 3

Which Language?

CHAPTER 6

Reaching Resolutions: Negotiating a Global English in a Multicultural Classroom

Simone Evans

◈ INTRODUCTION

As an ESOL teacher struggling with the implications of the globalization of English, I have found myself in a bind. Should I teach the discourse style or styles with which I am most familiar as the English-speaking norm? Or should I pretend that language is a norm-free, culture-independent entity that learners can use in any way they want without incurring negative consequences?

This concern was not simply theoretical. I had listened to learners' stories of out-of-class interactions that had been extremely frustrating or embarrassing for them. I had observed transactional talk in out-of-class contexts in which learners whom I knew to be well intentioned clearly offended those they were dealing with and, in turn, felt that they had been treated badly or with prejudice. I noticed in myself a tendency to react negatively to particular paralinguistic usage, even when a learner might be thanking me or making a request to which I was sympathetic. When, finally, I challenged another teacher on her claims that she knew that a learner was being sincere based on facial and other paralinguistic and extralinguistic behaviors, I realized that I needed to explore new approaches to the teaching of language and its accompanying norms. If teachers with experience in intercultural interaction and linguistics could still, at some level, respond negatively to different language usage, what hope was there for learners dealing with Australians and others in and outside the classroom?

This chapter discusses my attempt to explore a new approach. It describes a program I designed as part of my doctoral research aimed at increasing English learners' awareness of the many interactional and behavioral norms often present in a multicultural classroom. In the program, English was an explorative mechanism rather than the unmarked norm. The adult ESOL learners undertaking the course were encouraged to make choices about the discourse style they would use when speaking English in different contexts. At the same time, there was an emphasis on the learners' becoming aware of the choices and assumptions that other learners from different backgrounds might make. In this way, I hoped that their understanding and use of English would be global in nature, molded by Kachru's (1985) Outer Circle and Expanding Circle Englishes rather than by a native-speaking norm.

◈ CONTEXT

Educational Setting

The program took place at a private educational institution in Sydney, Australia. With approximately 250 learners, it is one of the larger language schools in the city, with a majority of its learner body being from North Asia and Brazil. At the time of the program delivery, however, there were increasing numbers of learners from Europe, other parts of South America, and Southeast Asia. Learners generally ranged in age from 17 to 35, with those over 22 years of age tending to be tertiary educated.

The classes on offer were, in the main, general intensive English classes. In addition to the weekly syllabus, each learner in these classes chose an option class 1 day a week that was intended to provide additional opportunities to extend language use in ways that were of interest to the learners and that may not have been pursued in regular classes. Option classes took a variety of forms: small-group projects, examination of different thematic or textual materials, or development of specific skills such as pronunciation or listening. One such option class was the program I delivered, Real-Life Negotiation for Business and University, advertised simply as a class that would facilitate the learners' ability to express themselves in problematic situations.

Learner Profile

The majority of the learners at the school were not intending to remain in Australia but had come for periods ranging from 2 weeks to 9 months. Following their study and some travel, most intended to return to their home country to find employment. Many took on low-paid, part-time work such as waiting or cleaning to support themselves while studying.

Nine learners chose to take my program (see Table 1 for their nationality, first language [L1], age, gender, and class level as well as an estimated speaking proficiency level at the time the course began). The learners' speaking ability varied considerably despite the class level, because, in the determination of proficiency levels, spoken proficiency often did not play a role, as a speaking test was optional,

TABLE 1. LEARNER PROFILES

Learner	Nationality	L1	Sex	Age	ACTFL (1998) level	Class
Russell	Japanese	Japanese	M	28	Intermediate—low	Upper intermediate
Graeme	Brazilian	Portuguese	M	19	Intermediate—high	Intermediate
Julia	Japanese	Japanese	F	23	Intermediate—mid	Intermediate
Milly	Russian	Russian	F	14	Advanced	Upper intermediate
David	Korean	Korean	M	28	Intermediate—mid	Upper intermediate
Kate	Czech	Czech	F	23	Intermediate—high	Intermediate
Stephanie	Colombian	Spanish	F	26	Advanced	Intermediate
Chad	Thai	Thai	M	22	Intermediate—mid	Intermediate
Sam	Brazilian	Portuguese	M	23	Intermediate—mid	Intermediate

unlike compulsory tests on reading, writing, listening, and English usage or grammar.

Learners gave a variety of reasons for undertaking the course, but three broad areas emerged from the brief comments on the forms they completed on enrollment, diary entries recorded and comments made to me during the program, and the interviews following the course.

First, learners expressed a broad interest in improving their speaking. This interest appeared to embody a desire to be able to express themselves with greater ease and in a manner more representative of their personality. They reported that they had found themselves panicking in certain situations and not knowing what to say, that they felt their English lacked subtlety in comparison with their L1 use, that they did not have strategies with which to approach certain situations, and that they were fearful of speaking on certain occasions due to a lack of confidence. These comments are representative of those made when learners compared their postcourse confidence with how they had felt before undertaking the course:

I learnt how to make strategy, strategies during conversation. Because [in the past] every time I said what I want to say directly but mm I can use indirect and I use strategy, I can think strategy. (Russell, Japanese, interview)

Before [in the past] I want to talk someone [unintelligible] scary about my mistake. I think oh maybe worry, something's wrong. But, but, yeah [unintelligible] because I think after this course if I say something wrong it doesn't matter my friends give help to me, tell me what is right and give help to me. (Chad, Thai, interview)

One day when I came late and, and Claudia was serious with me
   [Interviewer: This is your host mother?]
   Yeah that's my work, some money [for acting as nanny]. Then I tell her "my understanding is . . ." [laughter] and I expressed in very, very good. . . . I was relaxed when I finish because sometimes [in the past] I was "Oh my god, what I'm gonna say in this moment?" (Stephanie, Colombian, interview)

The second reason for taking the course was a desire to be able to participate in more authentic interactions with the broader community, or what the learners termed *real Australians*. They expected to do this in what they appeared to believe was real or nativelike English:

I'd like to learn real word which is said real Australian. (David, Korean, needs analysis)

I want to understand what people talking to me. (Chad, Thai, needs analysis)

I want to speak as a native speaker. (Kate, Czech, needs analysis)

Because I always feel shy to speak with native speakers. (Milly, Russian, needs analysis)

This expressed desire added to the list of issues I needed to address in my attempt to teach a global English, particularly because it was a wish shared by all the learners, regardless of the level of interaction they had with the community. Five of the learners participating in the program had part-time work. Three lived with homestay families; one learner was a live-in nanny. Half of the learners in the class lived with speakers of the same language and, as a result, reported having limited interaction with the Australian community or experience speaking English with others outside school hours.

Finally, three learners listed the benefit to their career as their major reason for undertaking the course. For this reason, and because only one learner was intending to undertake tertiary studies in Australia, the negotiation role plays given to learners during the course were set in a business context rather than an academic or a social one.

◈ DESCRIPTION

The program ran 1 day a week over 4 weeks. It involved both in-class and out-of-class tasks, and required learners to analyze their own discourse practices, those of other learners, and those of the speech community in which they were living at the time.

Negotiation Role Plays

At the heart of the program lay a series of dyadic, superordinate/subordinate, workplace-based negotiation role plays featuring a clear conflict of interest and an imbalance of power between the two negotiating parties. I developed these scenarios in a deliberate departure from the can-do spoken texts traditionally used in the ESOL classroom, which model and practice talk as if it is always unproblematic and conflict-free in the outside world (Burns, Joyce, & Gollin, 1997; Carter, 1997).

These negotiation role plays were videotaped before, during, and following the course. The first negotiation, filmed before the program began, formed the basis for the work done during the course (see the Appendix for the scenarios). Following each negotiation and every class, learners recorded their views of that learning experience and their evaluation of their own negotiation in a diary. Following their first negotiating experience, they identified what they wanted to learn how to do by identifying the problems that had arisen for them during the talk. These problems can be summarized as follows:

- losing control over the agenda
- forgetting their own objective
- being unable to find the right words to explain their position
- being unable to listen to the interlocutor because of a focus on their own argument
- being unable to understand the vocabulary used by the interlocutor
- expecting more direction from the boss
- expecting that the boss would be more authoritarian
- feeling defensive

Each lesson within the program then pursued a particular linguistic or paralinguistic theme related to conflict management negotiation as a *linguistic text*, defined by Fairclough (1995) as a whole piece of written or spoken language. These classes were aimed at raising learners' awareness of how their discourse practices differed from those of other learners and those of native English speakers.

Initially, in addition to examining their individual experiences of negotiation, learners explored the way such an encounter might be structured in their own culture and in an English-speaking environment, in terms of the generic stages a given interaction or text type typically passes through (Martin, 1985). In mixed language groups, they recorded the types of language and arguments they would put forward should such a scenario be undertaken in their own culture and language, and watched a video of two native speakers of English undertaking the same negotiation (again interacting without the use of scripted or prescribed dialogue) for comparative purposes. This revealed intercultural differences in such areas as

- how the talk might be opened and closed (Schegloff & Sacks, 1974)

- how topics were initiated (Schegloff & Sacks, 1974)

- how any hostility encountered might be managed (Ury, Brett, & Goldberg, 1988; Vuchinich, 1990)

- how these actions would be achieved via morphosyntax and lexis (Murphy & Neu, 1996), with one learner noting, "The strange thing is 'empathis[ing] with manager's position.' I don't think, in Japan, I say to my boss, 'I understand you [are] under pressure'" (Russell, Japanese, diary entry)

Indeed, the Japanese learners expressed doubts that a meeting in which a subordinate challenged a superordinate would even take place in their culture, an acknowledgment of difference supported by the literature (Yamada, 1990).

Additionally, the roles of pitch, intonation, and pace in politeness were covered briefly. I supplied examples of how two identical utterances could produce different meanings. The learners, in turn, experimented with the ways in which they conveyed emotion through their voice in their own cultures. Stephanie (Colombian) afterwards wrote in her diary: "Interesting: How the intonation and voice tone can change the idea of the conversation."

Awareness of How Emotions Are Conveyed

The second day of the course was aimed primarily at facilitating learners' awareness of how sincerity, politeness, and a variety of emotions are conveyed in their own culture. We then discussed how this might differ from the expression of the same emotion in the cultures of the other class members and in Australia.

This exploration took place through a series of small-group guessing games in which learners had to guess what emotion was being expressed and record exactly what the nominated learner was doing with his or her eyes, face, and voice. One learner discovered that he did not know how to manipulate his facial muscles to produce a frown. He recorded that "the most useful things I learnt today is expressions about my face, my face always smile but in English I'm to make serious face, it difference from my culture" (Chad, Thai, diary entry).

Chad's experimentation with his face created intense discussion among the learners regarding the acceptability or otherwise of displaying emotion, something that appears to differ greatly across cultures (Ekman, 1997). One learner commented,

It's really different from Russian even though use it with my sister, it's really different because when, when you see, I saw my father at the office, he just shouting and just because now he just tried not to lose his temper but he just shouting and [unintelligible].

[Interviewer: So you're saying that it's acceptable to shout? If you're angry, it's okay to shout?]

Yeah, it's okay. Maybe it's not okay but everyone do it, just and . . .

[Interviewer: So it's been very different for you [during this course]?]

When I was boss I just tried to, tried not to shout but huh, huh, huh [exhales to express frustration]. (Milly, Russian, interview)

The facial expression tasks were followed by an exploration of indirectness and politeness strategies more generally (Brown & Levinson, 1987). Learners completed a series of replacement and matching tasks that compared negative and positive politeness strategies and indirect and direct examples of language and expression. Interestingly, although the use of politeness strategies is said to differ greatly across cultures (Beal, 1990), the learners generally appeared to see this part of the class as an opportunity to bring their English more into line with their L1 usage rather than as an area of great cultural difference.

Following their experimentation with face and voice, I set learners an out-of-class diary task. This was primarily aimed at comparing their own discourse norms with those publicly on display in the surrounding community. This task, reproduced here, is followed by some cultural comparisons learners made after the activity:

Listening for Emotion

Listen for two people talking (in a train, bus, pub, your homestay). Wait until one person is doing most of the talking, and answer these questions:

1. What emotion is the person conveying?
2. What is his or her face/voice doing?
3. What is the story about (if you can understand it)?
4. How is the second person responding? Voice? Face? Words?
5. How is watching these people talk different from watching people talk in your country?

In Japan, we don't use our hand. Not so move our face. So it looks overstate for me. (Julia, Japanese, diary entry)

Most of [the people on the train] are contacting eyes when they are talking. In Korea we don't contact all the time. It means very rude and some times looks impudent manner. (David, Korean, diary entry)

In another out-of-class task, I asked learners to watch and analyze the video of their first negotiation. The learners' comments made it clear that they had previously been unaware of how their linguistic and paralinguistic behaviors appeared to others. This appeared to be a source of considerable surprise to them:

I was laughing all the time but I didn't know that before I saw the video. So I want to control my face more sirious when I speak my mistake or listen to manager's anger. (David, Korean, diary entry)

I have to speak more clearly because my voice is not clear and very low. Maybe, I think, maybe other people difficult to understand for my speech. I have to speak more clearly. (Russell, Japanese, interview)

Additionally, seeing their first negotiation appeared to give the learners a sense of how much greater their abilities to manipulate their linguistic behaviors had become.

Diary entries and anecdotes of their negotiating achievements began to appear about this time:

> I asked my boss if I can have more hours of working but it's quite difficult to talk to her. She started to be angry so I said "Ooh, don't be angry, I like this job, I want to continue . . ." [laughs] and ooooooohhh . . . so she interrupt her mood and she to be more friendly . . . yeah, yeah, maybe I used something from negotiation. (Kate, Czech, interview)

> I have used it [negotiation skills learned during the course] one time.
>   [Interviewer: Really? Tell me what happened.]
>   Flattery [laughter] 'cause my homestay don't like that sometimes I get home late for dinner or some meals so she was one day, I could see her face [imitates fear].
>   [Interviewer: Very angry?]
>   and I said "Oh I'm sorry, I know that you are a very good cook and your food is wonderful, but sometimes, I love your food but . . . I didn't get . . ." and she was "oh thank you, but don't do it again. . . ." (Graeme, Brazilian, interview)

> 3 days ago I went home very late and my sister yelled to me. She said that I will never go out again. I went to my room, read all the papers from our lessons, then came to my sister's room. I explained everything, how it was important for me and why I didn't call her. I used eye contack my voice were low and I use flattering. And . . . I won!!! Tomorrow I'll go out again with the same friend. (Milly, Russian, diary entry)

Viewing Each Other as Role Models

Toward the end of the program, learners undertook a negotiation role play in which they watched and were required to comment on the best aspects of each other's performances. As well as reportedly increasing learners' confidence, the activity appeared to mark a crucial turning point for the learners. From having previously relied on native-speaking models represented by their textbooks, teachers, and other contacts in Sydney, learners began to look to each other for language usage models:

> The most useful thing is that I watched another learner's negotiation. It was very instructive for me. When I find their good point, I can improve my skill. (Russell, Japanese, diary entry)

> The most useful thing I learnt from [Kate] today. Because of her face. It's wonderful how she can use flattering face. I want to do the same. (Milly, Russian, diary entry)

> [In the past] I didn't use body language [moving her arms from side to side and swaying] but I can use [it now], I think.
>   [Interviewer: Did you copy? How did you learn this? Who did you copy from?]
>   Stephanie. Her body language is so beautiful and goooood. (Julia, Japanese, interview)

> [Interviewer: You said you learnt from other students?]
>   Yes, I learnt from . . . copy acting, copy the word . . . it's fast to learn—just copy the person [makes gestures indicating many people]. . . . (Chad, Thai, interview)

Exploring Expressions of Power and Authority

On the last day of the course, the learners and I explored ways in which power and authority are conveyed through body motion and the use of space. Had there been time, a fuller exploration of proxemics, particularly in the area of furniture and its use, might have brought to light greater cultural difference in how territory is owned and controlled (Hall, 1966). This exploration would have been of particular value to learners operating in the globalized business world, where such seemingly trivial matters may play an important role in an interaction.

In any case, during this class it was increasingly obvious that the learners were making overt choices regarding whose behaviors they wanted to use themselves or whether they would maintain their own behaviors while negotiating. They were apparently also more accustomed to looking at and listening to the behaviors of others analytically—a skill I believe to be important because it is a resource for lifelong, independent learning in a way that many other skills taught within the ESOL classroom are not. As one learner noted following the course,

> When I ride on the train I listen the other people's dialogue. . . . Before people discuss I didn't listen the other people's dialogue but after this class . . . I manage to listen to what are they saying ah then if I can't understand [I think] what's the next stage? So other people's listening, I imagine what is saying. (David, Korean, interview)

Finally, we examined the use of facial expression and intonation rather than lexis or syntax in expressing agreement and disagreement, so critical when negotiating. This area is possibly the one in which I was most guilty of prescribing a native-speaking norm. I found it difficult to teach this aspect of communication in any other way, because the way ESOL learners are often taught to agree and disagree textbook style would appear to be unrepresentative of any culture's language usage.

Klippel (1984), for example, lists *OK* and *I (fully) agree with you* as means of agreement and *I don't agree* or *I don't think so* as typical ways to disagree (pp. 194–195). Not only are these utterances atypical, however (Davidson, 1984; Gardner, 2000; Pomerantz, 1984; Sacks, 1987; Schiffrin, 1987), but whether an expression such as *OK* indicates acceptance or rejection of the preceding utterance is dependent entirely on the pitch changes used to produce it. In other words, the lexis does not stand alone but requires paralinguistic interpretation.

Because this interpretation is culture or discourse-style specific, I was left with two options. I could have taught a list of formulaic expressions, such as those suggested by Klippel (1984), on the (false) assumption that focus on the literal utterance is sufficient for understanding the response of others. Alternatively, I had the option of teaching learners to identify the crucial role pitch may play in determining the meaning of such a response: a type of know-this-usage-is-out-there warning signal, or what Clyne (1994) has termed a *passive knowledge* of a discourse style. In pursuing the latter course, as I did, I risked giving the impression that it was the norm that all learners should pursue when speaking the language, regardless of the context. On the other hand, it certainly raised learners' awareness of one of the major pitfalls possible in intercultural communication. The task I used to highlight this feature is reproduced in Figure 1.

Following these tasks, and outside class, learners requested additional opportunities to watch themselves on video, which I provided. At the course's end, all learners reported an increase in their ability to understand the talk around them as well as increased confidence when interacting verbally. They attributed this variously to listening more critically to the public talk around them, to repeatedly undertaking the out-of-class pronunciation tasks, and, in the case of one learner, to the fact that she had been obliged to listen and understand people from other cultures:

[Interviewer: What are you most proud of?]

Listening, because it's very important and er sometimes I can't to listen somebody because I have to thinking about my problem and I can't er respond after so maybe listening, I think that

[Interviewer: So you mean you listen better now?]

Yeah, Yeah, I'm able to concentrate to speech of another, other people, person

[Interviewer: Right, oh that's great. Why is that? How did this happen?]

I think that it happened because of people from different cultures, and their pronunciation is difficult to understand and I have to concentrate er . . . er but I'm er I know how to . . . , I understand them now because I know their pronunciation and I know that somebody can't to pronounce some letter and now I know what does it mean without this letter. . . . (Kate, Czech, interview)

◈ DISTINGUISHING FEATURES

Several features of the program distinguish it from others that endeavor to teach speaking, discussion, or verbal interaction.

Decide whether these responses agree or disagree with the statement. Pay careful attention to voice and face as the responses are read.

1	2	3	4	5
Strongly disagree	Disagree	Neutral	Agree	Strongly agree

Your boss: "I tend to think we should give Sarah the job."

Response	Agreement
Absolutely.	_____
We could do that.	_____
Yeeeaaaaaah, yeah.	_____
Yeah, for sure. Her people management skills are good.	_____
Okay. Okay. Her people management skills are good.	_____
Hmm Hmm. What kind of training do you think she'd need?	_____
I'm not sure . . . . But she's probably the best person.	_____
Brilliant idea. What'll we tell Mark, though?	_____
Yeeeah, but what would we tell Mark?	_____
Weeell, that sounds fine.	_____

FIGURE 1. Agreeing and Disagreeing

Learner Choice

The program focused explicitly on the learners' choice of which language behaviors to use in a given situation, rather than their being determined by the teacher or syllabus. This element of choice is important given the debate surrounding which norms should drive a global English. Because of the diversity of discourse styles and the misunderstanding that they may create, there can be no single set of norms. Nor can comprehensibility alone be a guide because interlocutors may comprehend while still misunderstanding (Gumperz, 1995; Linell, 1995). Enabling learners to make context-specific choices would, therefore, appear to be a more viable approach for ESOL teachers in a multicultural classroom.

Focus on Pragmatics

Learners had choices available to them because of the program's emphasis on raising awareness of a multiplicity of discourse behaviors or practices. As Bennett (1986) has argued, the key to intercultural sensitivity is an acknowledgment of difference. If learners interact with people from other cultures while assuming commonality of social and linguistic behaviors, the interaction is unlikely to be successful. If, however, learners start with some expectation of difference and some experience of how that difference might be embodied in talk, the English they use will presumably become a more tolerant and, therefore, intercultural channel of communication.

The pragmatic features of language provide a key to this exploration of differing norms. Learners can and do assume an ability to translate the grammar and vocabulary of one language to another. It is much more difficult to do this with linguistic and paralinguistic behaviors. Difference is immediately apparent:

> Culture is strange and interesting and difficult to me. (Chad, Thai, diary entry)

> The strangest things were customs of Asian people to me. (Kate, Czech, diary entry)

However, the pragmatics of this course was not an interlanguage pragmatics that judges learners by their movement toward target-language norms. It was, rather, what Boxer (2002) has labeled a *cross-cultural pragmatics:* one that involved increasing awareness of the multiplicity of norms of the many others with whom a learner is likely to interact.

Learners as Models of a Global English

The course revolved around the use of English by culturally diverse members of the class. This emphasis was embodied in much of the task design itself, so that learners were constantly asked to observe, analyze, and provide (positive) feedback on the linguistic behaviors of other learners in relation to themselves. In this way, the learners became the language models. As a consequence, the English modeled was not the norm-driven variety spoken by a putative real Australian speech community but a global version created in and by a multicultural classroom.

❖ PRACTICAL IDEAS

In delivering this program, I was lucky to be working with a small number of highly motivated learners. I also had much more access to data generated by the learners on their own learning experiences than would ordinarily be the case. This situation strongly reinforced a number of concepts raised in the literature on language teaching and learning. More important, it allowed me to experiment with ways in which I could apply these concepts. Some of what I learned follows.

Put Choice Into the Learners' Hands by Using Video

Although learners have their own agendas in terms of what and how they learn (Breen & Littlejohn, 2000; Swain, 1995), I have felt, on occasion, that the demands of a school syllabus work against truly handing over control to the learners. During this course, however, various means of allowing learners to make decisions about their own language use in an informed manner became evident.

The most important of these means was the use of video. I discovered that repeatedly videotaping learners' language production and setting tasks that ask learners to evaluate themselves allows them to see how they appear to others and decide whether they want to change or maintain their language usage and behaviors. Instead of my assessing the learners, this process enabled them to assess themselves. In place of the umbrella learning plan of the program syllabus, each learner was able to develop, and develop reflectively, an individualized learning plan.

Make Better and More Varied Use of Diaries as Learning Tools

Diaries are not uncommon in ESOL classrooms. They have been used as an ethnographic tool (Bailey, 1991); as journals to develop writing fluency (Harmer, 1991); and as log books of lexis, structure, or other aspects of language garnered during classes (Di Pietro, 1987). The diaries the learners used during this course combined these functions, in addition to their use as a means of

- encouraging learners to reflect on and develop their own learning strategies

- motivating learners to observe and evaluate diverse language use and behaviors in the world outside the classroom

- providing an additional means for learners to communicate any concerns or achievements to me privately

❖ CONCLUSION

The program made use of the resource-rich environment of a multicultural classroom to teach a global or intercultural conception of English. It provided learners with immediate access to a number of the varieties of the language that they may interact with in the future. It raised their awareness of the many pragmatic elements that combine to make meaning as well as inhibit communication. In addition, with some knowledge of the effect their own discourse style may have on others, and of how the interactional behavior of others may affect them, successful intercultural communication is more likely than if learners were simply left to talk, unaware of the enormous cultural implications of such an act.

The program has run again since this case study was conducted. In its second iteration, greater emphasis was placed on the way in which culture influences understandings of appropriate business behaviors and expectations (Beal, 1990) and on demonstrating understanding of one's interlocutor, using reformulation techniques to ensure that learners were listening and responding rather than simulating polite understanding (Aston, 1986).

The different mix of the classroom as well as the learning styles of a different set of individuals meant that the program, too, was somewhat different. However, the basic approach remained unchanged. English sociolinguistic practices were explored critically and compared with those of the learners in the classroom with a view to increasing the range of linguistic behaviors available to learners in a variety of contexts. Similar misunderstandings were generated and later overcome. Similar, too, were the cries of astonishment from learners as they encountered the strange and interesting cultural and sociolinguistic practices of other learners.

◈ CONTRIBUTOR

Simone Evans was awarded her PhD by the University of New South Wales, in Australia, for the research on which this chapter reports. She has taught general English in Australia and Japan as well as business English and English for academic purposes.

◈ APPENDIX: NEGOTIATION SCENARIOS

"Public Humiliation" Precourse Scenario

Two days ago, you met with a client. Three people were at the meeting:

- you
- your boss
- the client (whose name is Jack Brown)

During the meeting, you gave the client wrong information with two results:

- It made your company look bad.
- It will cost your company money.

Your boss was furious. He or she told you *in front of the client* that

- you were incompetent
- he or she would be taking over the relationship with the client from now on

You know you made a big mistake, but you feel totally humiliated by his or her treatment of you.

Go and see your boss. The objective of your meeting with him or her is that he or she never speak to you like that in front of a client again.

"False Promises" Midcourse Scenario

You started a new job 6 months ago. It is a new industry for you, and you were very excited about joining the company.

You saw this job as a chance to start to use your new skills. You have just finished studying [Web design? sales? training? computing? personnel? management?]. Although your new boss said you would continue doing your old job initially, he or she also promised that:

- You would move into an area where you would be using your new skills very quickly.

- You would be first in line for this kind of job.

- You would only continue to do your old job for a while.

Last week a position in your study area came up. A colleague was given this position. You were not even told this position was available.

Go and see your boss. The objective of your meeting is to get a commitment to your starting in the promised role. You want a definite start time, and you want to know exactly what you have to do before then.

"Plagiarism" Midcourse Scenario

A month ago, a student in your class, John, borrowed an essay from you. John said he wanted to borrow it because he didn't know how to write essays well, and he wanted to look at yours. Without your knowing, he copied your essay and handed it in to the lecturer as if it were his. You handed in yours, too.

You got your essay back yesterday. A note from the lecturer said that he or she had given you a failing grade because the essay was plagiarized. You will fail the course because of this.

You asked John to go to the lecturer and tell him or her he had copied your essay. He refused.

Go and see your lecturer. The objective of your meeting is to persuade the lecturer that you didn't copy the essay—John did. You want the lecturer to give you the result you deserve.

"Losing the Tender" Postcourse Scenario

You are manager of marketing and tenders for a large call center company that provides services in billing and customer service for banks and utilities.

Your organization has just lost a tender worth millions of dollars annually. The reason is that the computer systems proposed by Information Technology (IT) did not meet the ABC Company's (your customer's) specifications written in ABC's Request for Tender.

Your tender was hundreds of pages long. You couldn't check everything—and you don't know a lot about computers anyway. You are furious because

- IT has lost the company a lot of money.

- You look bad.

- You never have enough resources to put together tenders properly. They are hundreds of hours of work.

- The head of IT, Janice Porter, has the same status as you. She doesn't have to do what you tell her, and she is very uncooperative.

You have a meeting with your boss. He or she is extremely disappointed, and your job is on the line. The objectives of your meeting are to

- explain your perspective (IT lost this contract, not me)
- get more resources for future tenders
- get guaranteed cooperation from IT in the future

PART 4

Which Standard?

CHAPTER 7

International English Myth and National Englishes Reality in EFL: A Learner Needs Perspective

Oleg Tarnopolsky

◈ INTRODUCTION

This chapter investigates a practical attempt to teach two national varieties of English in one program designed for adult and adolescent learners (from 14 years old) in an Eastern European country, Ukraine. In so doing, it evaluates practical ways of presenting learners of EFL with perspectives on different major national varieties of English. The focus is not on international English, which is considered a teaching myth rather than a linguistic reality.

International English could be considered the best variety of English to teach in EFL contexts, that is, where English does not have any official status—the so-called Expanding Circle countries (Kachru, 1986). The main goal of teaching and learning EFL is to provide learners with a lingua franca that gives them the easiest and broadest access to the most diversified international contacts. If some "internationally acceptable version of the target language" (Willis, 1996, p. 12) "rather than a native speaker variety" (Cook, 1999, p. 198) were taught to all EFL students the world over, it would greatly facilitate their international communication.

However, an internationally accepted and recognized international variety for EFL teaching does not yet exist, and no one can say what the peculiarities of such a variety might be. Currently, therefore, a practical EFL teacher cannot know or teach international English. Such a teacher has to choose a national, native speaker variety of English to teach—from the Inner Circle, not the Outer Circle (Kachru, 1986)— and may have to do so for many years to come. Harmer (2001), citing Svartvik (1998), argues in favor of just such an alternative, which seems reasonable because the varieties in question are the most widespread, accessible, and intelligible to the greatest number of English speakers, both native and nonnative. EFL teachers may either choose the native speaker variety they personally prefer or follow the students' needs, wishes, and requirements. The second is the only option in learner-centered EFL teaching (e.g., Nunan, 1988).

Course design may become complicated if needs analysis reveals that students prefer to learn two varieties of English rather than one. Nevertheless, whatever the difficulties of teaching an EFL course using the variety (or varieties) of English chosen on the basis of a needs analysis, such an approach is worth trying. Its potential for learner centeredness is too great to be neglected when the teaching of an international English is still a thing of the future.

◈ CONTEXT

The program that came to teach two national varieties of the English language has been functioning since 1993 in one of the largest Ukrainian cities, Dnipropetrovsk. I designed it for a commercial language school and developed it in such a way that students did not need to interrupt their work or studies to participate. Classes were held only in the evenings and on weekends—three times a week, 4 hours per class.

Preprogram Learners' Needs Analysis

To cater to the needs of the greatest possible range of potential students, the program design was based on an analysis of learners' needs. I interviewed 300 potential learners in Dniepropetrovsk during 1991–1992 and 225 during 1996–1997, all of whom had expressed interest in learning English. In 1991–1992 (see Tarnopolsky, 1999, 2000, 2003), they represented government employees, business executives, industrial workers, engineers, doctors, researchers in various fields of science and technology, and students of high schools and institutions of higher education. The interviewees' ages ranged from 16 to 50 years. One hundred made frequent trips to other countries for business or different personal reasons, and 97 others often found themselves in situations where they needed to communicate in English.

The questions in the interviews focused on what kind of English potential students preferred to learn—general (survival) English or some kind of English for specific purposes (ESP)—and on students' needs for different communication skills—speaking, listening, reading, and writing. The 1991–1992 interviews revealed that 70% of potential learners set some kind of ESP as their ultimate goal in learning English, with about 65% preferring business English. Therefore, the best solution seemed to be to develop a business English program. But all of the interviewees also wanted general, survival English to prepare them for foreign travel. Learning to write in English attracted very little interest (26% of potential students), as did reading (41%). A two-part program therefore seemed the most rational—the first devoted to survival (everyday, general) English and the second, to ESP (business English).

Program Structure

On the basis of the 1991–1992 interviews, I designed an oral/aural English program (consisting of a preparatory course for beginners, a course in everyday oral/aural communication, and a course in oral/aural business communication), which operated in Dnipropetrovsk for 4 years beginning in 1993. However, during the program the majority of learners (75%) began to feel the need to learn to read and write in English as soon as they had sufficiently mastered oral/aural communication.

These changes in the learners' perceived needs made the inclusion of reading and writing courses necessary, as did the results of the second needs analysis, in 1996–1997. The analysis, which was identical to the first (see Tarnopolsky, 2000, 2003), showed no changes in interviewees' attitudes to learning general English and ESP (business English), but the attitudes toward the four basic language skills were radically different. The overwhelming majority (85%) of potential learners of business English interviewed in 1996–1997 emphasized that they were in equal need of speaking, listening, reading, and writing skills. The difference in perceived needs was probably due to the change in the economic and political situation in Ukraine. As a result, I added reading and writing courses to the program.

The program now consists of seven consecutive, linked autonomous courses:

1. a 2-week preparatory course for beginning-level students

2. a 14-week course devoted to developing students' everyday speaking and listening communication skills and learning basic grammar and vocabulary for oral/aural communication

3. an 8-week course devoted to developing basic skills for writing in a specific field

4. a 10-week general course devoted to developing students' skills in reading texts of nonspecialized content (e.g., general issues of economics, public life)

5. a 14-week oral/aural business communication course, including a focus on conducting various kinds of business talks, negotiations, telephone calls, and meetings

6. an 8-week course devoted to business reading skills (e.g., reading specific texts such as legal documents, memos, and telexes)

7. a 10-week course devoted to developing skills in writing business letters and documents

◈ DESCRIPTION

Varieties of English in the Initial Program

The first version of the program, consisting of three oral/aural courses, was designed to teach British English. Traditionally, that variety of English is the only one taught in Eastern European countries, and the first interviews of potential learners did not ask about their preferences in that respect. However, the third course (business communication) included some American English, mostly in the area of vocabulary. For instance, some terms characteristic of British and American business English, such as the titles of senior business executives (e.g., *a managing director* [Br.] versus *a senior vice president* [Am.]), were introduced in parallel, but there was no specific focus on such differences.

Soon after the program began, however, the problem of language variety came to light. Because I was the principal and, for 2 years, the only teacher in the program, I had a great deal of contact with the majority of the learners, who started asking about the variety of English being taught and voiced their dissatisfaction with being taught only British English. As a result, I decided to conduct another learner needs analysis, this time devoted to the variety of the language to teach.

In 1994–1996, I surveyed 100 students in the three-course oral/aural communication program on the variety of English they preferred to learn (the age groups and professional groups in this survey mirrored those represented in the 1991–1992 interviews). The learners were asked three questions:

1. Would they prefer to learn international English or some native speaker, national variety?

2. If they preferred a national variety, what would it be—British English, American English, Canadian English, Australian English, New Zealand English, Irish English?

3. Would they prefer to learn two varieties of the language instead of one? If yes, what two varieties would they choose?

Learners asked for explanations of the term *international English*. After receiving explanations, only three learners chose international English as their preference. All the others indicated that they considered it artificial, useless for the practical goals that they were pursuing, and, as several learners put it, "not a real English at all." In their answers to the second question, the learners were divided almost equally in their preferences for British (44) or American English (42). The 3 learners who indicated their preference for international English also voted for British English (1) and American English (2). Of the remaining 14 learners, 9 opted for Canadian English, and 5 for the Australian variety (it emerged later that they planned to find jobs in Canada or Australia with the purpose of immigration). Nobody chose the Irish or New Zealand varieties.

The answers to the third question proved to be the most interesting. Seventy learners stated that they would prefer to learn two varieties of the language, British and American. Nine other learners, who had all voiced their preference for Canadian English in answer to the second question, chose the combination of the American and Canadian varieties. No other combinations were suggested by the learners.

The results led to two conclusions: first, that the learners were not psychologically ready for the notion of teaching international English and, second, that in this context, teaching two native speaker varieties of English—British and American—in combination would be desirable.

Varieties of English in the Current Version of the Program

The conclusions arising from the survey influenced the design of the seven courses described in the Context section. The preparatory course for beginners and the course in everyday oral/aural communication remained totally British English oriented to prevent difficulties for beginning- and elementary-level students (Harmer, 2001, p. 9). The courses in general writing and reading became totally American English based on course books and other teaching materials (including those for listening). I hoped that teaching different varieties in separate, autonomous courses would to some extent counteract the mixture of different varieties in learners' speaking and writing. At the same time, learners would be able to comprehend spoken and written texts in British and American English, thanks to exposure to both.

The oral/aural business communication course remained almost unchanged from its initial design (British English oriented with some American English). I simply provided additional materials in American English.

Finally, I designed the business reading and writing courses using British and American English in combination. Learners were required to read and listen to materials in both varieties of the language—often in the same class. For instance, the course on business reading used both American and British business newspapers (e.g., *The Wall Street Journal* and *Financial Times*) as reading material.

◈ DISTINGUISHING FEATURES

Program Design

The program design is characterized by three distinguishing features concerning the variety of English taught.

Two Language Varieties Taught Based on Learner Needs Analysis

The variety of English to teach was selected on the basis of learners' needs and requirements as determined from surveys. Based on the results, the program teaches two varieties (British and American).

Varieties Taught Separately

Two language varieties are introduced separately and gradually in the first half of the program, in which two courses focus on British English, and the two following courses teach American English.

The second half of the program (the three remaining courses) features combined, parallel use of both language varieties. In the same class, learners might read a newspaper article in American English, listen to a recorded text in British English, and speak or write using the variety of the language they prefer. (I introduce the British variety first only because it is the variety traditionally taught in Ukraine and is therefore more familiar to the learners. In other contexts, the sequence of varieties may be different.)

Emphasis on Intelligibility

The program emphasizes intelligibility as the underlying principle for setting teaching and learning goals and determining the minimum required level of learners' achievements in speaking, listening, reading, and writing.

In designing the program, I realized that if learners who were introduced to two varieties of the language had no possibility of achieving nativelike proficiency in either, both would remain less polished than one variety could be in a course of the same duration. In place of the unrealistic goal of nativelike proficiency, therefore, was the realizable goal of intelligibility—in other words, achieving relatively unhindered comprehensibility to native speakers and relatively unhindered comprehension of native speakers. This goal, which could be set as the minimum goal for any EFL program, supports teachers in assisting and encouraging learners to use English with its native speakers and as a lingua franca with nonnative speakers—arguably the purpose of an international English.

Students' Performance

The program as a whole appeared to be a success in developing learners' communication skills in speaking, reading, listening, and writing. This finding was borne out by end-of-course tests designed to determine learners' levels of achievement (see, e.g., Tarnopolsky, 1999, 2003, for the test results).

Learners' Use of American and British English

Through testing and observations during class, I made three discoveries about students' use of English. The first is that, in speaking, learners often used British and American English, particularly vocabulary, indiscriminately; that is, they confused the varieties. I did not manage to eliminate these kinds of errors until the end of the program. That was a disadvantage, albeit an expected and relatively minor one (see the Description section) when intelligibility is the key consideration.

On the other hand, I rarely observed the confusion of the two varieties in writing. Recall that in the first writing course (general writing), learners were taught to write in American English. The following courses (especially the course for business purposes) emphasized differences in writing in American and British English, and students rarely forgot about them in their own writing. The reason was probably that writing is a much more consciously controlled process than speaking, and the students' training allowed them to consciously choose one language variety.

Testing and observations also demonstrated that the students had no problems in reading texts written in either British or American English. Therefore, the approach proved to be an effective means of learning to read and to write in both varieties of English.

Success in Communicating With Native and Nonnative English Speakers

The adequacy of this approach in developing the students' speaking and listening skills could be determined only on the basis of analyzing students' contacts with native and nonnative speakers of English from different countries. Such contacts could not be organized sufficiently in the classroom to serve as a source of information.

The only possible sources were follow-up reports in which former students described their contacts with English speakers from other countries. I collected 47 such reports (mostly oral) over 3 years (1999–2002) from students who had interacted with English speakers from various Inner Circle, Outer Circle, and Expanding Circle countries (Kachru, 1986)—British, Americans, Canadians, New Zealanders, Australians, Czechs, Poles, Germans, Japanese, Maltese, Italians, and Cypriots.

These contacts were of different regularity, frequency, duration, and purposes (e.g., professional or business talks, everyday exchanges, occasional contacts, participation in different events, small talk, contacts while on holidays in foreign countries). Therefore, they cannot be used to draw any definite and statistically valid conclusions, but they give a general picture of the presence or absence of problems in understanding speakers of different varieties of English (including speakers with different accents) and in being understood by them.

The 47 students reported no serious problems of this kind, only occasional misunderstandings—with one exception. Maria (a homemaker, 39 years old) immigrated to New Zealand with her family in 2000. Before her immigration, she had achieved quite a good command of English, had passed her International English Language Testing System (IELTS) test with high scores, and had had frequent contacts with Australians and Canadians, reporting no problems of comprehension or of being comprehended. But in her first letters from New Zealand, she complained of serious difficulties in understanding the local accent. She was the only one of my former learners who came into contact with the New Zealand variety of the English language, and her difficulties could have related to the fact that she had rarely encountered a New Zealand accent.

These reports suggest that learning two varieties of English in combination had developed learners' abilities to communicate with native speakers of different varieties of the language and with nonnative speakers sufficiently and that they did not encounter any major problems in communication. And that, in turn, means that the suggested approach enabled learners to gain command of English for international use.

Furthermore, learners in the second version of the program (more than 200 between 1997 and 2001) were fully satisfied with the two-varieties-of-English approach and believed it met their needs and requirements. This was revealed in talks with them and interviews conducted in different groups in 1998–2001.

◈ PRACTICAL IDEAS

I can suggest four practical strategies to EFL teachers in Expanding Circle countries.

Choose a National Variety or Varieties of English

Do not look to a mythical international English as the variety to teach to all learners. Instead, select a variety of English on the basis of learners' requirements as clarified by a needs analysis. This strategy applies to the teaching of adult (and sometimes adolescent) learners, who can consciously formulate their choices. It also requires teachers who are capable of teaching different varieties of English and teaching materials written in such varieties.

Be Ready to Teach Two National Varieties of English

If the variety of English to be taught is selected from the perspective of learners' needs, teaching two varieties of English in the same program may be preferable. Anticipate this diversity, and be ready to teach more than one variety of English.

Teaching two varieties of English in one program has some predictable disadvantages. When learners are exposed to two varieties of the language, some degree of mixing in their own speaking and writing is inevitable. But I believe that to be a minor disadvantage because it does not necessarily make their speaking and writing incomprehensible to either native or nonnative speakers of English. As Harmer (2001) writes, quoting Svartvik (1998), "the differences between inner circle varieties, while notable, were not nearly so numerous as the underlying similarities" (p. 9).

Follow a Definite Sequence

Try to avoid difficulties for learners by following a definite sequence when teaching two national varieties of English in one program. Teaching two national varieties of English in one program is quite feasible if you take measures to avoid overburdening the learners. That is, teach one variety of the language to beginners, and switch to the second variety no earlier than the preintermediate or intermediate stage. The use of both varieties of the language in combination is better delayed until the upper intermediate or advanced stage of learning. But on reaching that stage, a combination is necessary to ensure that learners can comprehend spoken and written texts in either variety.

Adopt the Goal of Intelligibility

An intelligibility approach seems to be the most reasonable choice for EFL teachers until an internationally accepted form of international English (lingua franca) is established. Teaching two varieties separately at the initial stages will help learners avoid confusing the varieties in their own speech. However, even if learners can avoid this confusion in writing (a more conscious process), it will probably be noticeable in their speaking.

Teaching two varieties of English is therefore recommended not when the goal is nativelike proficiency in speaking but when teachers and learners adopt intelligibility in international use as the goal. This approach does not require learners to sound like native speakers but sets the goal of ensuring that they understand and are understood by the greatest possible numbers of native and nonnative speakers of English.

◈ CONCLUSION

The case outlined in this chapter suggests that, in EFL contexts, the variety of English to select as the standard for teaching should not necessarily be an *either/or* decision. A *both/and* decision is quite possible, meaning, for instance, the choice of both American and British varieties of English (or any others, depending on the learners' needs) as the objective of teaching and learning. In many cases, such an approach best meets the learners' needs and expectations, and allows them to be comprehensible to native and nonnative speakers of both varieties of the language. Learning more than one variety of English makes it possible for learners to comprehend speakers of other varieties of English without major difficulties. In practice, adopting these teaching objectives leads to learners speaking a mixed variety of English (e.g., American-British). But this inevitable drawback seems minor in view of a goal of international English and an approach aimed at intelligibility in English.

The intelligibility approach means that teachers see comprehensibility to both native and nonnative speakers as the goal of learning. Such an approach is probably the best solution until a real rather than mythical international English is available for teaching—if such a time arrives. Therefore, in EFL contexts, I highly recommend clarifying learners' needs in acquiring a particular variety or varieties of English and designing the course accordingly.

◈ CONTRIBUTOR

Oleg Tarnopolsky is a doctor of pedagogy and full professor at Dnipropetrovsk University of Economics and Law, in Ukraine, where he chairs the Department of Applied Linguistics and Methods in Foreign Language Teaching. He is the author of books and numerous articles on EFL teaching and has made numerous presentations at professional conferences worldwide.

CHAPTER 8

Who Chooses the Standard? English Language Norms and English Language Teaching in Macao

Mark N. Brock

◈ INTRODUCTION

In this chapter I focus on preservice and practicing teachers of English in Macao and, specifically, on their attitudes toward the varieties of English they view as normative models in their classroom teaching. Macao, the former Portuguese colony on the southern coast of Guangdong, China, which returned to Chinese sovereignty in 1999, is a small Special Administrative Region of China with a population of less than one-half million. It is situated on the southwest edge of the Pearl River Delta, approximately 40 kilometers from its larger and wealthier neighbor, Hong Kong, to the east. The economy of Macao is primarily service based, with gambling tourism serving as the prominent driver of economic activity.

◈ CONTEXT

Participants

The preservice teachers participating in this study were final-year students enrolled in the 4-year BEd (English) program at the University of Macau. (Note that the name of the university draws on the historic, Portuguese spelling, *Macau,* whereas the English spelling, *Macao,* is now preferred in many other contexts.) This program, which has an enrollment of approximately 100 students, is the only undergraduate teacher education program in Macao dedicated to the training of secondary school teachers of English.

The Faculty of Education at the University of Macau also offers a postgraduate certificate in education for in-service secondary school teachers of English and provides occasional noncredit in-service training courses in cooperation with the government's Department of Education for practicing teachers of English. Although other tertiary institutions in Macao offer courses in English language studies and teacher education, the University of Macau is the primary source of teacher education for local pre- and in-service teachers of English.

The practicing teachers who participated in this study make up a subset of local secondary school teachers of English in Macao. Macao's system of education is dominated by privately run schools, many affiliated with religious or philanthropic organizations. The government operates only 2 of 43 secondary schools in Macao. The private schools are operated by independent boards with little government influence on school policy, personnel, or curriculum. The government subsidizes teachers' pay and students' tuition, and evaluates and approves the qualifications of teachers seeking employment in local Macao schools. Macao, however, has no public examination system; no system of government review, approval, or recommendation of instructional texts; and no provision of government-approved guidelines for development of instructional goals and materials for the various subjects taught in Macao schools.

This lack of governmental influence on and control of education has created an interesting mix of curricula, textbooks, and school examinations in Macao schools. In teaching English, some schools have adopted textbooks, curricula, and even standardized testing instruments and procedures from China. Other schools have chosen the Hong Kong Certificate Examination as the standard to which they teach and have adopted textbooks published and approved for teaching English in Hong Kong. Still others have developed their own system or have geared their English teaching toward preparation for taking the English language section of university entrance examinations offered by specific universities in China or Taiwan or at the University of Macau.

At the two government-run secondary schools in Macao, students receive language instruction in English and Portuguese. Interestingly, by law, students enrolled in government-run schools must receive more hours of instruction in Portuguese than in other languages. Although there are curricular guidelines for teaching English in the government schools, these guidelines are almost exclusively grammar based, are written primarily in Chinese, and provide little practical assistance for teachers in developing classroom instruction. No texts or other teaching materials addressing these curricular guidelines are available for teachers' use, and, based on discussions with teachers at the government secondary schools, teachers neither are required nor choose to refer to the guidelines in developing instructional plans for the students. Indeed, the teachers with whom I spoke had never read the documents, and it seems clear that the guidelines are almost universally ignored.

English in Macao

The history of the English language in Macao is surprisingly long and interesting. When the modern era of trade with China began to develop some 200–300 years ago, Macao played an important role in providing a base of operations for merchant traders from Europe, the United States, and, most importantly, the United Kingdom. With British dominance rising both commercially and militarily in southern China, the importance of English grew in Macao along with Macao's importance as an entrepôt and seasonal rest stop for British, North American, and European traders. English-speaking Protestant missionaries also often transited through Macao, and, much later, a handful of these missionaries established Protestant schools and churches within Macao. With the establishment of Hong Kong in the mid-19th century, Macao's economic and strategic importance declined, but the importance and study of English was maintained by a segment of the population who saw the language as an important asset for economic and educational opportunity, primarily outside of Macao.

Although the role and influence of English in Macao today are significantly less than in neighboring Hong Kong, the importance of English is nonetheless evident and growing. English has no officially sanctioned role in Macao, the official languages being Portuguese and Chinese. The influence of Portuguese, however, is quickly declining, and the language is primarily confined to the courts and to government, which by law must publish all official communications in Portuguese and Chinese. Although before the handover in 1999 and, in particular, before the 1990s, it would not have been unusual for Westerners to be addressed in Portuguese by local, mainly Chinese, proprietors of markets, shops, and restaurants, today non-Chinese are much more likely to be addressed in English. Indeed, most Portuguese citizens have returned to Europe, and many, if not most, Macanese (members of the long-established community founded on Portuguese and Chinese intermarriage) have emigrated as well.

The decline of Portuguese since 1999 has seen a concurrent rise in the emphasis the government of Macao has given to the teaching of English. In 2002, for example, the government sponsored the first group of local primary and secondary school English teachers sent abroad, to the United Kingdom, for summer study focused on improving their English language and English language teaching (ELT) skills. Previous groups of teachers had been sponsored on trips to Portugal and elsewhere to enhance their skills in a variety of academic disciplines, but never in English or ELT. The group sent in 2002, along with groups of English teachers sponsored on study-abroad trips in subsequent years, marks a recognition by the government of the growing importance of English and ELT to Macao's educational and economic future.

As in many other cities in Asia, the influence of English is evident in the commercial and educational sectors of Macao. After Cantonese, the local Chinese language spoken by the majority of people there, English and Mandarin are the most important languages in the territory. English is a required subject in every primary and secondary school (although it is not introduced before the fifth year of government-operated primary schools), and in many secondary schools the teaching of English occupies 10 hours or more of classroom instruction per week. Indeed, at least five local primary and secondary schools offer an English section, in which textbooks and classroom instruction are primarily in English. There are also three small international schools established in Macao, two of which cater primarily to local families who want their children to receive their entire education through the medium of English. The University of Macau markets itself as an international institution where English is the primary language of instruction, a feature attracting more and more students from the neighboring Chinese mainland. Although Macao does not yet have an established English language newspaper—two attempts at establishing such a paper failed after a few months of publication—the *South China Morning Post,* the most popular English language newspaper published in Hong Kong, is widely available in Macao.

Language Norms and the Teaching of English

As S. McKay (1992) noted in her discussion of teaching English overseas, the context in which the language is taught often determines the variety of English presented in the classroom as the normative model toward which students should work. In settings where there is a strong historical link with one of the traditional branches of

English, primarily that of the United Kingdom or the United States, the model taught in schools is, in many cases, a standard variety drawn from the particular tree to which that country is closely linked (Strevens, 1992). In Puerto Rico, for example, American English is taught because of the island's close economic and political links with the United States (Crystal, 1997).

In other teaching contexts, close ties to a U.S. or British branch of the language have been broken, yet a local variety (or varieties) of English has been retained, nativized (Kachru, 1992a), and placed in a position of status as the normative model or variety to be taught in schools. India, Malaysia, and many countries in Africa and the Caribbean provide clear examples of this development (Augustin, 1982; Bokamba, 1992; Das, 1982).

Other classroom contexts fall outside of either of these situations. In countries with no dominant economic or political tie to one of the traditional branches of English or no historical impetus for the establishment of a local, nativized and standardized variety, teachers of English may face the difficult question of which normative model of English to teach (see Tarnopolsky, this volume). For some teachers, local or national departments of education answer this question. For other teachers, such as those in Macao, this question is more complicated and difficult to answer.

◈ DESCRIPTION

This study of practicing and preservice teachers' attitudes toward the role of English in Macao and English language norms was part of a larger, funded research project I undertook to investigate the attitudes of teachers of English in Macao toward their chosen profession (Brock, 2003). Data were collected with a survey and through interviews with practicing and preservice teachers.

Survey

First, a five-part, 75-item survey was distributed to teachers of English at all secondary schools in Macao and to all Year 4 preservice teachers enrolled in the BEd (English) program at the University of Macau. The survey focused on (a) teachers' beliefs about the role and importance of the English language in Macao, (b) their beliefs about language learning, (c) their beliefs about language teaching, (d) their beliefs about curriculum and planning of instruction, and (e) their views of ELT as a profession.

I focus here on responses to statements about the role of English in Macao and the normative model of English used in the classroom. The survey required teachers to rate their level of agreement or disagreement with 15 statements, on a scale of 1–4 corresponding to *strongly disagree, disagree, agree,* and *strongly agree* (see the Appendix for the questions in this section of the survey and the respondents' ratings).

I hand-delivered or mailed to each of the 43 secondary schools in Macao a packet containing a cover letter (in Chinese) addressed to the school principal, along with copies of the survey and separate cover letter for each English teacher employed at the school. The cover letter explained the purpose of the research and the focus of the survey, and requested that the headmaster pass copies of the enclosed survey to the school English panel chair for distribution to each English teacher in the school. A cover letter written in English and attached to the survey explained its purpose and requested that teachers complete the survey and hold it for collection by a research assistant who would return to the school in 2 weeks' time. A copy of the survey with an attached cover letter was distributed to each of the 33 Year 4 BEd (English) students enrolled at the University of Macau. Students were asked to complete the survey and return it to me.

Completed surveys were collected from 19 of 43 secondary schools in Macao. Of the 292 distributed to secondary schools, 101 were completed, returned, and tabulated for the study, and examined for trends in respondents' ratings. Twenty-eight of 33 Year 4 preservice B(Ed) English preservice teachers at the University of Macau completed and returned the survey.

Interviews

To explore further the question of English language norms, I interviewed five practicing teachers of English and five preservice teachers participating in the study. One of the teachers was employed in a government-run secondary school, and the other four were teaching in privately run secondary schools at the time the interviews were conducted. They had an average of 7 years' teaching experience in Macao schools. Each of the preservice teachers had completed one semester of practicum experience, observing and assisting a teacher of English in a local secondary school. They had each also completed two semesters of practice teaching during which they planned instruction and taught English classes in a local secondary school for 10 or more classroom hours each week. They were all enrolled in their final semester of study.

The interviews focused on the question of which variety of English, if any, should serve as the normative model for teachers and students in Macao secondary schools and on the role of the Macao government, if any, in determining which variety of English should be normative. The interviews were recorded, transcribed, and analyzed for similarities and differences in comments made by practicing and preservice teachers.

◈ DISTINGUISHING FEATURES

Here I summarize the views as expressed in the practicing and preservice teachers' responses to the 15 survey statements focusing on the role of English in Macao and preferred English language normative models (see the Appendix), and to the interview questions.

English Viewed as Increasingly Important

Respondents' ratings of survey statements regarding the role, importance, and future of English in Macao were similar. More than 70% of the practicing and preservice teachers agreed or strongly agreed that students viewed learning English as important for their future; almost 100% of the practicing and preservice teachers agreed or strongly agreed that it was important for the students to learn to speak English well. Both groups also agreed or strongly agreed, by an overwhelming majority, that English was growing more important in Macao and that learning English was more important than learning Portuguese, one of the two official languages in Macao.

These findings are not surprising, particularly in view of the growing role of Macao's gambling industry and, in particular, the rapidly expanding role of U.S. casino companies in Macao. Despite intermittent efforts by the previous government over many years, Portuguese in Macao never gained importance beyond the benefit it provided those seeking government employment.

Varying Views of the Importance of English Relative to Mandarin

Opinions on the importance of learning English relative to the importance of learning Mandarin, the official, standard Chinese language used widely in China and other parts of Asia, were more divided. Half of the practicing teachers responding to the survey disagreed or strongly disagreed that learning English was more important than learning Mandarin, but 35% of the preservice teachers disagreed or strongly disagreed with this statement. This difference may be a generational one, with the older, practicing teachers having more affinity with China and the official language. Indeed, a significant number of English teachers in Macao earned their undergraduate degrees from Chinese universities.

Varying Preferences for Variety of English to Teach

In considering normative varieties of English preferred for classroom teaching, practicing and preservice teachers alike disagreed or strongly disagreed, by overwhelming majorities (70% or more), with the suggestion that Asian varieties of English, including Australian, Hong Kong, Singaporean, and Filipino English, should be taught in classrooms in Macao. On the question of the two major varieties of English used in Asia and around the world, British and American English, the responses were less uniform. Over 80% of the practicing teachers agreed or strongly agreed that British English should be the variety of English taught in Macau. Among the preservice teachers responding to the survey, only 50% agreed or strongly agreed with adopting British English as the normative model for English classrooms. Over 70% of the practicing and preservice teachers, however, agreed or strongly agreed with the statement that American English should be the normative model taught in classrooms.

This preference is related to the teachers' and preservice teachers' exposure to the language. The majority of English language instructors with whom the preservice teachers studied at the University of Macau were from the United States, which certainly influenced the preservice teachers' preferences. This preference may also have been influenced by the growing influence of U.S. movies, music, and culture on youth culture in Macao.

Varying Views of the Government's Role

Responses to the suggestion that the government should impose the variety of English to be taught in Macao schools were divided between the two groups of teachers. Although 66% of practicing teachers agreed or strongly agreed with the suggestion that the Macao government should choose the normative variety of

English to teach, only 46% of the preservice teachers agreed or strongly agreed. Both the practicing teachers (90%) and the preservice teachers (64%) agreed with the statement that the government should develop a standardized, public examination of English as a means of enforcing English language standards in Macao schools.

Varying Views of a Normative Model of English

Practicing Teachers

Responses to the interview question about which normative model of English should be taught in Macao secondary schools were varied. Three of the teachers supported using British English as the normative model (as one stated, "It's pure, original English"), but the other two were opposed to adopting one particular model. The comments made by the teachers included the following:

I was taught British English. I like it best, so I teach it.

I think British English is most beautiful. It's so clear. I love to hear it.

This is not Hong Kong. This is not USA. We don't have to choose. If someone can understand me, that is enough.

English teachers in the schools come from Macao, from China, Philippines, even Europe. We speak our own way. That's OK.

Concerning the government's role in imposing a particular variety of English, three of the teachers interviewed were opposed to this idea, and two supported it. Some comments:

The government official can't even speak English. How could they choose?

We don't want the government telling us what to teach. However, we do want money from them [laughter].

No. No. The government would just mess it up. Just let me teach my own way.

Yes, I think the government should. Now there is no standard. Some schools are good, some bad.

I think the government could choose. Maybe we should just follow Hong Kong or China. But everyone should teach the same kinds of English.

Preservice Teachers

Of the five preservice teachers interviewed, two supported the use of American English, one supported a mixture of American and British English, and two opposed making a choice. Selected preservice teachers' comments follow:

Most of my teachers in FSH [Faculty of Social Sciences and Humanities] are American. I try to talk like them, especially Dr. [X].

I think my students like to go to the cinema. They watch American films. I think teaching American English will motivate them.

I want both British and American. When I teach reading and writing, it should be British. When I teach speaking and listening, I think American English is best.

We don't know what English we speak. We just speak. Don't ask me what it is.

I just say what I think is correct. I don't know if it is British English, American English, Hong Kong English. I don't know. I just try my best to use correct English.

Four of the five preservice teachers interviewed agreed that the Macao government should not impose a particular variety of the language on teachers of English in Macao; however, one saw a benefit in their doing so. Some of the preservice teachers' comments follow:

I don't think the government can do that. In Macao they can't do that. It's not legal for them.

Teachers should choose what to teach, how to teach. It's my students. How can the government tell me?

I don't trust the government. It's better now than before 1999, but I don't think they should tell me how to teach.

Maybe it's a good idea. In most schools, teachers don't even speak English in the classroom. They speak Cantonese to teach English. That's very bad. If the government says, "You must speak this kind of English," maybe teachers would pay attention.

◈ PRACTICAL IDEAS

Teaching English in an environment characterized by political, economic, and linguistic change, as Macao teachers of English have in recent years, presents a number of challenges. Whereas teachers of English in Macao tend to defend the independence they enjoy from government influence on school policy and classroom teaching, many feel a need for more guidance in determining the normative model of English they should teach and the learning standards by which students should be measured. Although government and economic leaders in Macao stress the importance of English and ELT, many teachers of English feel insecure about their own competence in the language. The findings of this survey suggest a number of practical steps that teachers and school officials working in similar environments should consider.

Provide Teachers With Opportunities to Develop Their English Language Skills

Teachers of English, particularly those teaching in environments where use of the language is not widespread but is growing, need opportunities to upgrade their English language skills. Training in language teaching methodology and classroom management is essential to teacher success, yet many teachers of English need opportunities to strengthen their own mastery and use of the language. Discussions about language norms and learning standards are indeed important, but for teachers struggling to use English as the primary language of instruction in their classrooms and working diligently to present an accurate and acceptable model of the language for the students they teach, language training and support may be more important than detailed curricular guidelines and standardized testing for students.

Since 1999, the government of Macao has taken important steps in providing language development opportunities for a number of practicing teachers of English. Many teachers want suggestions and guidance about the normative models of English they should introduce in their English classrooms. In many instances, however, the more important need is to develop teachers' competence in using the language in their classrooms.

Provide Guidance on Language Standards

Although freedom to teach in the way that is best for the students one works with is a cherished and necessary component of classroom teaching, many teachers of English want some guidance regarding the variety or varieties of English they should teach and the curricular goals that should guide their instructional planning. Because of the 1999 change of government in Macao, the role of Portuguese is quickly narrowing in the territory. Although English is not an official language in Macao, its role is expanding, and the government is working to expand support for English language teachers. Many of these teachers would welcome suggestions or noncompulsory guidelines from government education officials about the language standards toward which they should teach.

Consider Introducing Regional Varieties of English

English is a global language with a number of recognized varieties, including so-called nonnative varieties such as those spoken in Singapore, Malaysia, the Philippines, India, and elsewhere in Asia and around the world. Teachers of English in contexts similar to Macao's, where the importance of English is growing but the language does not enjoy official status and where strong historical or economic ties with the United States or the United Kingdom do not exist, may wish to introduce students to the varieties of English spoken in the regions where they live. Although findings from this research indicate teachers of English in Macao are unlikely to choose a regional variety as their normative classroom model, recognizing these varieties as legitimate may provide students who resist imposition of a U.S. or British standard with a motivating alternative.

Work to Influence Language Teaching Policies

Teachers of English in Macao need to work together proactively to influence language teaching policies rather than waiting for the government to develop and impose policies. Teachers have an opportunity to shape the future direction of ELT and language teaching policy in Macao. Because of legal restrictions on government interference in school curricula and government inexperience in developing policy and guidelines for the teaching of English, there is a lack of leadership in developing cohesive ELT policy and guidelines in Macao. It is in the best interest of English teachers and students for the teachers to form organizations through which they can share ideas, offer and receive professional support, and take the lead in shaping the standards of ELT for Macao schools. These teachers have the opportunity to largely shape how they teach the English language. It is an opportunity they should welcome and seize.

◈ CONCLUSION

With the opening in May 2004 of its first U.S.-owned and -operated casino, Macao's direction toward an ever-increasing use of the English language seems clearly set. Will a distinct variety of English emerge there, as, arguably, is the case in neighboring Hong Kong (Richards & Luke, 1981)? How will the teaching of English in China and Hong Kong influence the teaching of English in Macao and the normative models to which teachers of English in Macao refer?

Although English has long been taught and spoken in Macao, the role and function of the language is still evolving. For the moment, it is clear that, in the classroom, English teachers themselves will largely make the decision about the varieties of English they teach. That freedom and responsibility seems rightly theirs, as it is the classroom teachers of English in Macao who best know the students' needs and motivations.

◈ CONTRIBUTOR

Mark Brock has taught English and educated teachers of English in Macao, Hong Kong, and the United States. He is currently associate professor and director of ESL at Carson-Newman College, in the United States.

◈ APPENDIX: SURVEY QUESTIONS AND RESPONSES (%)

Statement and respondents	Strongly disagree	Disagree	Agree	Strongly agree
1. English is a difficult language to learn.				
Practicing teachers	3	60	36	1
Preservice teachers	2	64	17	17
2. My students believe that learning English is very important for their future.				
Practicing teachers	0	26	61	13
Preservice teachers	7	20	64	11
3. It's important that my students learn to speak English well.				
Practicing teachers	0	4	42	56
Preservice teachers	0	0	68	32
4. In the future, English will become more and more important in Macao.				
Practicing teachers	0	5	42	53
Preservice teachers	0	0	36	64

Statement and respondents	Strongly disagree	Disagree	Agree	Strongly agree
5. It's more important for my students to learn English than Portuguese.				
Practicing teachers	0	4	51	45
Preservice teachers	0	0	25	75
6. It's more important for my students to learn English than Mandarin.				
Practicing teachers	4	46	46	4
Preservice teachers	7	28	46	19
7. Proficiency in English is important for finding a good job in Macao.				
Practicing teachers	0	12	61	27
Preservice teachers	0	4	61	35
8. British English should be the variety of English taught in Macao.				
Practicing teachers	0	17	73	10
Preservice teachers	0	50	43	7
9. American English should be the variety of English taught in Macao.				
Practicing teachers	0	23	71	6
Preservice teachers	0	28	50	22
10. Australian English should be the variety of English taught in Macao.				
Practicing teachers	15	65	20	0
Preservice teachers	25	54	31	0
11. Hong Kong English should be the variety of English taught in Macao.				
Practicing teachers	18	54	28	0
Preservice teachers	21	64	25	0
12. Singaporean English should be the variety of English taught in Macao.				
Practicing teachers	19	67	14	0
Preservice teachers	29	71	0	0
13. Filipino English should be the variety of English taught in Macao.				
Practicing teachers	43	51	6	0
Preservice teachers	50	50	0	0

Statement and respondents	Strongly disagree	Disagree	Agree	Strongly agree
14. The government should set standards regarding the variety of English I teach.				
Practicing teachers	4	30	62	4
Preservice teachers	18	36	43	3
15. The government should develop a standardized examination to enforce English standards in Macao.				
Practicing teachers	5	5	58	32
Preservice teachers	8	28	32	32

PART 5

Which
Approaches?

CHAPTER 9

Learning to Learn: Perspectives From the Philippines English Language Teaching Project

María Luz C. Vilches

◈ INTRODUCTION

The increasing recognition of English as a worldwide language (see, e.g., Crystal, 1997; Graddol, 1997) serves as a major context within which the education of English teachers occurs, especially in second language contexts. This chapter discusses the experience of the Philippines English Language Teaching (PELT) Project and its contributions to teacher education from the viewpoint of teaching English from a global perspective.

◈ CONTEXT

English in the Philippines

Philippine English language teaching (ELT) is closely linked with the country's colonial history under U.S. rule (1898–1945), which established the public school system in which English was packaged as an essential component. In the postcolonial and multilingual Philippines, English has been accorded a privileged position as an official language on a par with Filipino, the national language (Gonzalez, 1997). Its use is widespread in the major domains of society and enjoys prominence in a flourishing body of Philippine literature in English. It is the medium of instruction in math, science, and English at all educational levels (see García, 1997; Gonzalez, Bernardo, Bautista, & Pascasio, 1998).

English language education is thus a significant part of the national agenda for development. A major rationale for this thrust is the conviction that the worldwide spread of English has made it an indispensable means of access to knowledge and, consequently, to worldwide opportunities for a country that aims to become globally competitive.

PELT

In view of the crucial role of English in education, the improvement of ELT has figured prominently in Philippine educational reforms (see the Presidential Commission on Educational Reform, http://pcer_ph.tripod.com/). Over the years, international aid projects in the country have supported such reforms (for details, see Asian Development Bank, 2004). ELT-related projects include the Secondary Education

Development Project (SEDP; 1988–1995), the PELT Project (1995–1999), and the Philippine-Australia Project in Basic Education (PROBE; 1996–2001; see AusAID, 2003; Government of the Philippines, 2005). In terms of geographical scope, the SEDP encompassed the entire Philippines, and the PELT Project focused on seven educational regions. PROBE concentrated on Mindanao, in southern Philippines. PELT, the subject of this case study, was developed with awareness of the SEDP as its main background context.

Funded by the World Bank, the SEDP supported the introduction of the New Secondary Education Curriculum in 1989. It included textbook development and teacher education for math, science, and English (*Project Completion Report,* n.d.). In ELT, it upheld such values as student centeredness, critical thinking, values education integration, and cognitive and affective development of the students (Bureau of Secondary Education, 1995). It also promoted a curriculum covering the four macroskills (listening, speaking, reading, writing) and literature as the main components (Bureau of Secondary Education, 1991) and reflected in the content organization of what were called the *SEDP textbooks.* To prepare about 30,000 secondary school English teachers to use the new curriculum via these textbooks (see Department of Education, Culture, & Sports [DECS], 1997), the SEDP launched teacher and trainer education programs nationwide, and focused on the development of strategies for teaching the four macroskills.

In 1994 and 1995, the Bureau of Secondary Education of DECS conducted an evaluation of the project, specifically in terms of student learning outcomes. The results indicated a slight increase in the level of students' performance within the subject areas. The SEDP's *Project Completion Report* (n.d.) points out the difficulty of ascertaining that the textbooks and teacher education provided by the project had had the desired effect on the students and acknowledges the influence of other factors. Thus, despite the SEDP's nationwide effort at redressing the perceived deterioration in the quality of English language use in the schools (Gonzalez, 1997; Gonzalez et al., 1998; Sibayan & Gonzalez, 1988), very little evidence of improvement emerged at this point, perhaps because it was too early to see any long-term effects of the educational change process.

The PELT Project

The PELT Project began at the close of the SEDP. It was the British government's response to the Philippine government's call for help in arresting the perceived deterioration of the quality of English use in the schools. Managed by the British Council in Manila, the project had support from the Philippine government through DECS and subsidies from in-country private funding agencies. Its programs were designed and implemented by Ateneo de Manila University via the Ateneo Center for English Language Teaching and by Lancaster University, in the United Kingdom, via the Institute for English Language Education—the latter acting as project consultant. PELT focused on English language teacher and teacher educator training in seven project regions (three from the main island of Luzon, two from the cluster of islands in the middle part of the country, and two from Mindanao, in southern Philippines), chosen by the director of the Bureau of Secondary Education on the basis of their long-term, limited access to educational opportunities. In this chapter, I describe only the teacher education component, as the issues there relate more directly to classroom practice.

Initial PELT Project data gathered from 15 full-length lessons observed across the project regions revealed four major characteristics:

1. The overall lesson structure typically consisted of reading materials with comprehension questions, listening and speaking exercises, grammar input, grammar drills, and writing practice. Though laid out in succession, these lesson parts were not necessarily smoothly linked.

2. In terms of cognitive challenge, the lessons usually exploited only a basic level of literal and inferential comprehension.

3. Student involvement was minimal because discussions were mainly teacher fronted and whole class.

4. Full-length lessons devoted to grammar alone usually began with the presentation of rules followed by sentence-level drills.

The observed teaching practices showed that the general trend in teaching English mostly addressed the students' basic level of affective and cognitive involvement. These main findings provided PELT's rationale for the emphasis on honing teachers' competency in understanding and promoting learning in the English language classroom.

The Teacher Education Program

Many English language teacher education programs, including SEDP, typically begin and end with seminar activities. Teachers are then left to implement what they learned in the seminar in the schools. More often than not, such types of training, which do not systematically build the connection between the seminar and the school setting, result in teachers' frustration with their inability to apply ideas that seemed to have worked well in the seminar (Waters & Vilches, 2000).

Recognizing this pitfall and based on consultation with school ELT managers, the project consultant and I (as project coordinator) aimed to avoid it by designing a program with the expressed goal of enhancing ongoing teacher learning in the schools (see Figure 1). This goal was in line with the PELT training theme of promoting language learning in the ELT classroom. Seeing this goal as the end result of the training, we worked backward by planning learning-centered seminars that included an orientation to the school-based follow-up development activity (SFDA). This activity was meant to act as the bridge between the seminar and the school.

Figure 1 illustrates this process-oriented design, showing the incremental development of the relationship between the school-based and seminar-based components of the training program. The seminar, which lies at the base, builds the foundation of teaching knowledge necessary for actualizing the teacher learners' potential for upgraded competency in their normal school setting. The school-based component of the training, shown at the top of the diagram, is the culmination of the process.

Sixty hours (10 days) of the seminar were devoted to building a foundation of knowledge of communicative language teaching. During April and May, 30–50 teachers participated in each of the seminars, which were taught by two or three teacher educators, of which I was one. Between 1996 and 1999, PELT staged approximately 60–70 seminars spread out among the seven project regions.

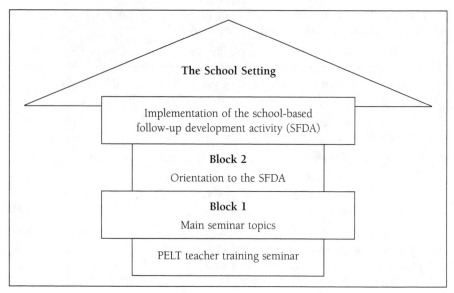

FIGURE 1. PELT Teacher Education Structure

Participants

The approximately 2,500 participants were mainly teachers in state secondary schools. Most were in their mid-30s and had had 5–8 years of teaching experience. Some (those in their late 20s) had been teaching for only 1–2 years. Also participating were a few teachers in their late 40s and mid-50s who were curious to learn about new ideas in the field.

Most of these teachers had participated in the SEDP, which had used demonstration teaching by the teacher educator as its chief strategy. It had promoted the mastery of selected strategies that teachers could then use to *cascade* or *echo* the training to their colleagues by holding local seminars on their return to their schools (*echo seminars* was the term used locally). In other words, most of the PELT participants had a training background that was basically teacher educator centered, input driven, and product oriented.

◈ DESCRIPTION

Unsurprisingly, the participants expected PELT to provide more of the type of training they had had in the SEDP. Instead, their experiences in PELT helped them expand their knowledge beyond their expectations. What follows is a description of the key concepts of PELT that underpinned these experiences.

Learning Theme

The subtext of the PELT teacher education program theme was that learning is the primary role of teaching and that the first learner is the teacher. The program proposed that the participants recognize two main levels of learning: (a) foundation building, or the basic level of knowledge achieved through such activities as whole-class, teacher-fronted input, literal comprehension, and rule-focused grammar; and (b) potential realizing, or the more creative exploitation and ownership of knowledge, which is triggered and encouraged by, for example, problem-solving tasks, meaning-focused grammar, and engagement with material and ideas that relate to students' personal lives and world (see Waters & Vilches, 1998, 2001, for a more detailed explanation of the concepts). The same two principles applied to the way PELT helped teachers learn how to teach through the two-tiered, seminar-based-to-school-based design.

Kolb's (1984) concept of the learning cycle (Figure 2) reflects this idea of learning as constantly building on existing knowledge. The cycle begins with immersion in experience (concrete experience), then moves toward analysis of this experience (reflective observation). This, in turn, leads to reflection (abstract conceptualization), the results of which become the basis for application and evaluation of the experience (active experimentation). In this model, learning—whether graphically illustrated as a two-tiered model or a cycle—is process oriented and multidimensional, and puts a high premium on practical experience as knowledge source and knowledge end.

The PELT seminars introduced this kind of learning through classroom practices that engaged teacher learners in doing classroom tasks that

- challenged them cognitively and involved them affectively in the lesson

- empowered them as learners

- helped them appreciate grammar as a way of enabling students to understand English structure for use in communication

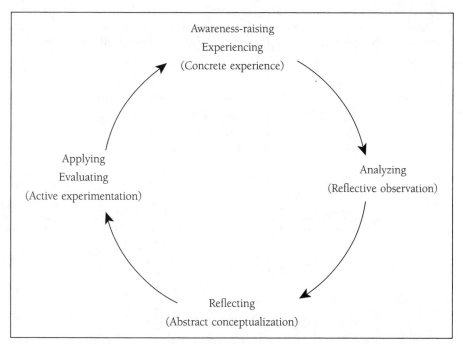

FIGURE 2. A Reinterpretation of Kolb's (1984) Learning Cycle

These key ideas were embedded in the main topics of the seminar-based training: Integrating Language Work (ILW), Levels of Thinking, Facilitating Learner Involvement, Small-Group Work, and Making Grammar Work More Creative.

Learning by Doing

The purpose of classroom tasks is to apply knowledge by using it in lifelike communication. This concept was introduced via a lesson-planning model—ILW—that aimed to show how a coherent lesson is made up of systematic and related parts or sequences that lead to meaningful communication. Figure 3 illustrates the elements of the learning-by-doing process (adapted from Hutchinson & Waters, 1987) in the context of the two-tiered learning scheme. The input forms the base of foundation building, and the task is the peak of potential realizing. The content focus and language focus elements are support structures to prepare the students systematically to perform the task. These two elements straddle the two tiers, depending on the kind of challenge they require of the student.

This model made a lot of sense to the teacher learners and thus gained immediate acceptance. It seemed to provide them with a recognizable solution to their need for more systematic lesson planning. Using their existing textbook lessons, they applied the model by first considering the task in mind and then working backward to choose the appropriate input and design the content and language focus activities that would help students accomplish the task. Through this exercise, they discovered that their textbook lessons generally consisted of 50% input, 20% content-focus activities, 25% language-focus activities, and 5% culminating tasks. Having become used to following such textbook lessons almost religiously, the participants had difficulty modifying them, especially when creating appropriate tasks. But the participants persisted in doing the practice exercises because they resulted in a sense of achievement. These experiences made the teacher learners appreciate the value of experiential learning, which also informs the ILW model.

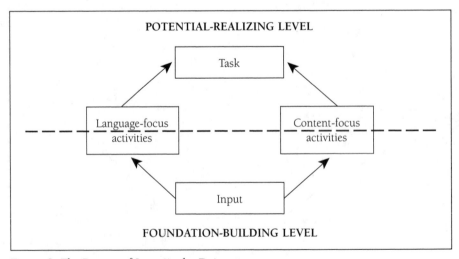

FIGURE 3. The Process of Learning by Doing

Levels of Thinking and Learner Involvement

Cognitive challenge and affective involvement refer to two related factors that promote learning. Recognizing the distinction between lower and higher level thinking (Bloom, 1956), the seminars introduced teaching strategies that could help the teacher learners promote students' higher level thinking skills through comprehension questions and activities that require analyzing, synthesizing, and evaluating ideas. We also noted that the motivation factor (Cook, 2001) in learning cannot be taken for granted and raised the question "What can help students want to learn?" The participants were introduced to strategies for using students' personal experiences, interests, and concerns as springboards for discussion.

To hone their skills in cognitively challenging and affectively involving students, the PELT participants critically reviewed their current practices when asking questions and using content-focus textbook activities. They discovered that their questioning processes often lacked gradual buildup toward critical thinking. In other words, questions moved straight from the literal level to the synthesis and evaluation levels, making comprehending the input a difficult task. The participants realized that this jump might be the source of students' lack of interest in the task and, perhaps, language learning in general. They then worked particularly on formulating inferential questions and feedback on their work focused on clarifying and practicing questions at this level.

The participants also explored the levels of thinking and affective involvement embedded in textbook activities. Doing this type of analysis seemed to be a new experience because they had been used to implementing textbooks endorsed by the Department of Education and had seldom questioned the underlying principles. The novelty of the PELT activity made them keenly interested in applying the ideas. What they found interesting was changing their teacher questions into activities. They saw that they could increase the students' enthusiasm by moving away from teacher-led tasks to tasks that students could complete more interactively with each other. The participants appreciated this experience as it gave them the opportunity to draw on their creative imagination while developing tasks systematically.

Empowerment via Small-Group Work

Empowering students refers to creating opportunities for developing autonomy. It pertains to recognizing that, ultimately, all learning must be done by the learner. We introduced a framework that would help participants achieve a balance in three areas: (a) in classroom interaction, between whole-class discussion and group work; (b) in language practice, between fluency and accuracy (Byrne, 1995); and (c) in teacher and student roles, between teacher-directed and student-directed learning (Wright, 1987).

Having been used to an input-driven and thus teacher-fronted classroom, the teacher learners appreciated the value of these ideas for promoting learner autonomy. However, they also felt uncertain whether they could feasibly make the changes in their classrooms. They were doubtful about the effective use of small-group work given their large classes (50–80 students) cramped in small classrooms; the thought of moving the students into groups discouraged them. Another concern was the level of noise that small-group work may create, thereby becoming a source of distraction for students in neighboring classes. In addition, they were concerned that students would speak in their own language rather than practice English. Some of the teacher learners had unsuccessfully attempted to implement small-group work ("It was chaos!"), and the suggestion to try it again provoked anxiety.

To help alleviate their anxieties, the teacher learners planned small-group work for a textbook task based on the following guidelines: rationale for the task, description of the task, expected output, instructions for the task, time limit, and mode of processing the output. What emerged from this exercise were interesting discoveries about small-group work. First, the participants realized that it was not simply a matter of putting students in groups—that it involved systematic and careful planning with clear procedures if students were to achieve the desired output. Second, they became aware of the importance of clear and well-staged instructions, which they had previously taken for granted. Third, they acknowledged that the reason some of them had had traumatic experiences of implementing small-group work tasks in the past was that they had overlooked proper planning and had given vague instructions.

The experience of setting up tasks lessened the teacher learners' anxiety about the practical application of group work. They realized that, although they could not change their class sizes, they could improve their application of small-group work through the insights gained from the training exercise.

System Building Through Creative Grammar Work

System building refers to fostering awareness that language is a system of rules and functions and that the student needs to create a mental network to make sense of the way the system works in meaningful communication (see Waters & Vilches, 1998, for a more detailed explanation). The teacher learners agreed with this line of thinking. The teacher educators asked them to review traditional, rule-based grammar teaching and communicative, task-based grammar teaching based on transcripts of lessons and to consider the advantages and disadvantages of each approach (see Table 1). They recognized that traditional grammar teaching provides classroom control. Its advantages for the teacher lie in ensuring a uniform orientation to learning grammar rules. Nevertheless, they also perceived the possible negative effects on student motivation and enthusiasm for language use. In relation to communicative language teaching, they pointed to the likelihood of maximizing students' language use in a more engaging and fulfilling manner. However, they also indicated that a communicative approach entails more planning and management of learning in the classroom.

The participants' assessment of these two approaches to grammar teaching indicated that they seemed ready to adapt to the task-based grammar teaching that PELT advocated. However, they were still unsure about how students could master grammar rules if the focus of the grammar lesson became the task instead of the language. The greater emphasis on language use also challenged the teacher learners' personal understandings of the uses of particular grammar points. For example, in addition to knowing how the present perfect is formed, they needed to know how it is used in real life in order to design a task with this language focus. They discovered, to their initial consternation, that their knowledge of grammar forms alone was no longer sufficient for them to teach grammar. Through collaborative practice exercises, they began to apply principles for making grammar work more creative

TABLE 1. PARTICIPANTS' OPINIONS ON ADVANTAGES AND DISADVANTAGES OF
TRADITIONAL AND COMMUNICATIVE GRAMMAR TEACHING

Approach	Advantages	Disadvantages
Traditional, rule-based grammar teaching	• Ease of preparation and following • Uniform orientation • Syllabus schedule • Controlled class • Easy-to-check tests • Security about knowledge of grammar rule	• Predictable • Mechanical • Boring • Detached from life • Lacking in real practice of language use
Communicative, task-based grammar teaching	• Element of surprise • Cooperative learning • Personal involvement • Maximized use of language structure in communication • Sense of achievement for learner • Understanding of grammar rule and use	• Difficult to prepare • Lacking in teacher control, leading to teacher insecurity • Difficult to measure achievement quantitatively • Time-consuming

and providing opportunities for learners to communicate using the language items in focus. The focus on language use was also linked with the notions of promoting cognitive challenge and affective involvement—ideas that they needed to consider in modifying existing grammar lessons. By focusing on the promotion of learning, we also enabled the teacher learners to examine their teaching practice critically in terms of (a) their teaching techniques and (b) their understanding of the nuances of the English language as a tool for meaningful communication.

At the end of the seminar-based training, the teacher learners worked on an action plan for the SFDA, which would allow them to apply systematically in the schools the ideas they learned in the seminar.

◈ DISTINGUISHING FEATURES

A Learning Orientation

PELT introduced a learning-centered training model, which complemented the macroskills approach promoted by the SEDP. The matrix in Figure 4 illustrates this relationship. The five PELT seminar topics (represented by horizontal lines) build on and intersect with the SEDP macroskills approach (represented by vertical lines).

Although previous training experiences (including the SEDP) had been input driven and inspired by demonstration teaching, PELT pioneered the introduction of a reflective methodology that challenged the teacher learners to drive the learning

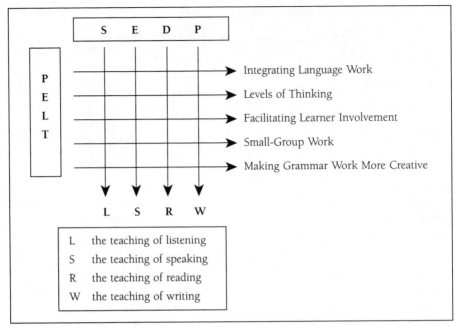

FIGURE 4. The SEDP-PELT Matrix

process in ways characteristic of successful communicative language teaching classrooms, where students are absorbed in problem-solving tasks.

Focus on Continuing Teacher Learning

The orientation to learning and process was not limited to the seminars. It was also dominant in the project's SFDA. This activity (see Waters & Vilches, 2000, for a detailed explanation) was conceptualized as a systematic strategy for teacher learning that continued from the seminar into the school.

When PELT was first introduced, it was met with skepticism by ELT managers who had seen enough projects that were completed without building in effective processes for continuity in the schools. The reliance on echo or cascade seminars—based on having teachers repeat for their peers the training they had received—had typically resulted in ineffective transmission of information that was not taken up in practice, and cascade training was losing its credence as a catalyst for teacher learning. The challenge for the project developers was to devise a system that aimed to integrate teacher learning in the seminar with teacher learning in the school. This system came in the form of the SFDA.

Systematically Structured, School-Based Follow-Up

The SFDA began in the seminar and ended in the school. It had three components: orientation, execution, and aftercare. Orientation, which was done in the seminar, clarified the principles, main components, and implementation stages of the activity. It also involved participants in preparing an action plan based on their choice of a specific aspect of a seminar topic. For example, if the topic choice were ILW, a possible focus would be *creating a communicative task to end the lesson*. Once the focus was identified, the teacher learners brainstormed execution issues.

The orientation to the SFDA in the seminar was followed by its execution in the school. It had four stages: preparation, implementation, review, and follow-up. The teacher learners began their preparation by informing their department head about the action plan in order to enlist support and help in its implementation. They also chose an instrument for gathering baseline data in their chosen area of focus and prepared experimental lessons. At the implementation stage, the teacher learners taught an experimental lesson and analyzed the impact on the students using the data they collected while teaching. At the review stage, they compared the baseline and impact data. Finally, at the follow-up stage, they decided whether to repeat the strategy—if the results had been unsatisfactory—or to share the outcomes with colleagues, if the plan had been successfully implemented.

The SFDA also encouraged teacher learners to repeat the cycle using a different topic until they had tried all the teaching strategies learned in the seminar. This repetition aimed to advance their teaching proficiency and create a learning orientation that would help teacher learners manage their teaching problems continuously. The monitoring and support of the ELT managers was an important aspect of the aftercare built in to the SFDA.

Emphasis on Teacher Participation

When the SFDA was launched, the teacher learners immediately saw it as a welcome alternative to the echo seminars. In practice, however, they ran into a number of difficulties. First, because action planning was a new idea for most of them, they found the discipline required in this phase quite tedious. Consequently, even if they had an action plan, they hesitated to begin it. Second, although support from the ELT manager was a necessary component of the SFDA, the teacher had to seek it, which was sometimes an impediment for teachers used to a culture of waiting to be told rather than of seeking help. Third, the time constraints stemming from the teacher learners' workloads distracted them from the activity focus.

Despite these constraints, most teacher learners persisted in carrying out their action plans. Based on 1996–1997 project data gathered through postal question-naires, group interviews, and discussions with ELT managers and teacher learners (see Center for English Language Teaching & Institute for English Language Education, 1997, 1998), those who carried out this phase benefited in terms of increased teaching competence, higher professional self-esteem, greater structure and direction, and improved working relations among colleagues and ELT managers. At a 1998 meeting in one project region, a successful implementer convincingly presented his experiences to a group of ELT managers who were hesitant about supporting the program in their schools. The conviction with which the teacher presented his work illustrated the kind of teacher learning that the PELT Project aimed to achieve. Anecdotal accounts such as this, told to numerous gatherings of teacher learners, highlighted the kind of support needed. These features of the program illustrate how PELT distinguished itself from previous educational innova-tions in Philippine ELT by building on what had already been achieved and by challenging the structures that impeded teacher and student learning.

◈ PRACTICAL IDEAS

Managing the PELT Project and running the teacher education program developed my insights about helping teacher learners learn how to learn. I offer two practical suggestions related to training procedures.

Build Incrementally on Teacher Learners' Knowledge and Experience

In teacher education, teacher learners may feel threatened by what they perceive as new ideas. The challenge for the teacher educator is to know how to help teacher learners manage the change process that will inevitably occur. What worked for me was to build incrementally on the teacher learners' existing knowledge and experience.

For example, in introducing task-based lesson planning via the ILW model, I first explored the teacher learners' concept of *integration*—a household term in their current lesson-planning practice. This exercise revealed that an integrated lesson meant the presence of listening, speaking, reading, and writing exercises as well as the inclusion of literature and values clarification. This formulation served as the background against which teacher learners could see ILW as an enrichment of their current lesson-planning practices. To deepen their understanding of the concept, they examined a textbook lesson and identified the parts that corresponded to the ILW elements: input, content-focused activities, language-focused activities, and task. Doing so made the newly introduced idea closer to their experience and less threatening. As a final exercise, they applied the principles of ILW to modifying the textbook lesson. Realizing that the ILW model did not entail starting a lesson from scratch made them feel more secure.

The procedure I used to introduce the ILW model may be summarized as follows:

- raising teacher learners' awareness of current practice (e.g., lesson planning, grammar teaching, asking questions, designing activities, managing classroom interaction)

- identifying an element of current practice that provides the link to the new idea

- showing how this new idea can enrich current practice and open up learning opportunities

- leading teacher learners toward the application of the new idea in a practice exercise

Give Teacher Learners Hands-on Experiences With Task-Based Lessons

PELT encouraged participants to see effective language teaching from the perspective of task-based lessons, which underpinned the ILW model. For the teacher learners, this view of language teaching was a *Eureka!* experience. It gave structures for developing cohesive lessons whose elements could build systematically toward a task with a communicative purpose.

Planning a lesson with a task in mind might seem to be common sense, but for teacher learners used to beginning with input, using a task-based approach can feel like turning a familiar world upside down. The following steps may help teachers overcome this difficulty.

Clarify the Concept of Task

Task in ILW is a culmination activity that simulates real-life communication. Based on this definition, an essay-writing exercise that asks students to compare and contrast two historical buildings in their hometown is not a task because it would not be found in the world outside the classroom. How, then, can teachers create a sense of real-life purpose in the English classroom so as to provide appropriate motivation for such a task? Answering this question leads to the formulation of the ILW task.

Explain the Importance of Task Context

In the language classroom, a task that is set up clearly should lead to an equally clear formulation of the task. Here is an example of a task context:

The Cultural Center of the Philippines is launching a "Know Your Locality" essay-writing contest open to students, in celebration of its golden anniversary as a center for Philippine culture, history, and life.

The requirements of the essay are as follows:

1. It must be about local culture, history, and life of a place or area fairly unknown and unwritten about.

2. It must be well documented.

3. It must have a clear focus about what it wants to say in general about the place: Is it the people? A significant person? The physical place? A custom/practice? Any significant event?

4. It must be three to five pages long, double-spaced, and typewritten in 12-point Times New Roman.

You have all been asked by your history teacher to participate in this contest. In groups of three, you will do research on a place of your choice. While you share your research data, each of you will write a different paper on an aspect of the gathered data.

Given this setting, the task can be formulated more specifically, perhaps, as follows:

When students write essays comparing and contrasting two historical buildings in the place of their choice based on the instructions given here, that is a decision students make as a result of the research and thinking processes that they will have gone through.

Provide Ideas for the Source of Input

Input could be anything that triggers communication and an exchange of ideas related to the task context. Possible input for the essay-writing task could include a play depicting historical highlights, an advertisement of a tourist site, or an editorial cartoon illustrating the banishment of a cultural tribe from its original place of residence.

Situate the Role of Content and Language Focus Activities

All input needs to be processed through content-focused activities that exploit the ideas presented. These activities prepare the students for the cognitive content of the task. The language-focused activities, on the other hand, enhance the students' linguistic ability to articulate ideas. The linguistic items the student would need to be able to write the assigned essay with grammatical accuracy are the main focus. Hence, one or two sets of linguistic items would suffice. A review of the past verb tenses and forms, for example, would be important for writing an essay that involves reporting observed and experienced events.

Focus on Implementation Issues

When all the lesson parts have been planned, the teacher can sequence the activities in view of other class factors, such as time allotment and the pace of the class. In the actual lesson, the teacher should evaluate the development of classroom events at each point and, in the process, observe and decide what is worth keeping from the original parts of the lesson, what needs modification, or what should be deleted. The basis for any of these decisions is the readiness of the students to carry out the task.

These practical applications of PELT ideas and insights, derived from the implementation of the training procedures, may be minimal, but they have had a wide-ranging and positive effect on language teaching and on teacher learner development in the Philippines.

❖ CONCLUSION

Doing a project case study is like telling a project story reflectively. That has been the aim of this chapter, with a specific focus on the flagship program of PELT—the teacher education component. As an initiative that came after a huge educational reform, PELT succeeded in creating a breakthrough in Philippine ELT. Its first major influence was in upgrading the language teaching competency of state secondary school teacher learners by introducing a learning-centered, process-oriented and task-based teaching methodology as a specific way of implementing communicative language teaching. In so doing, it advocated the restoration of the place of learning in the ELT classroom.

As a corollary to the first, its second major influence was in raising awareness about reflection as a key factor in teachers' continuing professional development. In promoting the teacher as a *reflective practitioner* (Schön, 1983), the project designed a cohesive teacher education program that aimed to integrate learning in the seminar with ongoing learning in the school.

Today, in the post-PELT period, the application of PELT ideas continues to flourish. I believe that, in the first instance, this is happening among the teachers who went through the project training. Although anecdotal evidence exists, a more systematic research effort is needed to identify the impact of the training. What I can attest to more confidently is the influence of PELT ideas on the activities undertaken by the Ateneo Center for English Language Teaching. The center has used the PELT model, with modifications as required, for other teacher education initiatives internally and elsewhere, and has applied the ideas by creating a task-based framework for syllabus and textbook design. At the time of writing, the most recent application of this framework was in the design and implementation of the 2003 nationwide mentor education program for teachers in basic education in Philippine state schools.

These developments indicate that although the original PELT project has ended, the underpinning principles of learning-centered and process-oriented training continue. They have been further tested and applied in various other contexts: trainer education, ELT management training, syllabus design, textbook project development, and others. In all these contexts, participants commonly feel that the training approach develops autonomous learning.

◈ CONTRIBUTOR

María Luz C. Vilches is an associate professor of English and the chairperson of the Department of English at Ateneo de Manila University in Manila, Philippines. She was the coordinator and lead local teacher educator for the PELT Project. Her research interests are in the fields of language and literature teaching and learning, teacher education and development, and ELT management.

PART 6

Which Texts?

CHAPTER 10

Reading the Wor(l)d: Exploring Global-Local Texts for the Malaysian Classroom

Moses Samuel and Saratha Sithamparam

◈ INTRODUCTION

In an age of globalization, teachers of English need to prepare learners to deal with new text forms arising out of technological innovations and cross-border culture flows. Satellite, cable, and mass communication have blurred the boundaries between local and global text consumption; hence our use of the term *global-local texts* in the title.

As new text forms, such as Web pages on the Internet, computer games, and digital messages on mobile phones, become part of the daily experiences of learners of English, ESOL teachers need to engage with and extend learners' textual repertoires. This chapter discusses how a TESOL postgraduate course, Reading in Schools, which we cotaught at the University of Malaya, addressed this need.

◈ CONTEXT

Participants in the MEd program at the University of Malaya are mainly teachers from schools and colleges, teacher educators from teacher education colleges, and officers from the Ministry of Education. This Malaysian postgraduate program is located in a milieu where English is a strong second language, widely used along with the national language, Malay, and other local languages, such as Mandarin and Tamil.

English in Malaysia, as in many postcolonial countries, serves global and local needs for international and intranational communication. An important link language between Malaysia and the rest of the world (M. Samuel, 2000), it is also widely used within the country in domains such as higher education, business, and the mass media. English is a vehicle for global flows of culture as words, images, and ideas seep across national boundaries. But because the language is also widely used locally, the global is not separate from the local.

Increasingly, in local environments in Malaysia, the literacy habitats of learners feature texts in English that are a result of globalization. The ubiquitous presence of consumer texts, such as signs and posters advertising McDonald's, Sony, and Nike, as well as texts from popular culture such as the *Star Wars* films (e.g., Lucas, 1977) and the cable network MTV in cinemas and on television, suggest a *glocalization* (Pakir, 1999) of such texts. Moreover, many teenagers have an *e-life* in which they surf the Internet, socialize in online chat rooms, and read texts in which the conventional printed word interfaces with graphics and images. As such, ESOL educators need to interrogate existing classroom practices so that learning and teaching take cognizance of cultural, social, and technological aspects of real-world literacy.

◈ DESCRIPTION

From our research on literacy in a Malaysian secondary school, we recognized a gap between school-based ways of teaching reading and the ways in which adolescents were experiencing texts outside the classroom. Our reading of the multiliteracies literature (New London Group, 1996) suggested how teacher educators could respond, and the lessons we drew are articulated in our philosophy for the Reading in Schools course.

Course Philosophy

Four cardinal ideas served as orienting principles:

1. Literacy acts of meaning making draw on word and image in multimedia and multimodal texts.

2. Literacy practices are situated in the lived experiences of learners, and educational programs have to be responsive to the needs of learners.

3. Although local lived experiences within the community are significant, texts provide access to diverse experiences beyond the immediate environment.

4. Literacy education has to be future oriented if school is to prepare learners for the future.

Course Structure

The official handbook describes the course as drawing on a foundation of current theories and issues in reading education to develop reading programs and materials. In our syllabus for the course, we chose to foreground a sociocultural orientation to designing literacy programs within a multiliteracies framework (New London Group, 1996). In helping teacher learners develop appropriate pedagogical approaches, we focused on the social situatedness of literacy (Street, 1984) and the changing nature of texts and literacy practices. We highlighted the use of multiple modalities, including the use of words and images (New London Group, 1996). In class, we used a metalanguage linked to these notions of literacy to promote ways of talking and writing about literacy. This metalanguage included terms used by the New London Group (1996), such as "multimodal" (p. 80), "designs of meaning" (p. 73), and "situated practice" (p. 85).

The course comprised two interconnected parts. Part 1, the ideas component, taught in the first half of the semester, introduced key concepts and issues. Part 2 explored implications for practice as teacher learners researched, designed, and trialed reading programs, and reflected on processes and outcomes. Part 1 was conceptual and issues oriented, and Part 2 focused on practice. Organizationally, therefore, as Figure 1 shows, this university course interfaced in-class course processes with on-site research and curriculum work; thus, the practical applications

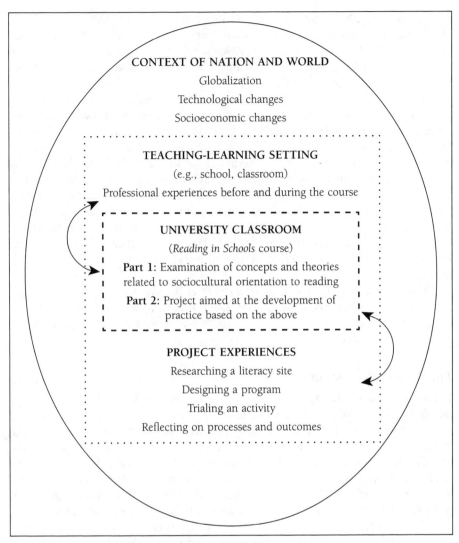

CONTEXT OF NATION AND WORLD
Globalization
Technological changes
Socioeconomic changes

TEACHING-LEARNING SETTING
(e.g., school, classroom)
Professional experiences before and during the course

UNIVERSITY CLASSROOM
(*Reading in Schools* course)

Part 1: Examination of concepts and theories related to sociocultural orientation to reading

Part 2: Project aimed at the development of practice based on the above

PROJECT EXPERIENCES
Researching a literacy site
Designing a program
Trialing an activity
Reflecting on processes and outcomes

FIGURE 1. Interrelated Dimensions of the Course

were located in the context of macrolevel developments, including globalization and technological and socioeconomic change in Malaysia.

The Ideas Component

Teacher learners read and discussed articles from the multiliteracies literature and other readings, and kept response journals. In putting together course readings, we juxtaposed concrete case studies with more abstract conceptual and theoretical pieces to facilitate theory-practice links. Thus, for instance, participants read Johns (1997) on the socioliterate classroom along with Heath's (1994) classic ethnography of home-school literacy links and Cazden's (2000) account of Puente classrooms; Kern (2000) and Goodman (2001) on textual designs and new text forms juxtaposed with Bromley's (2000) case study on reading *Beano* comics, which exemplified a child's meaning making with text design; and the section on critical literacy pedagogy in the New London Group (1996) article with Sylvester's (1997) account of the Sweet Cakes Town curricular initiative, which illustrated transformative practice in an inner-city classroom.

By moving between case studies and more theoretical readings, the teacher learners saw how abstract notions about literacy played out in a variety of contexts, for example, children learning to read in a family, young learners actively using literacy in a classroom simulation of running a town, and adolescents engaged in literacy practices in cyberspace. Furthermore, we shared with the teacher learners critical episodes from our school-based research on literacy curriculum design to illustrate how key literacy concepts played out in actual teaching-learning situations. We used photographs of the school and community as well as transcripts of interviews with learners as talking points to encourage the teacher learners to explore connections between learners' worlds and classroom practice. Class discussions helped the teacher learners critically examine their own experiences of literacy teaching.

These university classroom experiences thus became seedbeds where teacher learners explored notions of literacy pedagogy that they developed in the project component, which required them to research and design a reading program for students in a selected site.

The Project Component

For most of the teacher learners, our course involved making a transition from a psycholinguistic, skills-based orientation to a sociocultural orientation involving sensitivity to real-world texts and literacy practices. To achieve this, they needed to research the learners, the texts in their environments, and their textual practices in order to develop a pedagogy of literacy that would be relevant to the learners. The course therefore aimed at developing teacher researchers. We wanted the teacher learners to research and develop classroom practice that was theorized and grounded in local realities, taking into account developments in literacy education worldwide.

The research-based project comprised four main phases: (a) profiling learners and mapping literacy ecologies; (b) designing reading programs, including developing portfolios of texts and activities; (c) trialing text-based activities and recording outcomes; and, finally, (d) reflecting on the entire process. For their projects, some teacher learners chose to work with groups of learners; others worked with individuals. Although the teacher learners carried out their projects individually, they shared their experiences at each phase of the project during weekly class meetings. These shifts between fieldwork and class discussions allowed them to "move between two thought positions" (Kemmis & McTaggart, 2000, p. 590). They were insiders engaged in researching, designing, and teaching as well as outsiders examining and interrogating these processes within the space of the university classroom.

The teacher learners developed an anthropological stance on pedagogy by being responsive to learners and context. In researching the sites of their teaching, they mapped the literacy ecologies of their teaching-learning contexts, taking into account community literacy centers (e.g., libraries, cybercafés, and video rental stores) and texts in these environments (e.g., signs, billboards, and posters). In addition, they developed emic, or insider, perspectives of the situation by interviewing learners and other significant participants in the community (e.g., parents, video rental store owners, and librarians).

They collected data using various techniques. Teacher learners made observations, took photographs, interviewed learners, and examined samples of their work and the texts they read. For example, Adeline, a teacher learner, discovered that the learners she worked with were fans of J. K. Rowling's *Harry Potter* series and were familiar with the related cinematic text. Another teacher learner, Jugdeep, found that the 11-year-old learner she studied was exposed to a range of consumerist texts, such as advertisements in a variety of media and labels on various forms of packaging, whereas the learner Assunta wrote about was an adept player of computer games. Like other teacher learners on the course, these three systematically documented the texts in learners' life worlds.

What emerged was an awareness that many of the English texts (e.g., movies, advertisements, and computer games) that Malaysian adolescents engaged with reflected a larger culture of text production and consumption arising out of processes of globalization. These texts needed to feature in reading programs alongside other texts to provide continuity across various domains of adolescent experience, in and out of school.

◈ DISTINGUISHING FEATURES

As course instructors, we sought to connect processes in our university classroom with the social world, so that both readings and field experiences became resources for developing classroom practice. In class, teacher learners reflected on literacy teaching through journal writing and developed an awareness of new texts and a metalanguage for speaking about literacy. In the field, they researched texts in learners' life worlds and designed reading programs incorporating these texts. We draw on the teacher learners' projects to illustrate key features of the course.

Using Journals for Reflection

To implement reading programs with a sociocultural orientation to literacy, the teacher learners needed to see key concepts and issues introduced through the readings in terms of actual literacy environments. In our course, journal writing played a key role in enabling teacher learners to relate their readings on learners, the changing nature of texts, and textual environments as well as literacy practices to their own experiences.

For example, Gerard used his journal to reflect on Goodman's (2001) article on the analysis of visuals and the texts he encountered in his community. On the McDonald's billboard that he regularly drove past, he noticed that beside the letter *M* that was the McDonald's logo was the Malay word *makan,* which means *to eat.* The word was printed in the distinctive color and font of the McDonald's logo. Gerard observed,

> The huge yellow M . . . [also] stands for *makan* [eat]. How clever! The word *makan* is so very Malaysian and now when someone thinks of *makan* [eating] they might just think of McDonald's. (Masilamany, 2001, p. 11)

The word *makan* has a larger cultural significance in community life in Malaysia, where the meal provides a space for social interaction and bonding. What is especially significant about Gerard's observation about the advertisement is that a global text such as the McDonald's logo had assumed a local identity to appeal to a local audience. Although Goodman's article provided him with the necessary concepts as well as the language for thinking about texts, it was the process of journal writing that helped him situate his understanding and see its relevance in his own lived experiences.

Exploring Features of New Text Forms

Although the journal was useful for reflection and awareness raising, the project required teacher learners to consider ways in which they could help learners explore texts. As they worked with learners in actual teaching-learning situations, their hands-on experiences further contributed to their understanding of how different features of text worked to enable readers to make meaning.

For her project, Assunta explored 11-year-old Mischa's experiences with texts on Pearl Harbor. Mischa had found a computer game on Pearl Harbor difficult to understand because he did not have background information about the attack on Pearl Harbor in 1941. Responding to this need, Assunta planned a series of literacy activities. Together they examined a variety of texts: maps of the attack on Pearl Harbor, the Hollywood movie based on the historical event (Bay, 2001), a collection of war letters, the famous "Day of Infamy" speech by President Roosevelt, diary entries of survivors, and photographs of the event.

Details of text design were explored as Mischa compared the CD and DVD covers of the movie *Pearl Harbor*. Assunta reported,

> The CD and DVD covers were interesting. They were both of the same movie but were designed differently. . . . Concentrating on the front cover, [Mischa] pointed out that the same three faces appear [on both covers]. [Mischa concluded,] "They must be the main three characters in the story and Ben Afleck must be the main hero. This is because . . . in the CD version, only Ben Afleck's name is mentioned. He must have starred in other movies and must be famous too. This will make people want to see the show." . . . He said that in the CD version, below the *Pearl Harbor* title, [are the words] "From the Director of *Armageddon*." Mischa said he had watched *Armageddon* and it was a very, very good movie. So he feels *Pearl Harbor* will be a good movie too. People who have watched *Armageddon* will want to watch this. (Antonysamy, 2002, p. 12)

In talking about the two covers, Assunta said that she drew from Bromley's (2000) reading when she asked Mischa "questions similar to what Bromley asked her daughter about the *Beano* comics" (Antonysamy, 2002, p. 12). In their interrogation of the two covers, Assunta and Mischa read significance into information about the main actor and the director, as a marketing strategy to persuade potential movie watchers that this was a movie worth seeing. They drew on their understanding of the genre of the CD and DVD cover, and their knowledge of advertising and Hollywood. In incorporating genre awareness into her pedagogy, Assunta was drawing on her experiences in the Reading in Schools course.

Mischa also read the images together with the words and showed how they both worked to make meaning. Assunta wrote,

> [Both covers] seem to have the yellow and orange glow, with the seas dark, and the brown smoke. [Mischa] said that was the color of war, of fire. After all, the war message said they were attacked, so you can't have bright colors. "Why not red then, [I asked], blood is red?" [Mischa replied], "well, you can have red but it looks so yuks—more for horror movies. I think this yellow and orange color is better." (Antonysamy, 2002, p. 13)

CDs and DVDs, including their covers, are multimodal, multimedia texts, and Mischa was offering an interpretation of the significance of colors and the semiotic associations of the different hues. As the excerpt above demonstrates, part of his visual literacy involved developing an awareness of how the dimension of color serves as a resource for making meaning. With the increasing use of image and word in text construction, the course enabled teacher learners to interrogate texts and help learners develop an awareness of the grammar of the visual (Kress & van Leeuwen, 1996) as well as the verbal.

Developing Metalanguage to Speak About New Texts

As teachers of English, most of the teacher learners used print texts that were dominated by words rather than visuals to teach reading. As such, we felt that if new multimodal texts were to feature in their classrooms, these teacher learners would have to expand their repertoires of ways of speaking about texts beyond the notion of the word on the page. In order to prepare learners to read new texts, teachers of English needed a metalanguage, a vocabulary that would allow them to think and talk about these text forms.

For instance, to support the pedagogy of multiliteracies, the New London Group (1996) uses a metalanguage that "describes meaning in various realms. These include the textual and the visual as well as multimodal relations between different meaning-making processes that are now so critical in media texts and the electronic multimedia" (p. 24). The teacher learners explored the metalanguage of the multiliteracies literature for its relevance in theorizing about literacy and designing reading programs.

One concept that they grappled with in the readings by the New London Group (1996) and Kern (2000) was the notion of design. In breaking away from grammatical terms traditionally used to describe text form, the New London Group used the alternative term "design" (p. 73) of the text in much the same way one would use expressions like *the design of the car* to refer to the way in which it is constructed.

In designing texts, the New London Group (1996) envisaged language users drawing on what they label "available designs" (p. 74) to reproduce, redesign, or transform them to serve new communicative purposes. The term *available designs* initially appeared abstract and inaccessible to many teacher learners, especially when they first encountered it. In using her journal to clarify her understanding of this term in Kern's (2000) reading, Adeline wrote,

> I can almost see in my mind a Rolodex containing various index cards for the different available designs. Each time I read or write a text, I pick out a combination of available design index cards from my mental Rolodex that are suitable for the literacy task at hand.

Adeline used the metaphor of the Rolodex, a vivid visual image, as a heuristic for accessing the more abstract and somewhat enigmatic term *available designs*. The metaphor helped Adeline as a practitioner appropriate the term to guide her professional actions, as she drew from the theoretical literature to develop her personal theories. The metaphor of the Rolodex with its index cards also helped her explore the various elements of design comprising genres, images, vocabulary, and syntax.

In the readings in Part 1 and the project in Part 2 of the course, teacher learners used the metalanguage of multiliteracies as tools for talking about meaning making and textual representations. Not only were they exploring how texts were constructed, but, more importantly, they were learning to talk about texts, using metalanguage as building-block labels or concepts for their theorizing.

Researching New Texts From Learners' Life Worlds

As course instructors, we sometimes pushed against the grain of the undergraduate training that most of the teacher learners had experienced. Assunta wrote, "being so used/schooled into seeing literacy in terms of decontextualized skills and competencies, I am still grappling with the idea [of the] importance of literacy as social and cultural practice" (Antonysamy, 2002, p. 20). Although taxonomies of reading skills are useful in helping to facilitate ways to encourage readers to think about information in texts, the features of texts as well as purposes for reading need to be considered.

To move beyond generic, skills-based, cookbook-type practices centered on textbooks and workbooks that teacher learners like Assunta were familiar with, we needed to build into their practice a questioning stance: How useful were the activities in their reading lessons for literacy practices in real-world contexts? How relevant were the texts that they were using? To develop a socioculturally responsive reading pedagogy, the teacher learners had to be actively aware of authentic texts, purposes, and ways of reading.

To achieve this, they needed to develop a researcher stance of continually probing contexts and activities, and interrogating reading classrooms in terms of larger social realities. For reading in schools to be relevant to literacy practices resulting from globalization, teachers of literacy needed to be researchers of literacy. As Adeline put it, "it is not easy to wear two hats but it really needs to be done" (Liew, 2002, p. 23).

In her reflections on designing and teaching a reading program, Adeline described the synergy that comes from teaching and researching:

> The consciousness that I am wearing two hats—that of researcher, and that of teacher—has in a way forced me to look at the teaching-learning situation as objectively as possible, and to rigorously interrogate my teaching practices even as I interrogate my students' learning practices. Also, it has allowed me to . . . begin to understand my learners' context, to research their literacy practices, get a clearer picture of the place they come from and where they are

coming from culturally and socially. If a teacher did not take all these factors into consideration, she would be overlooking the significance of the situatedness of the teaching-learning situation. (Liew, 2002, pp. 23–24)

Teacher learners found that learners' life worlds constitute more than what initially meets the eye when they are examined through researcher lenses. The systematic and deliberate examination of context, learners, texts, and social practices provided nuanced readings of the situatedness of literacy within communities on which reading pedagogies could be premised. Technology, rapid communication, and the movement of multinational franchises across borders continually redefine *the local* in teaching-learning situations. The rapidity of the development of new text forms suggests that researching and designing are intrinsic to the processes of literacy teaching if the practices of school are to keep up with developments in the community.

Designing the Teaching and Learning of New Texts

As Stenhouse (1975) wrote, "the development of teaching can never be *a priori*" (p. 25). As the teacher learners researched texts, learners, and contexts, they came to see reading within a larger ecology of literacy. To play out the key pedagogical concepts of responsiveness and situatedness, the teacher learners developed reading programs at the sites of their teaching based on data about their learners and the texts in their environments. This development is illustrated through course projects from two domains of adolescent experience: consumerism and popular culture.

Reading Consumerist Texts: Fast Food Advertisements

In Malaysia today, globalization has brought into local markets a flood of consumer products packaged and advertised in glossy texts rich in image and word. In designing her reading program, the pervasiveness of advertisements in the world of the learner Jugdeep worked with led her to reflect,

> as members of a "consumer society" learners have to be taught to read the subtle messages behind words and pictures. In a world where texts are changing, where existing texts are being shaped not only into new forms but are being given new purposes, [learners] have to be taught . . . how to interpret the many visuals used in these texts, [as well as the] . . . words, print size, font, [and] color. (Kaur, 2002, p. 9)

Immersed in the textual environment of the learner she worked with, Jugdeep became sensitive to textual messages and their features. Although her aim was to ultimately develop a critical reading of these texts, she saw the need to scaffold the experience.

In designing to teach the reading of an advertisement of Kenny Rogers Roasters, a U.S. restaurant franchise in Malaysia, she began by situating the text in the learner's experiences by drawing on her knowledge of the menu, with which Winnie, the learner, was familiar. She then zeroed in on the text, highlighting its features. She reported, "I wanted so much to help her focus on the importance of words, as the next bit will show."

[Jugdeep:] Why do they use the word peppery so many times?
[Winnie:] Because it is Black Pepper Chicken.

[Jugdeep:]   So why do you think they have put all these words on the skin, the meat and even on the bone?

[Winnie:]   So people will know what is so great about it.

     . . .

[Jugdeep:]   Why are they telling you so much about this pepper chicken?

[Winnie:]   Because they want to introduce people to this chicken.

[Jugdeep:]   They are introducing this chicken to people. (Kaur, 2002, pp. 19–21)

With the text in front of them, she highlighted the placement of words in relation to image ("So why do you think they have put all these words on the skin, the meat and even on the bone?"), encouraging Winnie to integrate cues from this interfacing of words and visuals to make meaning. In the "talk around the text " (Jones, 2000, p. 71), Jugdeep also explored word coinages such as *pepped up* and *pepperific,* visual and graphological features, genre, and the intent of the text.

What Jugdeep sought to do was to help Winnie develop skills in both visual and verbal literacies. She also wanted Winnie to see the genre of the advertisement as part of social practice in an increasingly consumerist culture.

Reading Popular Culture Texts: Into the World of Harry Potter

When Adeline was discussing movies in English that the learners had seen, she reported that they "became extremely animated when they started talking about *Harry Potter and the Philosopher's Stone*" (Liew, 2002, p. 10). Young people in Malaysia are becoming increasingly active consumers of clusters of related texts comprising films, books, comics, Web sites, and sometimes games centered around popular culture. Examples of these clusters of texts include texts based on the *Star Wars* series of films (e.g., Lucas, 1977), Disney animation movies like *The Lion King* (Allers & Minkoff, 1994), and, more recently, the *Harry Potter* films (e.g., Columbus, 2001). Aggressive multimedia commercial campaigns to promote these products have resulted in their popularity among young audiences worldwide.

The adolescent appeal of *Harry Potter* and the fact that Adeline used the film experience as a bridge into more conventional texts like the storybook led her to develop a program drawing on a range of *Harry Potter* texts. Like Kincheloe and Steinberg (1998) she looked to "movies, video games, comic books, and other commercially produced youth culture or kinderculture" in addition to storybooks. In the activities she designed, these texts became "cultural artifacts to be examined around the questions of experience and identity" (p. 235). Although the *Harry Potter* stories were authored by British writer J. K. Rowling, Adeline felt that they could also be used to encourage her students to interrogate social issues of race and ethnicity that actively figured in the life worlds of her Malaysian Chinese students. She wrote,

In Book 2 and Book 3 of the *Harry Potter* series . . . J. K. Rowling deals with anti-Muggle sentiments and racial intolerance between magic folk and Muggles . . . or even issues of class consciousness where the haves (e.g., Draco Malfoy) often discriminate against the have-nots (Ron Weasley). By getting Mei Ee, Wei Hoong and Mei Kin to read chapters entitled "Mudbloods and Murmurs" (activity 2) and "The Dark Maze" (activity 3), I hope to get them to draw parallels between discrimination as it occurs in Harry Potter's world and discrimination as it occurs in the learners' own community and lifeworlds. [I want] the learners to distance themselves from their own cultural reality and look at it objectively, and then [talk] about it. . . . (Liew, 2002, p. 11)

The text allowed detachment from immediate circumstances so that issues such as "discrimination, bigotry and even snobbery" (Liew, 2002, p. 21) could be examined and analyzed. These activities encouraged the learners to make connections later with incidents reported in newspapers and television.

Guided exploration through intertextual links and connections with experience could, therefore, lead to contestation and critique (Unsworth, 2001). Used thus, the story world takes on local world significance as readers examine immediate circumstances anew and consider alternative possibilities.

◈ PRACTICAL IDEAS

We refashioned an existing course to meet what we saw as a critical need in ESOL teacher education to respond to the changing literacy terrain in Malaysia. We felt that a sociocultural orientation to literacy education would be sensitive to changing contexts, texts, and literacy practices in a globalizing world. As we asked ourselves what from our experiences for ESOL teacher education might be of practical value, we realized how critical course processes are in preparing teachers to handle the complexities of changing practice.

Facilitate Theory-Practice Links in Teacher Education

In designing our course, we worked to facilitate theory-practice links so that teacher learners developed informed pedagogies of reading relevant to diverse contexts of teaching and learning. Our experiences suggest that teacher educators can facilitate theory-practice links by

- developing course structures comprising an ideas component and an experiential project component
- selecting assigned readings comprising theoretical discussions and case studies of practice, so that interactions between the two can be explored
- promoting class discussions in which teacher learners share multiple perspectives from diverse classroom experiences to explore theory
- developing reflexivity through response journals
- facilitating the appropriation of metalanguage for thinking, talking, and even theorizing about practice

Encourage Teacher Research of Texts and Literacy Practices

With the presence of new texts, literacy ecologies are continually changing. For English language classrooms to remain responsive to the immediate and future needs of learners, we see teacher research into new texts and literacy practices in learners' life worlds as being critical to developing a growing knowledge base on which practice can draw. Preparing teachers to be researchers of literacy involves

- getting teachers to play the anthropologist, so to speak, by taking active note of texts and literacy practices, including their social purposes in the community

- helping teachers draw on a variety of sources and data collection techniques, including observations of classrooms and the community; interviews with learners, teachers, and others; photographs; and artifacts, including students' work

- enabling teachers to map textual ecologies and research features of diverse text forms, including the use of different media, modalities, and discourse strategies

Encourage Active Curriculum Development

Our course was located in a milieu where teaching in schools was driven by the national curriculum. In such a context, teachers are very often seen largely as curriculum implementers. However, in literacy education, where texts and what it means to be literate are constantly changing, we see the need for teachers to be actively and dynamically engaged in curriculum renewal so that school is relevant and responsive to learners' social futures. Teachers can develop as curriculum and program designers by

- finding spaces within existing curriculum frameworks to incorporate aspects of texts and literacy practices from the social worlds of students

- drawing on texts, literacy practices, and the social purposes of literacy from various domains of learners' experiences as curriculum resources

- establishing supporting professional networks to sustain curriculum renewal among teachers through school subject panels, professional associations, and discussion groups on the Internet

- establishing collaborative partnerships between schools and other agencies, including universities, to promote innovation for effective literacy education

- encouraging a spirit of innovation and a willingness to experiment with alternative ways of teaching

◈ CONCLUSION

Our experiences as university teacher educators suggest that ESOL teacher education is a dynamic field that constantly reinvents itself in response to changing circumstances arising from a larger dynamic, which may involve globalization, changing national policies, and changing ideas about what constitutes language and literacy, and what it means to be a user of English. In this case study, we focused on how we responded as teacher educators to a change permeating multiple domains of the Malaysian social and educational context: the increasing presence of multimedia, multimodal texts in English, and changing literacy practices.

Through the course processes, teacher learners in turn interrogated this phenomenon, drawing on course readings and their own experiences to develop understandings that would enable them to design reading programs that were responsive to their local circumstances. Understandings of the new demands of literacy education did not come easily. The teacher learners struggled with the readings and with the new ways of thinking about text and the teaching of reading as well as the messiness of dealing with classroom practice. The processes of active talk and journal writing as well as researching texts, teaching, and learning allowed them spaces to grapple with these processes within the supportive community of a graduate class. Although these experiences occurred on a particular course, the challenge remains to provide a similar milieu within the teaching profession so that the professional development of teachers can address the complexities of the globalization of English.

◈ CONTRIBUTORS

Moses Samuel and Saratha Sithamparam are associate professors in the Faculty of Education at the University of Malaya, in Malaysia. They teach undergraduate and postgraduate courses in ESOL teacher education and are involved in the continuing professional development of teachers. Their research interests include literacy education, ESOL teacher education, and language education in developing societies.

CHAPTER 11

Teaching the Literature of Global English

George R. Bozzini

◈ INTRODUCTION

Of particular relevance to TESOL is the fact that English has become an international literary language of extraordinary reach and diversity, and—given the proliferation of literary works in English from all around the world—a literary language of astonishing vigor. Unfortunately, many serious discussions of English as a global language overlook this fact (see Crystal, 1997, 1999; Wallraff, 2000).

I would maintain that, given its widespread cultural importance, the literature of global English merits a place at the TESOL table of English for specific purposes, along with content-based ESOL courses in business, science, medicine, and other disciplines. In this regard, no less a literary figure than Rushdie (1991) has advocated that

> if all English literatures could be studied together, a shape would emerge which would truly reflect the new shape of the language in the world, and we could see that [literature in English] has never been in better shape, because the world language now possesses a world literature, which is proliferating in every conceivable direction. (p. 70)

Making the case for teaching literature in general in ESOL is a considerable body of articles and other writings. I would cite S. McKay (1982), Spack (1985), Gajdusek (1988), and Oster (1989); Talib (1992), who addresses specifically the teaching of international literature in ESOL; Widdowson's (1982) plenary presentation; and doctoral dissertations by Stern (1985) and Zou (1991).

Arguments in favor of teaching literature in ESOL include the following:

- Literature plays a positive role in developing language competence.

- Literary texts present vocabulary and syntactic structures in a rich variety of contexts that reflect actual language use.

- An integrated approach to teaching literary texts incorporates all four language skills—reading, speaking, listening, and writing.

- Analysis and discussion of literary texts sharpen students' critical skills.

- Reading literature makes learning a language both interesting and enjoyable, thus appealing to both the intellectual and the affective domains in the learning process.

- Literature, with its universal themes, is entirely relevant to many other subjects in the students' academic experience, to the extent that they deal in one way or another with the human condition and humankind's quest for discovering and telling truth.

◈ CONTEXT

The Course

The course from which I draw this case study, English 11-15, is a special section for international students of a credit-bearing course that satisfies the second-semester institutional requirement in English composition at The George Washington University (GW) in Washington, DC, in the United States. (The course was subsequently moved to the EFL Department and renamed EFL 011.) Undergraduates in all but the School of Engineering must complete English 11. Second language (L2) students were formerly *mainstreamed*, that is, required to take their second semester of English composition in the English Department. This often proved to be problematic, as the GW composition program—unlike those at many U.S. colleges and universities—does not follow a standard syllabus. Rather, virtually every section of composition focuses on its own topic, usually literary, and is designed generally for native speakers having an ample cultural and literary background in English.

Having taught sections of English 11 to classes of mostly first language (L1) students and to mixed classes of L1 and L2 students, as well as having taught literature in advanced-level EFL, I was able to create special sections of English 11 for international students that would not compromise English Department standards.

The students in the course come largely from Asia—China, Indonesia, Japan, Malaysia, Thailand—and the Arab Middle East. They typically have TOEFL scores of 550 and above. They study a variety of majors in the schools of business, international affairs, arts and sciences, and health sciences. At GW, they have access to state-of-the-art instructional technology such as online syllabi, a well-stocked library database, and the Internet. Like many of my colleagues at GW, I chose to put my syllabi online, using the course management system Prometheus (replaced since then by Blackboard [see http://www.blackboard.com/], a similar system), which I describe below. However, the literary syllabus would be equally as enriching with no more than a traditional chalkboard for technology, an instructor who enjoys introducing international students to literature in English, and eager and attentive students.

Texts on Family, Heritage, and Community

This case study focuses on a unit for teaching literary texts on family, heritage, and community. The texts include short stories, poems, and memoirs by authors of diverse nationalities: English, Irish, American, Canadian, Jamaican, New Zealander, Malaysian, Indian, and Sri Lankan. Even within these nationalities, there are authors of diverse ethnicity: for example, Japanese British, Pakistani Canadian, Maori New Zealander, and Chinese American. All the texts are contemporary, that is, written in the past 50 years, and most in the past two decades. All of the texts referred to here are contained in Bozzini and Leenerts' (2001) *Literature Without Borders*.

The unit in this study is one of several units in a one-semester, 14-week syllabus. Other units might vary from semester to semester and include themes such as coming of age; immigration; societal alienation, or *othering,* as described in an ESOL context by W. K. Johnson (1999) and Kubota (1999, 2001); colonization; war and, it is hoped, peace and reconciliation; and nature, faith, and spirit. A unit is designed for 3 weeks' work, with 3 hours of class meetings weekly, student group discussions outside class, and ongoing teacher-student conferences.

An essay test is given at the end of the unit. Students are asked to write an essay of one to one and one-half pages for each of four questions. They are reminded to cite information from the text to support their main ideas and to indicate the paragraph number where the citation is located. They may refer to the textbook, to their class or home notes, and to an L1 or bilingual dictionary. They have the whole 75-minute period to complete the test.

The test is intended to be selective rather than comprehensive, and students are given many choices, as evinced in questions such as *Discuss the literary devices—both stylistic and structural—used to tell one of any of the stories that we have read in this unit* or *Discuss a social or historical issue that drives the story in two of the texts that we have studied.*

◈ DESCRIPTION

An effective approach for teaching literature provides a uniform framework in which to study individual texts. And within such a framework, each of the various types of exercises makes particular assumptions about teaching and learning literature.

The process-based approach used in the course incorporates five types of exercises: (a) reading readiness, (b) scanning the text, (c) close reading, (d) thinking and talking about the text, and (e) writing about the text. In my syllabus, I have designated these exercise types as Perspectives, Charting the Text, Considerations of Style, Afterthoughts, and the Writer's Craft, respectively.

Perspectives

Reading readiness activities assume that the students have developed in their life experience a fundamental knowledge of their own world, well-defined cultural values, and a burgeoning world view. Thus, these activities prepare them to read meaningfully by first probing their experience with and their feelings about central issues that will be addressed in the text. When familiarity with an issue might be lacking—and in many cases I assume it will be—I encourage the students themselves to research the issues in the campus library or over the Internet. I invite them to share their ideas in a class discussion—usually in small groups—before we analyze the text.

Charting the Text

Getting students to scan the text assumes that, to be appreciated fully, a literary text must be read carefully, deliberately, and interactively from beginning to end. Thus, questions about the text should be shaped to address, in addition to the comprehension of ideas, a text's meaningful divisions, its narrative or poetic structure, and the power of its ideas to engage the reader. I further encourage students to put themselves into the text and to interact with it, manifestly by marking and annotating it and responding to it while they read. Students are expected to chart the text for homework with the help of the Plan for Literary Analysis grid, described below.

Considerations of Style

A closer reading of the text invites students to focus their attention on the literary devices that give the text—be it narrative or poetic—its lifeblood: images, symbols, sound patterns, an attitude. My major assumption here is that exploring the nuances of language is essential to fully appreciating and delighting in a work of literature. Students are asked to review the style exercises for homework but are reminded that these will be discussed in class as well.

Afterthoughts

Having read between the lines of the text, having reflected on it, and having put it in perspective with their self-experience or with other texts, students are presumably prepared for stimulating, sensitive, and participatory discussion that transforms the classroom into a forum of ideas.

The Writer's Craft

A final assumption underlying the approach discussed here is that, in the study of literature, reading and writing are necessarily interconnected, and the one reinforces the other. To this end, I offer students a variety of writing tasks, such as retelling part of the story from another point of view, writing a critical or argumentative essay on a poignant issue in the text, or comparing the treatment of an issue in two or more texts. Typically, I strive to make the texts meaningful in the ongoing personal narrative of the students themselves by having them chronicle their own experiences vis-à-vis the events in the texts.

Prometheus: The Online Syllabus

The online syllabus, available through GW's Web-based course management system, Prometheus (see http://www.prometheus.com/), gives my students ready access to a great deal of course information even before they register, such as a course description, the course objectives, method of instruction, due dates for assignments throughout the semester, and method of evaluation.

The course outline lists meeting dates and the topic for each session, such as

Sep-03-01 Session 1 FATHERS AND SONS
Sep-05-01 Session 2 FATHERS AND SONS
Sep-10-01 Session 3 MOTHERS AND DAUGHTERS
Sep-12-01 Session 4 MOTHERS AND DAUGHTERS
Sep-17-01 Session 5 ACROSS THE GENERATIONS
Sep-19-01 Session 6 ACROSS THE GENERATIONS
Sep-24-01 Session 7 WORKSHOP ON THE PERSONAL NARRATIVE
Sep 26-01 Session 8 TEST ON THE FAMILY AND HERITAGE UNIT

I can create, delete, or reorder sessions in the outline, as appropriate—for example, if we miss a scheduled class day, if I choose to devote a session to a relevant, recently discovered video, or if I sense the need to extend the workshop another day. Handily, when changes are made online, students have immediate access to a fresh version of the syllabus.

By clicking on the session in the outline, the student accesses the Assignment Page for the session, which indicates the topic, a class plan, assignments due, and required readings (see Figure 1 for a typical Assignment Page). Students typically work in preassigned groups on specific questions that will be part of the class discussion. Students are also asked to write a one- to two-page response— individually or in a group—to each of the texts assigned for the session. Through Prometheus, the instructor and the students are able to send messages to individuals, small groups, or the whole class.

Additional readings can be posted in the Files component of Prometheus. For example, before reading Silko's (2001) poem, I would have students download a file called Questions for Poetry Analysis, which would introduce them to the four elements that distinguish poetry from prose: rhythm, pattern, image, and sound (RPIS). Silko's poem is particularly good for showing the difference between the rhythm of a poem and a prose narrative—a difference made evident when the poem is written in prose form and both versions are read aloud.

Original version (excerpt):

It was a long time before
I learned that my Grandma A'mooh's
real name was Marie Anaya Marmon.
I thought her name really was "A'mooh."

Monday, September 17, 2001

Session 5

Topic: ACROSS THE GENERATIONS

Class Plan: Discuss Silko's poem and Lam's short story per the group assignments below.

Group I: Compare and contrast the speaker's and the narrator's intergenerational experiences with your own.

Group II: What are some contemporary issues in American society that Silko's poem and Lam's story address?

Group III: How, where, and—do you suppose—why is humor imbued in Lam's narrator's telling of his grandmother's death? How do imaginative and autobiographical fiction work together in this narrative?

Assignments due: Your written responses to Silko's poem and Lam's story.

Required readings:

"[It was a long time before]"—poem by Leslie Marmon Silko

"Grandma's Tales"—story by Andrew Lam

FIGURE 1. Typical Assignment Page

I realize now it had happened when I was a baby
and she cared for me while my mother worked.
I'd been hearing her say
"*a'moo'ooh*"
which is the Laguna expression of endearment
for a young child
spoken with great feeling and love. (pp. 3–4)

Reconstructed version in prose:

It was a long time before I learned that my Grandma A'mooh's real name was
Marie Anaya Marmon. I thought her name really was "A'mooh." I realize now
it had happened when I was a baby and she cared for me while my mother
worked. I had been hearing her say "*a'mooh,*" which is the Laguna expression
of endearment for a young child, spoken with great feeling and love.

In assigning students a personal narrative based on a relationship with a
grandparent or older relative, I give students the option of using poetic or prose
form. In either case—and the poetic form is a popular choice—the assignment
generates some very fine personal narrative writing.

Charting the content of this simple narrative poem is pretty straightforward, as
the speaker recalls her Laguna Pueblo great-grandmother from her own infancy to
the old woman's death. Each of the five stanzas presents a vignette from the two
women's shared lives—each one as graphic as a photograph from a family album. In
fact, the poem is contained in a miscellany, *Storyteller* (Silko, 1981), which includes
family history, fiction, photographs, and poetry.

Relevant links to Silko's poem might include information on the Laguna Pueblo,
the multicultural setting of Silko's native New Mexico, or the treatment of the aged
in Western and other cultures, per the study question assigned.

The following excerpts are from "Grandma's Tales" (Lam, 2001):

The day after Mama and Papa took off to Las Vegas, Grandma died. Nancy
and I, we didn't know what to do, Vietnamese traditional funerals with
incense sticks and chanting Buddhist monks not being our thing. We have a
big freezer, Nancy said. Why don't we freeze her. Really. Why bother Mama
and Papa. What's another day or two for Grandma now anyway? (p. 19)

Nancy's older than me, and since I didn't have any better idea, we iced her. (p.
20)

In presenting "Grandma's Tales" as the first short story in the course, I post a file
for students to download, Plan for a Literary Analysis, a grid on which students fill
out the elements of a narrative: setting characters, plot, theme(s), point of view, tone,
irony, language use, foreshadowing, imagery, and symbolism. The grid, shown
completed in Figure 2, is assigned thereafter for all narratives, fictive and nonfictive,
and serves as a good point of departure for discussion of the text.

Relevant links to the content of "Grandma's Tales" might include articles on
Vietnamese immigrants in the United States, including from Lam's own reporting for
the Pacific News Service or his commentaries on National Public Radio, in which his
real-life grandmother often figures. Another relevant link would be an article on
Buddhist notions of reincarnation—to lend plausibility to the reappearance of the
late grandmother in the story, 40 years younger and speaking excellent English.

TEXT	"Grandma's Tales"
AUTHOR	Andrew Lam
SETTING	(time, place, social context) contemporary San Francisco; middle-class Vietnamese immigrants
CHARACTERS	narrator, sister Nancy, narrator's boyfriend Eric, Grandma, parents
PLOT	Grandma dies; narrator and daughter freeze her till parents return from Las Vegas. Narrator tells Grandma's story of war and hardship in Vietnam. Grandma is briefly and humorously reincarnated. Last scene depicts her traditional Buddhist funeral.
THEME(S)	differing ways of making cultural connections—with homeland, with adopted land—among generations of immigrants
POINT OF VIEW	that of narrator, first-generation American, sympathetic toward Grandma, sensitive to hardships of Vietnamese immigrants of her generation
TONE	satirical, playful, but ultimately sadly touching
IRONY	[Its apparent lack here may engender discussion of what irony is and is not.]
LANGUAGE USE	narration, dialogue, contemporary slang
NARRATIVE DEVICES	shifting time lines: for example, the death scene revisited twice; flashback to Grandma's life in Vietnam; the reincarnation fantasy; the descriptive funeral scene at the end, with flashback to family home in Vietnam
FORESHADOWING	The narrator's sensitive telling of Grandma's story after describing the bizarre freezing of the dead body suggests that the story might end on a serious note.
IMAGERY	death scene; party scene; funeral scene [Describe which words convey sense impressions and, in turn, emotional responses in each scene.]
SYMBOLISM	reincarnation as self-reinvention

FIGURE 2. Plan for a Literary Analysis

As the course progresses, I ask students themselves to find relevant articles to post for the whole class. As a prelude to this activity, we search together for articles in the university library's database, as an alternative to the Internet.

In selecting texts for each session, I attempt to look for those which are especially comparable. Like the great-grandmother in Silko's (2001) poem, "It Was a Long Time Before," Grandma in Lam's (2001) story is a rich repository of tradition, language, and heritage culture for the younger generations growing up in an anglophone, Euro-centered America. Also like Silko, Lam speaks of his beloved elder with deep affection and respect—and a finely honed sense of humor, which she clearly shared with him.

The other Across the Generations session in this unit was devoted to "Ah Mah," a poem by Malaysian-born Lim (2001) about her Chinese grandmother who has had her feet bound, and "Grandfather at Noon: Lahore, 1957," a memoir by Pakistani-born Canadian J. Samuel (2001) about his family's emigration from Pakistan to England.

Lim's poem can open the way to discussions of footbinding and other physical confinements of women in Chinese and other cultures. A relevant link here is selected scenes from the play *The Waiting Room* (Loomer, 1998), which questions the way women have been bodily manipulated by the male-dominated medical and fashion industries. The three principals, who meet in the waiting room of a doctor's office, are an 18th-century Chinese woman whose bound feet have caused her toes to become gangrenous, a 19th-century woman who suffers from so-called hysteria caused by painful corseting, and a contemporary U.S. woman whose silicone breast implant has gone awry.

For this session, students have contributed articles on footbinding, corsets, the chastity belt, female genital mutilation, and neck stretching as illustrations of historical confinements of women.

For J. Samuel's (2001) memoir, some useful links include articles relating to the memoir's setting in time and place, such as the 1947 partition of India and Pakistan, and Web sites about Lahore, a sophisticated, arty, and progressive city—often called *Lollywood* or the *Los Angeles of Pakistan*. In this regard, I ask students to find cinematic aspects of the memoir's style (Samuel is a documentary filmmaker as well as a writer), such as color images, cross-cutting, and shifting point of view.

Fathers and Sons dyads include the poems "The Gift" by Chinese American author Lee (2001) and "Digging" by the Irish poet Heaney (2001), both of which portray warm, loving memories that the speakers have of their respective fathers. On the other hand, the short stories "Goalie" by Western Canadian Thauberger (2001) and "A Family Supper" by the Japanese British Ishiguro (2001) portray conflicted relationships between father and son.

Similar dyads can be created for the Mothers and Daughters sessions. Affectionate relationships ultimately emerge in Indian Deshpande's (2001) story "Why a Robin?" and Canadian Munro's (2001) story "Friend of My Youth," while somewhat darker relationships figure in Kinkaid's (2001) story "My Mother" and Sri Lankan Wijenaike's (2001) monologic story "Anoma."

◈ DISTINGUISHING FEATURES

The Online Syllabus

Although the basic methodology of presenting literary texts in this ESOL case study can be said to be fairly standard, the mode of delivery online through Prometheus is one of its two distinguishing features. Using technology in general appeals to international students and thus may allay fears or concerns that they might have at the thought of studying literature in a foreign language.

Additionally, Prometheus enables students to communicate efficiently both synchronously (using the Discussion component) and asynchronously (using the

Message component) with each other and with the instructor. Such out-of-class discussion also enhances their readiness to engage with challenging literary texts in the class sessions, to respond both personally and critically to them, and to think and write about issues germane to those texts.

Focus on Global English

Technology aside, the most distinctive feature of the program illustrated in this case study is its focus on contemporary international literature in English at a time when the world as a whole has become interconnected by English. However, the global syllabus discussed here deemphasizes notions of British or U.S. cultural hegemony, or of colonial or postcolonial nation-states, and celebrates instead a world literature that for all its diversity exhibits both uniqueness and oneness.

◈ PRACTICAL IDEAS

In selecting texts for a global ESOL syllabus in your own practice, I offer several criteria. In general, select texts that are contemporary, that are shorter rather than longer, and that deal with issues familiar to students. Additionally, I would note four specific criteria relating to global representation, gender diversity, diversity of genre, and level of difficulty.

Select Writers From the Various Categories of English-Speaking Countries

Categories of English-speaking countries include the historic center (England, Ireland, Scotland, Wales); the settler nations (e.g., Australia, Canada, Jamaica, the United States); and the postcolonial nations (e.g., Ghana, India, Kenya, Nigeria, Pakistan, the Philippines, Singapore). In fact, I would argue that the purpose of a global literature syllabus is to blur such distinctions or, at least, to deprive them of any hierarchical significance.

Within national literatures, seek also regional, ethnic, and social diversity. For example, check out texts by both Black and White writers in South Africa, regional writers in Canada, local and diasporic writers from India, and ethnic immigrants in any of the anglophone countries.

In looking for a diversity of texts on the Internet, I have found useful sites such as the home page of the journal *ARIEL: A Review of International English Literature* (University of Calgary, 2003, http://www.english.ucalgary.ca/ariel/ariel.htm), which is devoted to "the critical and scholarly study of the new and the established literatures in English around the world" (n.p.) and particularly welcomes articles on the relationships among them. Two other sites are those of the International Association for World Englishes (http://www.iaweworks.org/) and of the International Association of Teachers of English as a Foreign Language Global Issues Special Interest Group (n.d., http://www.countryschool.com/gisig.htm).

Among useful reference works is the two-volume *Encyclopedia of Post-Colonial Literatures in English* (Benson & Conolly, 1994), which contains articles on genres and major subjects (e.g., women's writing, travel literature, or anthologies), critical biographies of writers, and articles on the literatures of specific countries or regions, and Ross's (1991) *International Literature in English: Essays on the Major Writers.*

A great deal of geographical overlapping and cultural fusion exists among writers in English around the world. For example, Salman Rushdie was born in Bombay, lived briefly in Pakistan and was educated in England; however, his Indian identity is still a strong presence in his writing. Edna O'Brien, a quintessentially Irish writer, left her homeland in 1954 and moved to London, where she still lives and writes—mostly about Ireland and the Irish. Bharati Mukhergee was born in Calcutta, studied in India and the United States, married a Canadian, became a Canadian citizen, taught English at McGill University in Toronto—where she began writing fiction—and later moved to the United States, became a U.S. citizen, and now teaches at the University of California at Berkeley. Likewise, Malaysian Shirley Geok-Lin Lim, Indian Anita Desai, Cameroonian Ba'bila Mutia, and Saint Lucian Derek Walcott are all academics at U.S. institutions.

Seek to Represent Male and Female Voices Equally

Because literature addresses the whole human condition, male and female voices should be equally represented. Moreover, women writers in particular figure very prominently in addressing the critical global issues of today: peace, social justice, human rights, racism and sexism, and the environment.

An excellent reference source in which to find contemporary women writers is Sage's (1999) *The Cambridge Guide to Women's Writing in English,* which "aims to consolidate and epitomise the re-reading of women's writing that has gone on for the last 25 years" and "reflects the spread of literacy, the history of colonization, and the development of post-colonial cultures using English and changing the English language" (cover).

Include a Variety of Genres, Though Not Necessarily an Even Number of Each Genre

I tend to include short stories, poems, and memoirs in the majority; then a short play or two, a few essays, and a short novel. On the whole, I find that teaching multiple shorter texts offers students a rich variety of voices, styles, structures, vocabulary, and social contexts. It also makes them aware of all the wonderful literature in English that is, simply, out there.

As Walcott (1987) has said in "Tomorrow, Tomorrow,"

To have loved one horizon is insularity;
it blindfolds vision, it narrows experience. (p. 79)

Memoirs—fictive and nonfictive—are good models for student narrative writing, which I assign often, based on the assumption that people write best about what they know best, and sharing personal feelings and observations contributes in a major way to making the classroom a community of writers.

Notwithstanding my love of the theater, I limit the number of full-length plays because they take up a lot of time in the syllabus, though I occasionally have students rewrite scenes from stories as dramatic dialogue or have them declaim a poem as a performance piece. I also limit essays—which tend to be more sophisticated and less accessible to L2 students than a good story is—unless the essays are thematically relevant to the unit.

Poetry may seem daunting for L2 students, but many poems are quite accessible, and poetry in general has a singular compactness, conciseness, elegance, and power. I have enjoyed good success in teaching poems by first getting students to understand the basic elements that distinguish poetry from prose—rhythm, pattern, image, and sound—for which I use the acronym RPIS, as I noted in the Description section. After that, we unpack the content. Also, I find that teaching a story, a memoir, and a poem that share a common theme helps make the poem more accessible.

Consider Especially Lexical, Rhetorical, and Cultural Difficulty

In the 1960s and 1970s, lexical and syntactic difficulty was often determined by word frequency lists, *t*-unit analyses, and analyses of average word and sentence length. Nevertheless, such quantitative methods have proved to be neither efficient nor effective and probably would not be even today if they were conducted with a computer.

Snow (1994) noted that 77% of the L2 students she surveyed found language to be the most difficult aspect of studying literature in English, and of these, 44% cited vocabulary as the biggest stumbling block. After many years of teaching literature to L1 and L2 students, I certainly concur with those findings, although my repeated polling of students as to unfamiliar vocabulary items that they (a) did not understand at all or (b) could guess the meaning of from context resulted in such diverse responses as to render them statistically unreliable. Nevertheless, in *Focus on Vocabulary in Teaching Literature* (Bozzini, 1998), I advocated teaching lexical sets that refer to the various literary components of the text—for example, setting/sense of place, descriptions of characters, cultural references, the vocabulary of imagery and mood, and specific verbs that could be used to summarize the plot. Thus, each text's particular lexical possibilities are studied within the common framework of literary analysis. I would also emphasize that exercise types tend to be idiosyncratic to a particular text rather than standardized, as in the examples shown in Figure 3.

A text's rhetorical complexity can be determined by careful charting, as noted in the Description section. In particular, note the text's meaningful divisions. For example, a story may be divided into sections marked by visual breaks, with each section typically divided into paragraphs. In some cases, however, the scenes of a narrative may not correspond with section or paragraph divisions. The same holds true for a poem, in which section and stanza divisions may belie other meaningful rhetorical divisions.

The cultural difficulty of a text is addressed initially in the Perspectives, or reading readiness, exercises—noted earlier—and is further addressed in lexical exercises such as those shown above, as well as in the textual analysis in the Charting the Text exercises and in discussion engendered by the Afterthoughts exercises.

❖ CONCLUSION

In this case study, I have attempted to relate a literary ESOL syllabus to the rapid globalization of the world today, based on the premise that although globalization has controversial hegemonic aspects, the globalization/internationalization of literature in English seeks to create a common intellectual locus for peoples of the world formerly divided by such hegemonies.

Which of the words in the right-hand column suggest the *mood* of the subject or the speaker in the sentences in the left-hand column? Indicate which words in the sentence convey the mood.

a. Mr Abe bellowed, "Hello, young man!" (12).	1. sad
b. It had me going (17).	2. proud
c. His face beamed (19).	3. excited
d. That was the last I saw of Abe-san (19).	4. friendly

Helene and Hector often express their feelings through *gestures* or other types of body language—communication with the body rather than with words. Indicate the unspoken meaning of the italicized words below, using the words in the right-hand column.

a. Helene *raised her eyes to the ceiling* (5).	1. agreement
b. Hector *nodded* (8).	2. unhappiness
c. "I don't get it," Hector *whined* (10).	3. impatience

Butler uses very specific words to describe his characters' actions and moods. Which of the following italicized words—as used here—refer to *physical* states, or actions, and which refer to *emotional* states, or moods?

	Physical	Emotional
a. Sometimes I sound pretty *bitter* (2).	_____	_____
b. I watched him *slouch* around the yard one Sunday (6).	_____	_____
c. There was a certain *suspicion* in his voice (7).	_____	_____
d. He was *squirming* a little bit (15).	_____	_____

FIGURE 3. Vocabulary and Mood, Tone, or Attitude

I have reiterated here the case for teaching literature in ESOL and attempted to reflect its arguments in my teaching methodology. I have suggested as well criteria for selecting texts for a global syllabus. Finally, I have shown how technology can be used to deliver such a syllabus, and make it accessible and highly interactive.

◈ CONTRIBUTOR

George R. Bozzini is an associate professor emeritus of English and EFL at The George Washington University, in the United States. He was the founding director of the university's Program in English for International Students. He has conducted teacher education workshops sponsored by the former United States Information Agency in the Americas, Western and Eastern Europe, and Asia.

CHAPTER 12

Consuming With Caution: Local Responses to Global Messages

David Cooke

⬙ INTRODUCTION

The world came into the course, called Dealing With Viewpoint, in every important domain. The students came from many different parts of the world, often intending to lead an international career and life after getting their degrees. The subject matter of the course was world issues, such as the international impact of environmental damage, in the context of globalization. The medium of the course, and its goal, was English, the world's lingua franca. A major source of information was internationally available media, notably in this case, BBC World Service radio, heard around the world, and its accompanying Web site (http://www.bbc.co.uk/). A key element of the course was critical appraisal of the use of English.

Dealing With Viewpoint had one other important international dimension: Students brought an awareness of differing cultures from around the world that played valuably into course discussion and analysis of texts and message.

⬙ CONTEXT

Language in Canada is a highly charged entity, given the uneasy coexistence of English and French communities, made more complex by strong and continuing immigration after World War II. Language issues are especially pressing in the light of the threat that francophones feel from the dominant English language and cultures of Canada and the United States. One of the centers of such dominance is Toronto, a large, multicultural city of over 3 million, with a diverse population that includes socially aware sectors that intervene noticeably in public life.

The University

Within Toronto, York University is one of three public universities and one with a track record of social concern among its academic and teaching profile. ESL courses at York have for many years concentrated on content at least as much as on language. For the past 25 years, ESOL courses at York's smaller campus, Glendon College, have explicitly focused on content (hence courses like English Nonliterary Texts, Media, The Nature of Language, English Varieties, Modes of Communication, and Studies in English Literature). Content teaching has a rich history in the literature (see Brinton,

Snow, & Wesche, 1989; Hunter & Morgan, 2001; Mohan, 1986; Richard-Amato & Snow, 1992; Snow & Brinton, 1997).

Some of the courses listed above have focused on social issues at the local, national, or international level. Doing so has called for a questioning approach to the subject matter—critical thinking on the part of instructors and students. It has also called for some awareness of world events, recent history, earlier history, and global forces.

Glendon College is a bilingual French-English liberal arts college of approximately 1,500 students within a much larger "multiversity" of about 40,000 students. Located on a separate campus, Glendon has had the opportunity to develop its own academic culture, including its language programs, deemed to be essential to the fulfillment of its bilingual mission. ESOL courses, offered through the English department, all grant credit toward the undergraduate degree, which provides majors in disciplines such as economics, English, French, history, psychology, and sociology.

York's language courses assume that second language (L2) students are quite capable of dealing with academic subject matter provided they benefit from suitable support in language and academic content. Language can indeed be a barrier to study, and that is where the ESOL courses come in. But these courses treat the academic content with respect, maintain scholarly standards, and demand evidence of university-level performance in course requirements. This is as it should be in university courses, but this orientation has added significance given the global spread of English and its power to set agendas worldwide.

The Course

One course in particular, Dealing With Viewpoint, offers a case study in the impact of World English. Typically, students in the course are a very diverse group. Because of Glendon's bilingual orientation, the class includes Quebecois and other fluent speakers of French from France and various francophone countries. There are nationals of countries in Africa, Europe, the Middle East, Latin America, and Southeast Asia, to name a few parts of the world. Many contend with disrupted and often heart-rending backgrounds. Some are refugees, with grim stories of survival. A familiar pattern is an Iranian student who was obliged to move to Germany, then to Britain, then to Canada—and therefore was a perhaps permanently uprooted speaker of three or more languages with experience of several contrasting cultures.

The students' educational backgrounds vary greatly. Some are visiting students who plan to relocate after completing their degrees. Others are immigrants or citizens of Canada, with long-term plans for residence there. All of them matter-of-factly assume that English is an inevitable part of their lives and is likely to be so in international settings.

When asked what they need from the course, students typically say they want to know how to write an essay, increase their vocabulary, acquire advanced grammar, read and understand academic texts, and come to grips with the opportunity and challenge of English in their lives and their futures. Instructors say students need to know how to write an essay, interpret texts, develop an academic argument, and deal with the pervasive presence of English in their lives and around the world.

In this advanced-level course, students are relatively fluent in English, often impressively so in oral skills, but need strong assistance in academic writing. Most can speak volubly on a range of different topics, though they often need to work on how to build an effective argument. They perform rather differently from each other in dealing with text, some proving much more proficient than others in grasping the subtleties, nuances, and possible interpretations of text. At the same time, they come with interesting backgrounds that weave their way through the course. On social issues of local, national, and world concern, they bring informed perspectives from differing cultural groups and international experiences, and wry commentaries on how they are seen in English-speaking Canada. They are conscious not just of the extensive spread of English but of its power to shape local and global discourse and debate, along with the way in which English advantages those who are fluent in it and disadvantages those who are not. When offered the chance to challenge ideas, they do so with gusto, including, disconcertingly, those of the instructors and some of the arguments in texts that the instructors happen to agree with. Not surprisingly, students themselves are often very effective instructors in the course. In discussion and debate, they can respond sharply and thoughtfully to the views that swirl around the table. Their responses, for instance, frequently challenge questionable cases, put matters in necessary context, and extend arguments in productive ways, in much the way instructors would like to when they are on form.

◈ DESCRIPTION

Dealing With Viewpoint focuses on the nature of argument, drawing on topics and texts of social significance such as the environment, use of resources, biodiversity and sustainability, globalization and structural adjustment, nuclear war, education, and work. It meets 3 hours a week for 12–13 weeks, with large amounts of reading, reflecting, and writing beyond class, including accessing of relevant Web sites. The course draws exclusively on authentic materials subjected to critical analysis.

Over time, the course has studied oppositional and differentiated texts selected from such sources as the BBC's Reith Lectures 2000 (a series of prestigious presentations delivered annually on critical world topics by selected speakers; see BBC, n.d.); speeches and press releases by Canadian and U.S. political figures; media reports and commentaries; a briefing document for the Asia Pacific Economic Community (APEC; Republic of Korea, 1997); and statements from business, labor, and social activism. It draws on print publications, broadcasts, Web sites, and audiovisual sources on global issues.

Aspects of Globalization

The content of the course can change from year to year. One version of the course has concentrated on globalization and structural adjustment as international issues that are promoted and sustained to a large extent through the English language. In very simple terms, *globalization* is taken to mean the spread of business interests worldwide, and *structural adjustment* to mean the creation of a market economy, as happened in New Zealand, for instance, in the 1980s and 1990s, when it jettisoned much of the previously existing welfare state.

The goal in the course is to explore ideas and assumptions that shape debate on these contentious issues, investigate questions of ideology and belief, evaluate how arguments are constructed, and build sound cases in response to the issues posed. The course draws on the materials listed in Appendix A.

Reading 2 (Republic of Korea, 1997), the APEC position paper from Korea on restructuring education for the needs of business and work, is an illustration of how English is used to carry the case for globalization. In its own distinctive form of English, it advocates the values of global market forces in economies and education, in terms like the following:

> Another driving force is globalization. And, in some member economies, the way to economically grow was through globalization, and these two forces caused structural changes in their industries. The globalization of economies show up as the following. The present business strategies focus on cultural integration. All economies are in the race with different economies to gain and develop new markets. (p. 4)

Building on the extensive reading required for the course, classes typically focus on at least four main elements: the context of texts, the background to texts, ideas in the texts, and the strength of the arguments made. To clarify ideas, instructors commonly need to detail the background to content areas, especially for topics like globalization, which lie outside many people's consciousness. A common difficulty for university students by definition is that they are required to deal with unfamiliar bodies of knowledge. It is hard to make sense of an article or find something serious to say about a topic that one does not really understand. Hence an important part of exploring the ideas of a text is to fill out the background to a set of issues. In the course on globalization, students need clarification of fundamental terms and concepts like *globalization* and *structural adjustment* (themselves matters of some debate); free trade agreements; and the role of international agencies like APEC, the Organization for Economic Cooperation and Development, and the World Trade Organization.

A particular dimension of globalization is the use of English in disseminating information around the world. A case in point is the BBC's Reith Lectures for 2000, entitled Respect for the Earth (see BBC, n.d.), which formed a sizable part of one version of Dealing With Viewpoint. Throughout the course, students accessed the print versions of the lectures on the Web, which in itself is another sign of the globalizing of English.

Analyzing the lectures meant that students from up to 10 different countries were dealing with the international topic of the environment and biodiversity, presented in the program from the differing perspectives of British, North American, and Indian contributors. In the conduct of the course, this experience led to the critique of three issues: the role and power of English, questions of ecology, and globalization (see Appendix B for samples of course content). The Reith Lectures provided differentiated texts that contrasted with each other in focus, orientation, and outlook, and some spawned oppositional viewpoints (see, e.g., Prince of Wales, 2000; the response by Connor, 2000; and some of the audience commentary on the lectures, BBC, n.d.). Overall, the different texts of the course offered a range of arguments on given topics.

English does more than just increasingly disseminate information on a worldwide scale. As the above topics indicate, it carries message and viewpoint, values, opinions, and assumptions. For consumers constantly bombarded with information in this dominant language, there is a strong case for approaching texts with a questioning framework, or, to put it in other terms, from a critical thinking perspective.

Critical Thinking

"The essence of critical thinking is informed skepticism. . . . It is active inquiry rather than passive acceptance of tradition, authority, or 'common sense,'" says Cornbleth (1985, p. 13). Cornbleth elaborates her point:

> Critical thinking involves *questioning the ideas we encounter.* It is, therefore, a dynamic process of questioning and reasoning, of raising and pursuing questions about our own and others' claims and conclusions, definitions and evidence, beliefs and actions. (p. 13)

Cornbleth's views are part of an extensive body of thought about thinking, summed up succinctly by McPeck (1990) as "reflective skepticism" (p. 42) and providing a challenging framework for the ESOL course in question. "A critical thinker," says McPeck, has "both the disposition (or propensity) and the relevant knowledge and skills to engage in an activity with reflective skepticism" (p. 21). In the same spirit, Brookfield (1987) claims, "People who are reflectively skeptical do not take things as read" (p. 9).

There are several major reasons for incorporating critical inquiry into the course. Instructors assume that Western university academic life rests on a base of inquiring into knowledge, that the essence of scholarship involves questioning ideas in the process of constructing knowledge. Furthermore, they see such knowledge as rooted in social context, in other words, as socially constructed. It follows that both the academic world and the social world in which it exists are areas of critical inquiry, and thus English in academic settings has social significance. English is highly sought after, and so is the information it conveys. But neither the language nor the content is neutral, so part of the function of the course is to promote an ability to critique and reflect on topics of world importance.

Assignments

The intent of course assignments is to reinforce the search for meanings and the appraisal of argument presented throughout the course work. Separate papers follow a progression that develops from reacting to others' arguments to presenting one's own case:

- giving possible interpretations of a text
- responding to a case (stated in the assignment description as "giving your own view of the information in the text")
- analyzing different viewpoints (stated as "comparison of several conflicting texts in the course")
- giving a critique of an argument (stated as "analysis and critique of the way an argument is constructed")
- constructing a reasoned case

Papers are evaluated on argument, content, and organization. Language use (e.g., vocabulary and grammar) is marked but not graded, on the assumption that the essence of the course is the focus on ideas. At the same time, marking inevitably takes into account the interaction of content and expression.

Writing is a very contentious issue in tertiary education, greatly debated in the literature and the language teaching profession (e.g., Dias, Freedman, Medway, & Pare, 1999; Giltrow, 1995; F. Smith, 1982; Tobin, 1993). The course takes the position that there is no magic formula for writing papers (e.g., the five-paragraph theme, complete with thesis statement). It holds that academic papers should evolve organically from the kind of argument or treatment being created, based on the notion that the ideas are the driving force and therefore create the shape of the paper.

The course routinely provides a guide to making an argument (see Appendix C). Separately, it also gives samples of language used in argument (see Appendix D) and, when appropriate, the language of specific topics. There is attention to relevant aspects of grammar, structure, lexis, and semantics, usually centered on given texts. Tutors respond to students' writing in some detail, usually in contrast to class discussions, in which the emphasis is on encouraging students to speak without the interruption of instructors' feedback on their accuracy.

◈ DISTINGUISHING FEATURES

International Texts

The course deals with international texts from a variety of sources. At the same time, it uses local and national texts whenever appropriate for the course topics, thereby providing relevance to the country and setting of the course. It can also motivate students to realize that they can make connections between international developments and the local scene. One of the features of international texts is that their content can resonate worldwide—the subject matter can be local and global at the same time, as shown in this brief extract from the start of Shiva's (2000) Reith lecture:

> Recently, I was visiting Bhatinda in Punjab because of an epidemic of farmers [sic] suicides. Punjab used to be the most prosperous agricultural region in India. Today every farmer is in debt and despair. Vast stretches of land have become water-logged desert. And as an old farmer pointed out, even the trees have stopped bearing fruit because heavy use of pesticides have killed the pollinators—the bees and butterflies. . . .
>
> Seattle and the World Trade Organisation protests last year have forced everyone to think again. Throughout this lecture series people have referred to different aspects of sustainable development taking globalisation for granted. For me it is now time radically to reevaluate what we are doing. For what we are doing in the name of globalisation to the poor is brutal and unforgivable. This is especially evident in India as we witness the unfolding disasters of globalisation especially in food and agriculture. (p. 1)

A key aspect of the course was to identify the arguments of writers like Shiva, capturing the particular concerns of speakers in relation to different parts of the world, considering the general significance of their remarks and tracing the implications for other countries and communities. The global significance of local developments is a theme that Lovejoy (2000) states quite explicitly in the introduction to his Reith lecture on biological diversity and ecological sustainability:

> I chose to come to California to give this lecture rather than somewhere else, because of an exciting experiment with biological diversity. I believe it may well help us in the global quest to maintain the biological underpinnings of

sustainability, but I will turn to the story of the California Gnatcatcher later in this talk. (p. 1)

In Canada at the end of the 1990s, a national issue was privatization of various structures of society, a question taken up in the annual report of the Canadian Union of Public Employees (CUPE, 1999). Privatization in this case was taken to be an expression of structural adjustment or neoliberal social and economic reform, in other words, a national and local form of certain globalizing trends, and a process that had been fostered by both successive federal governments and several provincial governments, such as Alberta's and Ontario's. During the course, it was helpful to locate this national concern in the context of privatization elsewhere in the world and in relation to the overall forces of globalization, as revealed in national and international texts studied (e.g., Clarke, 1997; Martin & Schumann, 1997; Republic of Korea, 1997).

Varieties of English

The course draws on a few geographical varieties of English, mostly standard English, though not exclusively so (see Republic of Korea, 1997). Given the accessibility of information worldwide now, it would be very easy to provide numbers of different varieties of World Englishes. An extract from the APEC paper (Republic of Korea, 1997) illustrates some slight variations from standard English, which students noticed but took in their stride:

> The dichonomic view on school and work is no longer appropriate. The emphasis on education for itself or on education for good members of a community without a large emphasis on preparations for the future work are no longer appropriate. (p. 5)

Although we noted some of the language variation in this text, part of the point of reading it was to realize that the class as a whole could process a different form of L2 English in a satisfactory way and move on to interpreting and critiquing the discussion, which related to proposals for connecting education squarely to the world of work.

World Issues

As is evident from various of the texts cited above, the course deals with significant (nontrivial) content that is of world concern, such as the environment and, notably, the topic of globalization. The term *globalization* is subject to various different interpretations and constructions, ranging from relatively benign (the global village and shrinking boundaries; see Waters, 2001) to relatively malign (corporate control of the world; see Korten, 1995). Course discussion moved between these two poles trying to identify the range of different viewpoints in the texts under analysis.

To clarify the major contrasting positions here, on the one hand, a widespread optimistic view of globalization sees it as an inevitable and positive process for the world. By this thinking, globalization is the product of modern technology; ease of travel and communications; sharing of resources; and harmonization of business, trade, commerce, culture, education, and other key sectors of society. On the other hand, a sharply critical view holds that various extremely powerful corporations seek to dominate world business and many other sectors of the globe, overriding or removing national sovereignty wherever necessary and establishing policies of liberalization through such mechanisms as free trade pacts and the like (see Clarke, 1997; Dobbin, 1998; Kelsey, 1995; McMurtry, 1998). The task for the course and the class was to interrogate texts, propose appropriate interpretations of them, try to situate the texts on the continuum from supportive to critical views of globalization, investigate the way language was used in the texts, develop responses to each of these activities, and, not the least, construct arguments of one's own in relation to world developments. In doing so, the students and I hoped that we were engaging in reflective inquiry.

Critical Inquiry

The course emphasizes critical scrutiny of texts, messages, and meanings (see Siegal & Carey, 1989). "Critical thinking," says F. Smith (1990), "is an attitude, a frame of mind" (p. 103). Such an approach is increasingly relevant as English becomes the dominant medium for carrying information of crucial concern around the world and also a language for nominating topics, framing issues, and promoting certain discourses. (A case in point would be the Iraq war of 2003, carried and driven massively in English. At the same time, it was subjected to widespread analysis in English, e.g., the BBC World Service program *Spinning to Win,* Lustig, 2003, which focused on world events such as war, international leaders, and world media.) Neither the language nor the content of the subjects studied is neutral, so Dealing With Viewpoint tries to promote the ability to critique and reflect on topics of world importance, in the process exploring the nature of argument and the construction of reasoned viewpoint. As Cornbleth (1985) puts it, "Our conceptions and forms of reasoning both reflect and shape how we think, talk about, study, and act on our world" (p. 12).

The course holds that it is important for students to realize that the world of English is laden with message. Throughout the course, we try to analyze such familiar items as the content of media; the statements of politicians, world leaders, and others who behave politically (as most people do at different times in their lives); the social policy decisions made in our name; and the utterances and actions of powerful institutions of society like governments, corporations, education, parliament, law courts, police, and the local city council. Such analysis often requires the suspension of belief followed by some close examination of message. "Critical thinkers," say Siegel and Carey (1989), "do not accept facts at face value; instead, they challenge the status of facts as given" (p. 16).

In the course, part of the examination was to try to identify the outlook of different speakers and writers, then to trace the bases of their viewpoints. Brundtland (2000), for instance, seemed to portray a liberal attitude of mind, with great compassion for suffering:

> I want the fight against poverty to be our global cause as we straddle the millennium. Our goal must be to create a world where we all can live well fed and clothed, and with dignity. We must do this without undermining future generations' ability to do the same.
>
> Tonight I want to suggest a fresh way of joining this fight. I will argue that poor people will only be able to prosper, and emerge from poverty, if they

enjoy better health. I want health to be at the heart of our struggle for sustainable development. (p. 1)

It was plain that Brundtland was greatly moved by poverty:

The poor really do die young.
     Poverty has a woman's face; of the 1.3 billion poorest, only 30% are male. Poor women are often caught in a damaging cycle of malnutrition and disease. This plight stems directly from women's place in the home, and in society: it often also reflects gender bias in health care. Women from poor households are more than a hundred times more likely to die as a result of childbirth than their wealthier counterparts. . . . (p. 1)

Yet her graphic description seemed to concentrate more on illustrating the outcomes of poverty than on analyzing contributing factors: "These are not so much territorial disputes as they are rooted in general misery, the aftermath of humanitarian crises, shortages of food and water and the spreading of poverty and ill-health" (p. 1).

By contrast, Shiva (2000), in her pointed critique of globalization, is eager to identify cause and effect: "The devaluation of women's work, and of work done in sustainable economies, is the natural outcome of a system constructed by capitalist patriarchy. This is how globalisation destroys local economies and destruction itself is counted as growth" (p. 4).

Then again, the Prince of Wales (2000) charts a distinctly different spiritual course that differs in interpretation from the other speakers, despite obvious points of contact with them on the current condition of the world:

So, although it seems to have become deeply unfashionable to talk about the spiritual dimension of our existence, that is what I propose to do.
     The idea that there is a sacred trust between mankind and our Creator, under which we accept a duty of stewardship for the earth, has been an important feature of most religious and spiritual thought throughout the ages. (pp. 1–2)

Such dimensions of text and their interpretation were key features of the seminar discussions and analyses in the course. As part of the process, we explored the different stances of oppositional and parallel texts (see Morgan, 1998, pp. 118–123), for instance, in relation to genetically modified organisms (GMOs) (see Appendix B). The students entered with gusto into the interrogation of texts, exercising their own critical thinking about the various texts. A case in point was the annual report of CUPE (1999), referred to above. Although the case made was similar to that of many of the texts encountered in the course, some students considered the argument lacking in adequate development and evidence, a sign perhaps that they were engaging in precisely the kind of inquiry required for a course of this nature.

Use of Language

Unpacking texts and topics involves examining the way language is used for different interests and purposes. Any of the contentious subject matter of this course would illustrate the point, including, for instance, the marketing of globalization, the debate around GMOs, or conflicts over ecology and the environment. An example was a transcript of an address by the Ontario minister of education (Snobelen, 1995) arguing the need to change systems. As students pointed out, throughout the in-house speech to his ministry, he never once actually referred to education. The point of the presentation, it seemed, was to put the case for change per se, during a period of intense structural adjustment that the provincial Tory government initiated in the mid-1990s. It was a telling example of language used for the particular purpose of moving to a market economy, introduced in the following terms:

> A long time ago—or what seems like a long time ago, with the compressed air around here—I personally took on a commitment to doing whatever it was that I could do to enable people to act powerfully. There was some possibility of our province, and country, and world working a different way if people would all act powerfully. And by "powerfully," I mean the rate at which your intentions become reality. So that, if you will, is the context in which I've been working in the last decade, or so. . . .
>
> It seems to me that there are three useful places to look. One of those is in the nature of organization, and one of those is in the whole area of change, the last is leadership. Those are themes that run through the work you're doing, and I'd like to just visit a little bit about each of those for a moment or two this morning. (n.p.)

A course of this nature inevitably looks closely at how language is used, during which process students can develop strong sensitivity to language, meaning, the construction of argument, and the effects of text.

❖ PRACTICAL IDEAS

A number of key practical ideas arose from the course.

Look for Topics of International Social Significance

Topics like the environment, GMOs, health, education, and energy are ones that students can relate to. They are part of students' consciousness, if for no other reason than that they appear in the media that envelope people's lives. More importantly, they have social and international impact. Beyond a superficial analysis, they affect people's lives in dramatic ways, as became apparent with several of the globalization issues studied in the course described. What is more, students themselves contribute richly to the debate because they are consistently adept at finding relevant information on the Internet and bringing it to class.

Meanwhile, one dimension to bear in mind is the need to provide context for many of the topics dealt with. Members of a class have a varied grasp on given items and often need the background, setting, and history of an issue for it to be usefully accessible. In this respect, it was interesting to see the ways students could help each other with necessary background, over and above the teacher's contribution.

Explore Language and Content

There is sometimes a jarring contrast between university ESOL courses and the other disciplines that students take in their undergraduate programs. ESOL can seem empty of content, focusing instead on language forms, while the rest of their program is packed with weighty theoretical and conceptual subject matter. But content language courses can introduce serious issues worthy of intellectual inquiry while exploring the language that carries the content. Studying issues of work and employment, the fast-food industry, the world of business, and biodiversity is rewarding. In so doing, the ESOL course is a preparation for disciplinary study at university through a process of learning by doing.

There is always the risk, of course, that students may not warm to seemingly remote topics like globalization. In such cases, the challenge for the teacher is to make the links to people's everyday lives, provide necessary localized context, and promote exploration of topics in ways that make the subject matter immediate, real, and meaningful for learners. Sometimes the bridge for students lies in encouraging them to engage with viewpoint—developing a reasoned position, becoming emotionally or intellectually committed to a point of view, challenging an opposing outlook, or relating to a human interest story that illustrates the issues embedded in a concept or debate.

Search Out Multiple Sources of Texts

Many sources of text are available to teachers—for example, journals, newspapers, academic papers and chapters, audio- and videotapes, and the Internet—with differing viewpoints and orientations (see below). If possible, you and the students should decide on topics at the start of a course, allowing for a realistic time frame to find and prepare suitable materials. As a result, students' choices can usually only appear in a later segment of the course. However, students can also bring their own materials, texts, and documents to class, which results in enriched information and viewpoints.

An array of global resources is available, including international radio and TV, the Internet, publications, and media from different countries. One point to bear in mind is that even though vast amounts of information are accessible on the Internet, some (e.g., the BBC's materials) require consent and payment in order to be reproduced as class sets.

Find Oppositional Texts and Parallel Texts

The course included a rich array of contrasting texts on GMOs (see Appendix B), ranging from government sources that seemed to favor them fairly consistently to academic and journalistic critiques. In a course of this kind, it was natural to compare these various texts, analyzing their standpoints, charting the way they develop their case, and interpreting and categorizing their use of language. (On parallel texts, see, e.g., Morgan, 1998, pp. 118–123.)

Explore Meaning, Both Literal and Inferred

Texts are subject to various interpretations and evaluations (Cooke, 2004). One of the fascinations of this kind of course is to explore the interaction of text and context, asking how given texts might be seen from different viewpoints. Gee, Hull, and Lankshear (1996) make the point energetically:

> Furthermore, any text can be read in *different* ways. Here we need an example. Consider the following sentences from a brief story in which a man named Gregory has wronged his former girlfriend Abigail: "Heartsick and dejected,

Abigail turned to Slug with her tale of woe. Slug, feeling compassion for Abigail, sought out Gregory and beat him brutally."

In one study (Gee, 1989, 1996) some readers, who happened to be African Americans, claimed that these sentences "say" that Abigail told Slug to beat up Gregory. On the other hand, other readers, who happened not to be African Americans, claimed that these sentences "say" no such thing. These readers subsequently claimed, in fact, that the African Americans had *misread* the sentences. The African Americans responded: "If you turn to someone with a tale of woe and, in particular, someone named 'Slug,' you are most certainly asking him to *do* something in the way of violence and you are most certainly responsible when he's done it." (p. 2)

The point is that these different people read the sentences in different ways and thought that others had read them in the "wrong" ways.

Content courses of the kind described here provide an ideal forum for inviting different interpretations from the class. You can prompt debate by presenting different interpretations followed by commentary on them.

Provide Reading Guides

Give students reading guides, outlines of content and issues, and reflective questions for discussion and analysis (see Appendix E for an example). The challenge here is to avoid the trap of presenting the reading guide as a set of fixed rules that allows for only one right interpretation, especially in light of the discussion in this chapter.

Emphasize Critical Scrutiny of Material

Problematize ideas and issues, thereby giving scope for students' powers of thinking. The point is to interrogate texts, assess information, evaluate arguments, and identify orientation in a text.

Universities prize critical thinking. Dealing With Viewpoint explicitly promotes the concept, analyzing others' arguments and developing one's own, in the spirit of Siegal and Carey (1989) that "critical thinking is always a search for meaning and not for enduring truth" (p. 26).

Analyze the Uses and Orientation of Language, Text, and Discourse

Encourage students to consider the possible effect of texts on different kinds of readers, and examine the way language is used to advantage or disadvantage different groups. Then develop responses to various uses of language, and build a frame of mind for advancing one's own best arguments.

◈ CONCLUSION

Dealing With Viewpoint requires ESOL students to think carefully about topical and often weighty subjects of world significance and impact. It puts students in touch with English used in a number of international and local domains, and aims to prepare learners for the texts, discourses, and messages they will be subject to in accessing English. It tries to put students on guard for the ways in which English can be used for a range of different outcomes, from benefiting to disadvantaging selected groups and individuals. It demands analysis of material and some distancing from content, in order to develop an understanding of argument. It has an overriding concern: to foster the habit of reflection in continuing to deal with global English.

❖ CONTRIBUTOR

David Cooke has taught language education and teacher education in Britain, Canada, Cuba, Mozambique, New Zealand, Nicaragua, and the People's Republic of China. He is a senior lecturer in the School of English and Applied Linguistics, Unitec New Zealand. He is interested in language education and critical thinking, education and globalization, and immigration to Western countries.

❖ APPENDIX A: CLASS READINGS ON GLOBALIZATION AND STRUCTURAL ADJUSTMENT

General

1. Martin, H.-P., & Schumann, H. (1997). The 20:80 society. *The global trap* (pp. 1–11). Montreal: Black Rose Books.

2. Republic of Korea. (1997, May). *The provisional themes for the 2nd APEC Human Resources Development Ministerial Meeting (part 1).* Concept paper presented at the 10th Meeting of the APEC Education Forum, Montreal, Quebec, Canada.

3. Reiter, E. (1994). The fast food industry: Putting the family to work. In W. Giles & S. Arat-Koc (Eds.), *Maid in the market: Women's paid domestic labour* (pp. 96–102). Halifax, Nova Scotia, Canada: Fernwood.

4. Richardson, B. (1996, March). Surviving the "miracle." *Canadian Forum,* 12–15.

5. Barlow, M., & Campbell, B. (1995). The hostile takeover. In *Straight through the heart: How the Liberals abandoned the Just Society and what Canadians can do about it* (pp. 48–68). Toronto, Ontario, Canada: HarperCollins.

6. Clarke, T. (1997) Global managers. In *Silent coup: Confronting the big business takeover of Canada* (pp. 39–69). Toronto, Ontario, Canada: Lorimer.

Education

7. Kuehn, L. (1994). Globalisation, NAFTA & education. *Our Schools/Our Selves, 6*(1), 9–19.

8. Canadian Union of Public Employees. (1999). Consuming classrooms. In *Hostile takeover: Annual report on privatization 1999.* Ottawa, Ontario, Canada: Author. Retrieved April 16, 2004, from http://www.cupe.ca/www/ARP1999/45289

9. Calvert, J., & Kuehn, L. (1993). NAFTA and education: A Pandora's box of nasty surprises. *Our Schools/Our Selves, 4*(2), 6–20, 29–32.

10. Natale, C. (1998). Social Darwinism comes to the classroom: The career education scam. *Our Schools/Our Selves, 9*(1), 26–42.

The Multilaterial Agreement on Investment

11. Joint NGO statement on the Multilateral Agreement on Investment (MAI), October 27, 1997. (1997, November 7). *Inside U.S. Trade,* pp. 16–17.

12. *NGOs reject any proposal for moving the MAI or an investment agreement to the WTO* [Press release]. (1998, May 17). Geneva, Switzerland: World Trade Organization.

13. Huner, J. (1998, October 29–30). *Trade, investment and the environment.* Paper presented to the Royal Institute for Internal Affairs, Chatham House. Retrieved January 5, 2005, from http://www.web.net/cela/

14. Lalumiere, C., & Landau, J.-P. (1998, September). *Report on the Multilateral Agreement on Investment: Intermediary report, September 1998.* Paris: Government of France.

15. Clarke, T., & Barlow, M. (1997). The emergence of global corporate rule. In *The MAI (Multilateral Agreement on Investment) and the threat to Canadian sovereignty* (pp. 30–54). Toronto, Ontario, Canada: Stoddart.

◈ APPENDIX B: REITH LECTURES: RESPECT FOR THE EARTH

The Environment

1. Suzuki, D. (2000, September 12).We don't need cheaper gas, we need options. *Globe & Mail.*

2. Lovejoy, T. (2000). *Biodiversity* (Reith Lectures 2000: Respect for the Earth). http://news.bbc.co.uk/hi/english/static/events/reith_2000/lecture2.stm

3. Brundtland, G. H. (2000). *Health & population* (Reith Lectures 2000: Respect for the Earth). http://news.bbc.co.uk/hi/english/static/events/reith_2000/lecture4.stm

4. Diemer, U. (2000). Contamination: The poisonous legacy of Ontario's environmental cutbacks. *Canadian Dimension, 34*(4), 33–35.

Genetically Modified Organisms

1. American Council on Science and Health. (2000, September). *Health panel affirms the many benefits of modern food biotechnology.* http://www.acsh.org/press/releases/biotechnology092000.html

2. Canadian Food Inspection Agency, Office of Biotechnology. (2000, September 21). *Agricultural products of biotechnology: A brief status report.* http://www.cfia-acia.agr.ca/english/ppc/biotech/gen/statuse.shtml; http://www.inspection.gc.ca/english/sci/biotech/gen/statuse.shtml

3. Canadian Food Inspection Agency, Office of Biotechnology. (n.d.). *Agricultural products of biotechnology: What are the benefits?* http://www.cfia-acia.agr.ca/english/ppc/biotech/gen/bene/shtml

4. Canadian Food Inspection Agency, Office of Biotechnology. (2000, September 21). *How many genetically modified food products are permitted in Canada?* http://www.cfia-acia.agr.ca/english/ppc/biotech/gen/safsal/novalie.shtml

5. Canadian Food Inspection Agency, Office of Biotechnology. (1997, August). *Biotechnology and agriculture in Canada.* http://www.cfia-acia.agr.ca/english/ppc/biotech/gen/canadae.shtml

6. Prince of Wales. (2000). *A royal view . . .* (Reith Lectures 2000: Respect for the Earth). http://news.bbc.co.uk/hi/english/static/events/reith_2000/lecture6.stm

7. Connor, S. (2000, May 20–21). Artificial, synthetic but still necessary. *Weekend Herald* (Auckland), p. B7. [response to Prince of Wales, 2000]

8. Revington, M. (1999, August 26). The gene genie. *The New Zealand Listener,* 16–20.

9. Coghlan, A., MacKenzie, D., & Concar, D. (1999, October 16). It's that man again. *New Scientist,* 6.

10. Agence France Presse. (2000, March 16). Cloned piglets raise "silent virus" concerns. *New Zealand Herald,* p. B2.

11. Whither GM corn? (1999, December 1). *Environment, 41*(10), 9.

12. Bt maize and its regulatory context. (1999, December 1). *Environment, 41*(10), 11.

13. Coghlan, A. (1999, October 16). How safe is safe? *New Scientist,* p. 9.

14. Howard, P. (2000, July–August). Genetic modification of foods and seeds: Is it inherently dangerous? *Canadian Dimension,* 5–6.

15. Strauss, S. (2000, September 16). Food, food, not-so-glorious food. [Review]. *Globe and Mail,* p. D14.

Globalization

Shiva, V. (2000). *Poverty and globalisation* (Reith Lectures 2000: Respect for the Earth). http://news.bbc.co.uk/hi/english/static/events/reith_2000/lecture5.stm

◈ APPENDIX C: GUIDE TO CONSTRUCTING AN ARGUMENT

Prepared by Judy Hunter.

Ask yourself, think about	Write
Introduction	
1. What's the controversy? What are you going to talk about?	Define and explain the issue.
2. a. How much does the reader know about it? How does your specific issue fit the reader's knowledge?	Contextualize your issue for the reader.
b. How does the topic relate to a wider area of knowledge or enquiry?	
3. What's your opinion?	Present the main point, your position.
Discussion	
4. What exactly do you mean? What are the implications?	Explain and clarify your point for the reader.
5. Is it believable? Why do you have this opinion?	Give supporting points, reasons, evidence.
6. How does the evidence support your views?	Explain your line of reasoning.
7. How does the evidence fit together, how is it all related?	Make explicit links between your points.
8. What about the other sides of the issue?	Acknowledge and respond to opposing views in terms of your position.*
Conclusion	
9. What do you want to stand out in the reader's mind when s/he finishes reading?	Reemphasize your main point (or summarize your argument if it's lengthy).
10. What effect do you want to have on the reader? How do you want the reader to respond?	Stress the importance and significance of your position.

*You may integrate this into your introduction and supporting points or deal with it separately.

◈ APPENDIX D: LANGUAGE OF MAKING AN ARGUMENT

1. Agreeing

I agree with [that] [X]; I support [X]; I'm in favour of [X]; I go along with [X]
That's right; [informal/colloquial: Right on!]

2. Distinguishing

I take your point [+/− but . . .]; you've got a point there [+/− but . . .]

3. Arguing a Case

I would argue that . . . ; I [would] feel that . . . ; my feeling is . . . ; my view
is . . . ;
I propose/suggest/advocate/recommend that . . .

4. Disagreeing

I would argue against . . . ; I want to argue against [X]; I can't/don't agree
with this line of thought; I'm opposed to this line of thought; I'm [somewhat/
a bit/strongly] opposed to [X]; I disagree with . . . ; I'm not in favour of . . .
[informal] I don't go along with [X]; I'm not with this

5. Refusing/Negating a Position

5.1. Politely Differing in Opinion

With (all) (due) respect, we can't accept this point of view
We have difficulty with this position; We are troubled by this view
We find it hard to accept [X]; We are unable to accept [X]/agree to . . .
We do not entirely agree with [X]
We tend to differ [somewhat/slightly/a bit/a lot] on this
We can't quite accept/agree to/go along with [X]

5.2. Expressing a Relatively Neutral Position

I wouldn't put it that way; I would put it differently
I would put it another way; I prefer not to comment [on . . .]

5.3. Rejecting a Position

We do not hold/take [this position/line]/support/endorse/align ourselves
with [X]
We differ/depart/diverge from this point of view
We take exception to [X]; I strongly/completely/totally reject [X]/resent [X]
We reject [X] [outright]; We refuse/repudiate [X]
We categorically deny/refuse/reject [X]
We take a contrary point of view; we take the opposite point of view
This position is not acceptable

◈ APPENDIX E: TEXT GUIDELINE FOR BROWNE (2000)

Outline of talk: introduction, Browne's response, process, critics, the future

1. Introduction

the debate on progress, including the issue of industrialisation
("Or is one strand of progress—industrialisation—now doing such damage to the environment . . .")
asks, "So are we just then rerunning history . . . ?"
contrasts USA and Europe: Europe losing faith in progress ("America still remains predominantly optimistic . . .")
speculates on causes of pessimism: population growth; urbanisation; water shortages; environment challenges; a world without certainty

2. Browne's Response

Business is constructively engaged: technology and the global economy (". . . the means to deliver genuine progress").
Business is contributing to sustainable development ("Business . . . has a fundamental role in delivering sustainable development").
Business wants to stay in business ("Most want to do business again and again over many decades"). Compare those in natural resources ("extracting and developing the world's natural resources"). Role of "technical advances." The economy and new technology: the "connected economy" of networks. (". . . a network of multiple and simultaneous linkages").
Relationship of the connected economy to environment challenges?

    a. "the shift in productivity"
    b. the role of knowledge in a global economy (in paragraph, "But, and this is the second point")

with respect to climate change and air quality

Climate Change

a. reducing emissions: flares; transfer of crude oil; Kyoto Agreement
b. natural gas: methane in Wyoming and New Mexico project; reducing greenhouse gas emissions; gas-fired power station in Norway

Air Quality

a. technology and clean fuels (e.g., refining technology)
b. substitute natural gas for other fuels
c. produce cars that eliminate emissions
d. alternatives: e.g., photovoltaic power

3. Process: Accountability

relationships with employees, customers, shareholders/public, governments

employees working for business they believe in: therefore commercial targets concerned with environmental and ethical objectives

transparency through reporting

relationship of companies to governments (paragraph "It is said . . .", and following)

concludes: "trust companies to deliver sustainable development"

4. Critics

the business incentive questions progressive initiatives

response: "the enlightened company" sees "good commercial reasons" for environmental progress

5. The Future in History

importance of the green revolution, sewerage, clean water

For Discussion and Analysis

1. Browne's own belief in progress (what is it and what does it come from?)

2. Browne's belief in technology

3. Browne's belief in the global economy

4. a belief in ethical business practices?

5. Browne's argument in relation to Suzuki, Lovejoy, Shiva (possibly others in course kit): How does he compare?

the strengths and possible flaws in Browne's case

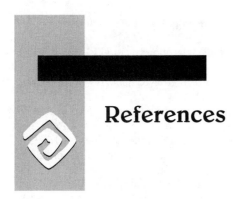

References

Allers, R., & Minkoff, R. (Directors). (1994). *The lion king* [Motion picture]. United States: Walt Disney Pictures.

American Council on the Teaching of Foreign Languages. (1998). *ACTFL guidelines: Speaking*. Retrieved December 23, 2004, from http://www.sil.org/lingualinks/LANGUAGE LEARNING/OtherResources/ACTFLProficiencyGuidelines/ACTFLGuidelinesSpeaking .htm

Antonysamy, A. C. (2002). *The new way the world learns to read*. Unpublished course project, University of Malaya, Kuala Lumpur, Malaysia.

Archer, D. (Producer), & Silver, J. (Director). (1991). *A world of gestures* [Videotape]. Berkeley: University of California Extension Center for Media & Independent Learning.

Asian Development Bank. (2004). *Philippines: Secondary education development and improvement*. Retrieved January 3, 2005, from http://www.adb.org/Documents/Profiles/LOAN /25182013.ASP

Aston, G. (1986). Trouble-shooting in interaction with learners: The more the merrier? *Applied Linguistics, 7,* 128–143.

Augustin, J. (1982). Regional standards of English in peninsular Malaysia. In J. B. Pride (Ed.), *New Englishes* (pp. 249–258). Rowley, MA: Newbury House.

AusAID. (2003). *Philippines-Australia vulnerable groups facility*. Retrieved January 3, 2005, from http://www.ausaid.gov.au/business/publications/incentives/mv_vgf.pdf

Bachman, L. F. (1990). *Fundamental considerations in language testing*. Oxford: Oxford University Press.

Baik, M., & Shim, R. (2002a). *A course in teaching English as a world language*. Retrieved December 13, 2004, from http://tewol.edufuture.com/

Baik, M., & Shim, R. (2002b). Teaching World Englishes via the Internet. *World Englishes, 21,* 427–430.

Bailey, K. M. (1991). Diary studies of classroom language learning: The doubting games and the believing game. In E. Sadtono (Ed.), *Language acquisition and the second/foreign language classroom* (pp. 60–102). Singapore: SEAMEO Regional Language Centre.

Bamgbose, A. (1998). Torn between the norms: Innovations in World Englishes. *World Englishes, 17,* 1–14.

Bardovi-Harlig, K. (1996). Pragmatics and language learning: Bringing pragmatics and pedagogy together. *Pragmatics and Language Learning, 7,* 21–39.

Barton, D., Hamilton, M., & Ivanic, R. (Eds.). (2000). *Situated literacies*. London: Routledge.

Batchelder, D., & Warner, E. (1977). *Beyond experience: The experiential approach to cross-cultural education*. Brattleboro, VT: Experiment in International Living.

Baxter, J. (1980). How should I speak English? American-ly, Japanese-ly, or internationally? *JALT Journal, 2,* 31–61.

Bay, M. (Director/Producer). (2001). *Pearl Harbor* [Motion picture]. United States: Touchstone Pictures.

BBC. (n.d.). *Reith lectures 2000: Respect for the Earth.* Retrieved January 4, 2005, from http://www.bbc.co.uk/radio4/reith2000/

Beal, C. (1990). "It's all in the asking": A perspective on problems of cross-cultural communication between native speakers of French and native speakers of Australian English in the workplace. *Australian Review of Applied Linguistics, 7*(Series S), 16–32.

Bennett, M. J. (1986). A developmental approach to training for intercultural sensitivity. *International Journal of Intercultural Relations, 10,* 179–196.

Bennett, M. J. (1993). Towards ethnorelativism: A developmental model of intercultural sensitivity. In M. Paige (Ed.), *Education for the intercultural experience* (2nd ed., pp. 109–135). Yarmouth, ME: Intercultural Press.

Bennett, M. J. (1998a). Intercultural communication: A current perspective. In M. J. Bennett (Ed.), *Basic concepts of intercultural communication* (pp. 1–34). Yarmouth, ME: Intercultural Press.

Bennett, M. J. (1998b). Overcoming the golden rule: Sympathy and empathy. In M. J. Bennett (Ed.), *Basic concepts of intercultural communication* (pp. 191–214). Yarmouth, ME: Intercultural Press.

Bennett, M. J. (Presenter). (2002). *Better off together than A-P-A-R-T: Intercultural communication, an overview* [Videotape]. Newtonville, MA: Intercultural Resource Corp.

Benson, E., & Conolly, L. W. (Eds.). (1994). *Encyclopedia of post-colonial literatures in English.* New York: Routledge.

Berns, M. (1990). *Contexts of competence: Social and cultural considerations in communicative language teaching.* New York: Plenum Press.

Bhawuk, D. P. S., & Triandis, H. C. (1996). The role of culture theory in the study of culture and intercultural training. In D. Landis & R. S. Bhagat (Eds.), *Handbook of intercultural training* (2nd ed., pp. 17–34). Thousand Oaks, CA: Sage.

Blommaert, J. (1991). How much culture is there in intercultural communication? In J. Blommaert & J. Verschueren (Eds.), *The pragmatics of international and intercultural communication* (pp. 13–31). Amsterdam: John Benjamins.

Bloom, B. (1956). *Taxonomy of educational objectives: The classification of educational goals.* New York: Longman.

Bokamba, E. G. (1992). The Africanization of English. In B. B. Kachru (Ed.), *The other tongue: English across cultures* (pp. 125–147). Urbana: University of Illinois Press.

Boxer, D. (2002). Discourse issues in cross-cultural pragmatics. *Annual Review of Applied Linguistics, 22,* 150–167.

Bozzini, G. R. (1998, March). *Focus on vocabulary in teaching literature.* Paper presented at the 32nd Annual TESOL Convention, Seattle, WA.

Bozzini, G. R., & Leenerts, C. A. (Eds.). (2001). *Literature without borders: International literature in English for student writers.* Upper Saddle River, NJ: Prentice Hall.

Braine, G. (Ed.). (1999). *Non-native educators in English language teaching.* Mahwah, NJ: Erlbaum.

Braithwaite, D. O., & Braithwaite, C. A. (2000). Understanding communication of persons with disabilities as cultural communication. In L. A. Samovar & R. E. Porter (Eds.), *Intercultural communication: A reader* (9th ed., pp. 136–145). Belmont, CA: Wadsworth.

Breen, M. P., & Littlejohn, A. (2000). The significance of negotiation. In M. P. Breen & A. Littlejohn (Eds.), *Classroom decision-making: Negotiation and process syllabuses in practice* (pp. 5–38). Cambridge: Cambridge University Press.

Brinton, D. M., Snow, M. A., & Wesche, M. B. (1989). *Content-based second language instruction.* New York: Newbury House.

Brislin, R. W., Cushner, K., Cherrie, C., & Yong, M. (1986). *Intercultural interactions: A practical guide.* Beverly Hills, CA: Sage.

Brock, M. N. (2003). *Teaching English in Macao: The state of the profession.* Unpublished paper, the University of Macau.

Bromley, H. (2000). "Never be without a *Beano!*" Comics, children and literacy. In H. Anderson & M. Styles (Eds.), *Teaching through texts* (pp. 29–42). London: Routledge.

Brookfield, D. (1987). *Developing critical thinkers: Challenging adults to explore alternative ways of thinking and acting.* San Francisco: Jossey-Bass.

Brown, K. (1993). World Englishes in TESOL programs: An infusion model of curricular innovation. *World Englishes, 12,* 59–73.

Brown, K. (1995). World Englishes: To teach or not to teach. *World Englishes, 14,* 233–246.

Brown, K. (1997). A world language perspective: English, French, and Spanish. In K. Bardovi-Harlig & B. Hartford (Eds.), *Beyond methods: Components of second language education* (pp. 137–151). New York: McGraw-Hill.

Brown, K. (1999). *Internationalizing the university: A concept paper.* Unpublished policy paper, Portland State University, Portland, OR.

Brown, K. (2002). Ideology and context: World Englishes and EFL teacher training, *World Englishes, 21,* 445–448.

Brown, K., & Peterson, J. (1997). Exploring conceptual frameworks: Framing a World Englishes paradigm. In L. Smith & M. Forman (Eds.), *Literary studies East and West: Vol. 14. World Englishes 2000* (pp. 32–47). Honolulu: University of Hawaii Press.

Brown, P., & Levinson, S. (1987). *Politeness: Some universals in language usage.* Cambridge: Cambridge University Press.

Browne, J. (2000). *Business* (Reith Lectures 2000: Respect for the Earth). Retrieved January 4, 2005, from http://news.bbc.co.uk/hi/english/static/events/reith_2000/lecture3.stm

Brundtland, G. (2000). *Health and population* (Reith Lectures 2000: Respect for the Earth). Retrieved January 4, 2004, from http://news.bbc.co.uk/hi/english/static/events/reith_2000/lecture4.stm

Brutt-Griffler, J. (1998). Conceptual questions in English as a world language: Taking up an issue. *World Englishes, 17,* 381–392

Brutt-Griffler, J., & Samimy, K. K. (1999). Revisiting the colonial in the postcolonial: Critical praxis for nonnative-English-speaking teachers in a TESOL program. *TESOL Quarterly, 33,* 413–433.

Bryan, B. (1994). English in its place. In M. Hayhoe & S. Parker (Eds.), *Who owns English?* (pp. 98–107). Oxford: Oxford University Press.

Bureau of Secondary Education. (1991). *Desired learning competencies: English.* Manila, Philippines: Department of Education, Culture, & Sports.

Bureau of Secondary Education. (1995). *Education in the Philippines: Focus on secondary education.* Manila, Philippines: Department of Education, Culture, & Sports.

Burns, A. (1999). *Collaborative action research for English language teachers.* Cambridge: Cambridge University Press.

Burns, A., & Coffin, C. (2001). *Context, use and analysis of the English language: A global perspective.* Distance learning materials prepared for master's in applied linguistics/master's in education courses, Macquarie University, Sydney, Australia, and The Open University, Milton Keynes, United Kingdom.

Burns, A., Joyce, H., & Gollin, S. (1997). Authentic spoken texts in the language classroom. *Prospect, 12*(2), 72–86.

Byrne, D. (1995). *Techniques for classroom interaction.* Harlow, England: Longman.

Canadian Union of Public Employees. (1999). Consuming classrooms. In *Hostile takeover: Annual report on privatization 1999.* Ottawa, Ontario, Canada: Author. Retrieved April 16, 2004, from http://www.cupe.ca/www/ARP1999/4528

Canagarajah, A. S. (1999a). Interrogating the "native speaker fallacy": Non-linguistics roots, non-pedagogical results. In G. Braine (Ed.), *Non-native educators in English language teaching* (pp. 77–92). Mahwah, NJ: Erlbaum.

Canagarajah, A. S. (1999b). *Resisting linguistic imperialism in English teaching*. Oxford: Oxford University Press.

Canagarajah, A. S. (2002). Globalization, methods and practice in periphery classrooms. In D. Block & D. Cameron (Eds.), *Globalization and language teaching* (pp. 134–150). London: Routledge.

Canale, M. (1983). From communicative competence to communicative language pedagogy. In J. C. Richards & R. W. Schmidt (Eds.), *Language and communication* (pp. 2–27). London, England: Longman.

Canale, M., & Swain, M. (1980). Theoretical bases of communicative approaches to second language teaching and testing. *Applied Linguistics, 1,* 1–47.

Candlin, C. (1997). General editor's preface. In B. Kenny & W. Savage, *Language and development: Teachers in a changing world* (pp. xii–xvii). New York: Longman.

Carter, R. (1997). Speaking Englishes, speaking cultures, using CANCODE. *Prospect, 12*(2), 4–11.

Caulk, N. (1998). Intercultural faculty meetings. In J. C. Richards (Ed.), *Teaching in action* (pp. 132–136). Alexandria, VA: TESOL.

Cazden, C. B. (2000). Four innovative programmes: A postscript from Alice Spring. In B. Cope & M. Kalantzis (Eds.), *Multiliteracies: Literacy learning and the design of social futures* (pp. 321–348). Melbourne, Australia: Macmillan.

Center for English Language Teaching & Institute for English Language Education. (1997, September). *PELT project bulletin no. 6*. Retrieved January 3, 2005, from http://acelt.faithweb.com/publish/PELT/pelt.htm

Center for English Language Teaching & Institute for English Language Education. (1998, March). *PELT project bulletin no. 7*. Retrieved January 3, 2005, from http://acelt.faithweb.com/publish/PELT/pelt.htm

Chiba, R., Matsuura, H., & Yamamoto, A. (1995). Japanese attitudes toward English accents. *World Englishes, 14,* 77–86.

Clarke, T. (1997). Global managers. In *Silent coup: Confronting the big business takeover of Canada* (pp. 39–69). Toronto, Ontario, Canada: Lorimer.

Clyne, M. (1994). *Inter-cultural communication at work: Cultural values in discourse*. Cambridge: Cambridge University Press.

Columbus, C. (Director). (2001). *Harry Potter and the sorcerer's stone* [Motion picture]. Burbank, CA: Warner Bros.

Connor, S. (2000, May 20–21). Artificial, synthetic but still necessary. *Weekend Herald* (Auckland), p. B7.

Cook, V. (1999). Going beyond the native speaker in language teaching. *TESOL Quarterly, 33,* 185–210.

Cook, V. (2001). *Second language learning and language teaching*. London: Arnold.

Cooke, D. (2004). What can a text mean? *New Zealand Journal of Adult Learning, 32,* 52–65.

Cope, B., & Kalantzis, M. (Eds.). (1999). *Multiliteracies*. London: Routledge.

Cornbleth, C. (1985). Critical thinking and cognitive processes. In W. B. Stanley (Ed.), *Review of research in social studies education: 1976–1983* (pp. 11–63). Washington, DC: National Council for the Social Studies.

Corson, D. (1995). World view, cultural values and discourse norms: The cycle of cultural reproduction. *International Journal of Intercultural Relations, 19,* 183–195.

Cortazzi, M., & Jin, L. (1999). Cultural mirrors. In E. Hinkel (Ed.), *Culture in second language teaching and learning* (pp. 196–219). Cambridge: Cambridge University Press.

Crystal, D. (1997). *English as a global language*. Cambridge: Cambridge University Press.

Crystal, D. (1999, March). *The future of English: A Welsh perspective*. Plenary address at the 33rd Annual TESOL Convention, New York.

Crystal, D. (2001). *Language and the Internet*. Cambridge: Cambridge University Press.

Curriculum Council. (1998). *National curriculum standards reform for kindergarten, elementary school, lower and upper secondary school and schools for the visually disabled, the hearing impaired and the otherwise disabled: Synopsis of the report*. Tokyo: Ministry of Education, Culture, Sports, Science, & Technology. Retrieved January 12, 2003, from http://www.mext.go.jp/english/news/1998/07/980712.htm

Dalton, C., & Seidlhofer, B. (1994). *Pronunciation*. Oxford: Oxford University Press.

Damen, L. (1987). *Culture learning: The fifth dimension in the language classroom*. Reading, MA: Addison-Wesley.

Das, S. K. (1982). Indian English. In J. B. Pride (Ed.), *New Englishes* (pp. 141–149). Rowley, MA: Newbury House.

Davidson, J. (1984). Subsequent versions of invitations, offers, requests, and proposals dealing with potential or actual rejection. In J. M. Atkinson & J. Heritage (Eds.), *Structures of social action: Studies in conversation analysis* (pp. 152–163). Cambridge: Cambridge University Press.

Davies, A. (1995). Proficiency or the native speaker: What are we trying to achieve in ELT? In G. Cook & B. Seidlhofer (Eds.), *Principle and practice in applied linguistics* (pp. 145–158). Oxford: Oxford University Press.

Department of Education, Culture, & Sports. (1997). *Facts and figures on Philippine education*. Pasig City, Philippines: Author.

Deshpande, S. (2001). Why a robin? In G. R. Bozzini & C. A. Leenerts (Eds.), *Literature without borders: International literature in English for student writers* (pp. 25–30). Upper Saddle River, NJ: Prentice Hall.

Dias, P., Freedman, A., Medway, P., & Pare, A. (1999). *Worlds apart: Acting and writing in academic and workplace contexts*. Mahwah, NJ: Erlbaum.

Di Pietro, R. J. (1987). *Strategic interaction: Learning languages through scenarios*. Cambridge: Cambridge University Press.

Dobbin, M. (1998). *The myth of the good corporate citizen: Democracy under the rule of big business*. New York: Stoddart.

Dobler, A. L. (1998). Instructor-student interaction: Teacher, friend, or other? In J. C. Richards (Ed.), *Teaching in action* (pp. 121–124). Alexandria, VA: TESOL.

Edge, J. (Ed.). (2001). *Action research* (Case Studies in TESOL Practice Series). Alexandria, VA: TESOL.

Ekman, P. (1997). Should we call it expression or communication? *Innovation, 10*, 333–344.

Ellis, G. (1996). How culturally appropriate is the communicative approach? *ELT Journal, 50*, 213–224.

Escobar, A. (1995). *Encountering development: The making and unmaking of the Third World*. Princeton, NJ: Princeton University Press.

Fairclough, N. (1995). *Critical discourse analysis: The critical study of language*. London: Longman.

Fantini, A. E. (Ed.). (1997). *New ways in teaching culture*. Alexandria, VA: TESOL.

Farrell, T. S. C. (1998). Communicating with colleagues of a different culture. In J. C. Richards (Ed.), *Teaching in action* (pp. 125–128). Alexandria, VA: TESOL.

Financial Times. (2001, June 4). *Financial Times executive education ranking*. London: Author. Retrieved February 13, 2005, from http://www.ft.com/

Ford, A., Silverman, A., & Haines, D. (1983). *Cultural encounters*. Oxford: Pergamon Press.

Fowler, S. M., & Mumford, M. G. (Eds.). (1999). *Intercultural sourcebook: Vol. 2. Cross-cultural training methods*. Yarmouth, ME: Intercultural Press.

Gajdusek, L. (1988). Toward wider use of literature in ESL: Why and how. *TESOL Quarterly, 22*, 227–257.

Gannon, M. J. (2000). Irish conversations. In L. A. Samovar & R. E. Porter (Eds.), *Intercultural communication: A reader* (9th ed., pp. 247–254). Belmont, CA: Wadsworth.

Gao, G. (1998). "Don't take my word for it": Understanding Chinese speaking practices. *International Journal of Intercultural Relations, 22,* 163–186.

Garcia, E. (1997). The language policy in education. In M. L. S. Bautista (Ed.), *English is an Asian language* (pp. 73–86). Sydney, Australia: Macquarie Library.

Gardner, R. (2000). Resources for delicate manoeuvres: Learning to disagree. In E. A. Soler & J. R. Guzman (Eds.), *Discourse and language teaching* (Annual Review of Applied Linguistics, Series S), pp. 31–47. Cambridge: Cambridge University Press.

Gee, J. (1989). Literacies and traditions. *Journal of Education, 171,* 26–38.

Gee, J., Hull, G., & Lankshear, C. (1996). *The new work order: Behind the language of the new capitalism.* Boulder, CO: Westview Press.

Giltrow, J. (1995). *Academic writing: Writing and reading across the disciplines* (2nd ed.). Peterborough, Ontario, Canada: Broadview Press.

Gonzalez, A. (1997). The history of English in the Philippines. In M. L. S. Bautista (Ed.), *English is an Asian language* (pp. 25–40). Sydney, Australia: Macquarie Library.

Gonzalez, A., Bernardo, A. B. I., Bautista, M. L. S., & Pascasio, E. M. (1998, July). *The social sciences and policy making in language.* Paper delivered at the Fourth National Social Science Congress, Manila, Philippines.

Goodman, S. (2001). Visual English. In S. Goodman & D. Graddol (Eds.), *Redesigning English* (pp. 38–105). London: Routledge.

Govardhan, A. K., Nayar, B., & Sheorey, R. (1999). Do U.S. MATESOL programs prepare students to teach abroad? *TESOL Quarterly, 33,* 114–125.

Government of the Philippines. (2005). *Educational development project implementing task force.* Retrieved January 3, 2005, from http://www.gov.ph/cat_education/o_edpitf.asp

Graddol, D. (1997). *The future of English?* London: The British Council.

Graddol, D. (2001). English in the future. In A. Burns & C. Coffin (Eds.), *Analysing English in a global context: A reader* (pp. 26–37). London: Routledge.

Granger, S. (2003). The international corpus of learner English: A new resource for foreign language learning and teaching and second language acquisition research. *TESOL Quarterly, 37,* 538–544.

Green, M. (2003). The internationalized campus: A strategic approach. *International Educator, 12*(1), 13–21.

Green, M., & Olson, C. (2003). *Internationalizing the campus: A user's guide.* Washington, DC: American Council on Education.

Gudykunst, W. B. (1998). *Bridging differences: Effective intergroup communication* (3rd ed.). Thousand Oaks, CA: Sage.

Gumperz, J. J. (1995). Mutual inferencing in conversation. In I. Markova, C. F. Graumann, & K. Foppa (Eds.), *Mutualities in dialogue* (pp. 101–123). Cambridge: Cambridge University Press.

Hall, E. T. (1966). *The hidden dimension: Man's use of space in public and private.* London: Bodley Head.

Hammer, M., & Bennett, M. (1994). *Intercultural Development Inventory* (Version 1). Portland, OR: Intercultural Communication Institute.

Hammer, M., & Bennett, M. (1999/2001). *Intercultural Development Inventory* (Version 2). Portland, OR: Intercultural Communication Institute.

Hamnett, M., Porter, D., Singh, A., & Kumar, K. (1984). *Ethics, politics and international social science research: From critique to praxis.* Honolulu: University of Hawaii Press.

Harmer, J. (1991). *The practice of English language teaching* (2nd ed.). London: Addison Wesley Longman.

Harmer, J. (2001). *The practice of English language teaching* (3rd ed.). Harlow, England: Longman.

Heaney, S. (2001). Digging. In G. R. Bozzini & C. A. Leenerts (Eds.), *Literature without borders: International literature in English for student writers* (pp. 92–93). Upper Saddle River, NJ: Prentice Hall.

Heath, S. B. (1994). What no bedtime story means: Narrative skills at home and school. In J. Maybin (Ed.), *Language and literacy in social practice* (pp. 73–95). Clevedon, England: Multilingual Matters.

Holliday, A. (1994). *Appropriate methodology and social context.* Cambridge: Cambridge University Press.

Honey, J. (1997). *Language is power: The story of standard English and its enemies.* London: Faber & Faber.

Hunter, J., & Morgan, B. (2001). Language and public life: Teaching multiliteracies in ESL. In I. Leki (Ed.), *Academic writing* (Case Studies in TESOL Practice Series, pp. 99–109). Alexandria, VA: TESOL.

Hutchinson, T., & Waters, A. (1987). *English for specific purposes.* Cambridge: Cambridge University Press.

Hyde, M. (1994). The teaching of English in Morocco: The place of culture. *ELT Journal, 48,* 295–305.

Ichikawa, Y., Yasuyoshi, I., Kobayashi, C., Shiokawa, H., Hagino, S., & Hestand, J. R. (2003). *Unicorn English reading.* Kyoto, Japan: Buneido.

Ishiguro, K. (2001). A family supper. In G. R. Bozzini & C. A. Leenerts (Eds.), *Literature without borders: International literature in English for student writers* (pp. 105–113). Upper Saddle River, NJ: Prentice Hall.

International Association of Teachers of English as a Foreign Language Global Issues Special Interest Group. (n.d.). *Global issues in English language (EFL/ESL) education.* Retrieved June 30, 2003, from http://www.countryschool.com/gisig.htm

Iwata, Y., Ogawa, M., Wen, Q., Sakamoto, E., Takarada, M., Horio, A., Muto, K., & Mogi, R. (2002, March). Kyoukasho kara mita ibunka to no kakawari [Exposure to different cultures through English textbooks]. *ASTE Newsletter, 46.* Retrieved August 14, 2002, from http://www.bun-eido.co.jp/aste/aste46.html

Jenkins, J. (2000). *The phonology of English as an international language.* Oxford: Oxford University Press.

Johns, A. M. (1997). *Text, role and context.* Cambridge: Cambridge University Press.

Johnson, F. L. (2000). Discourse consequences: Where language and culture matter. In *Speaking culturally: Language diversity in the United States* (pp. 245–296). Thousand Oaks, CA: Sage.

Johnson, W. K. (1999, October/November). Observations of the anti-other: An avenue to self-censorship. *TESOL Matters, 4.* Retrieved June 24, 2003, from http://www.tesol.org /pubs/articles/1999/tm9910-04.html

Jones, K. (2000). Becoming just another alphanumeric code. In D. Barton, M. Hamilton, & R. Ivanic (Eds.), *Situated literacies* (pp. 70–90). London: Routledge.

Kachru, B. B. (1985). Standards, codification and sociolinguistic realism: The English language in the outer circle. In R. Quirk & H. G. Widdowson (Eds.), *English in the world: Teaching and learning the language and literatures* (pp. 11–30). Cambridge: Cambridge University Press.

Kachru, B. B. (1986). *The alchemy of English: The spread, functions and models of non-native Englishes.* Oxford: Pergamon Press.

Kachru, B. B. (1988). Teaching World Englishes. *ERIC/CLL News Bulletin, 12*(1), 1–8.

Kachru, B. B. (1992a). Models for non-native Englishes. In B. B. Kachru (Ed.), *The other tongue: English across cultures* (2nd ed., pp. 48–74). Urbana: University of Illinois Press.

Kachru, B. B. (Ed.). (1992b). *The other tongue: English across cultures.* Urbana: University of Illinois Press.

Kachru, B. B., & Nelson, C. L. (2001). World Englishes. In A. Burns & C. Coffin (Eds.), *Analysing English in a global context* (pp. 9–25). London: Routledge.

Kachru, Y. (1994). Research Issues: Monolingual bias in SLA research. *TESOL Quarterly, 28,* 795–800.

Kamhi-Stein, L. (1999). Preparing non-native professionals in TESOL: Implications for teacher education programs. In G. Braine (Ed.), *Non-native educators in English language teaching* (pp. 147–157). Mahwah, NJ: Erlbaum.

Kaur, J. (2002). *Stretch learners' minds in new directions: A case for the combined use of visual images and the printed word to develop critical thinking skills.* Unpublished course project, University of Malaya, Kuala Lumpur, Malaysia.

Kelsey, J. (1995). *The New Zealand experiment: A world model for structural adjustment?* Auckland, New Zealand: Auckland University Press with Bridget Williams Books.

Kemmis, S., & McTaggart, R. (2000). Participatory action research. In N. K. Denzin & Y. S. Lincoln (Eds.), *Handbook of qualitative research* (pp. 567–605). Thousand Oaks, CA: Sage.

Kenny, B. & Savage, W. (1997). *Language and development: Teachers in a changing world.* New York: Longman.

Kern, R. (2000). *Literacy and language teaching.* Oxford: Oxford University Press.

Kincheloe, J. L., & Steinberg, S. R. (1998). Making meaning and analyzing experience—student researchers as transformative agents. In S. R. Steinberg & J. L. Kincheloe (Eds.), *Students as researchers* (pp. 228–246). London: Falmer Press.

Kinkaid, J. (2001). My mother. In G. R. Bozzini & C. A. Leenerts (Eds.), *Literature without borders: International literature in English for student writers* (pp. 73–77). Upper Saddle River, NJ: Prentice Hall.

Kiryu, N., Shibata, T., Tagaya, H., & Wada, T. (1999). An analysis of Monbusho-approved textbooks for English Course I: From the perspective of World English. *The Language Teacher, 23*(4), 21–24.

Klippel, F. (1984). *Keep talking: Communicative fluency activities for language teaching.* Cambridge: Cambridge University Press.

Kohls, L. R., & Knight, J. M. (1994). *Developing intercultural awareness* (2nd ed.). Yarmouth, ME: Intercultural Press.

Kolb, D. (1984). *Experiential learning.* Englewood Cliffs, NJ: Prentice Hall.

Kornblum, H., with Garshick, E. (Ed.). (1992). *Directory of professional preparation programs in TESOL in the United States, 1992–1994.* Alexandria, VA: TESOL.

Korten, D. (1995). *When corporations rule the world.* West Hartford, CT: Kumarian Press.

Kramer, S. (Producer/Director). (1991). *Awakenings* [Videotape]. Burbank, CA: RCA/Columbia Pictures Home Video.

Kramer, S. (Producer/Director). (1995). *Guess who's coming to dinner* [Videotape]. Burbank, CA: Columbia TriStar Home Video. (Originally produced 1967)

Kramsch, C. (1998). The privilege of the intercultural speaker. In M. Byram & M. Fleming (Eds.), *Language learning in intercultural perspective: Approaches through drama and ethnography* (pp. 16–31). Cambridge: Cambridge University Press.

Kramsch, C., & Sullivan, P. (1996). Appropriate pedagogy. *ELT Journal, 50,* 199–212.

Kress, G. (2000). Multimodality: Challenges to thinking about language. *TESOL Quarterly, 34,* 337–340.

Kress, G., & van Leeuwen, T. (1996). *Reading images: The grammar of visual design.* London: Routledge.

Krishnaswamy, N., & Burde, A. (1998). *The politics of Indians' English.* New Delhi: Oxford University Press.

Kubota, R. (1999). Japanese culture constructed by discourses: Implications for applied linguistics research and ELT. *TESOL Quarterly, 33,* 9–35.

Kubota, R. (2001). Discursive construction of the images of U S classrooms. *TESOL Quarterly, 35,* 9–38.

Lam, A. (2001). Grandma's tales. In G. R. Bozzini & C. A. Leenerts (Eds.), *Literature without borders: International literature in English for student writers* (pp. 19–23). Upper Saddle River, NJ: Prentice Hall.

Lee, L.-Y. (2001). The gift. In G. R. Bozzini & C. A. Leenerts (Eds.), *Literature without borders: International literature in English for student writers* (pp. 83–84). Upper Saddle River, NJ: Prentice Hall.

Levine, D. R., Baxter, J., & McNulty, P. (1987). *The culture puzzle.* Englewood Cliffs, NJ: Prentice Hall Regents.

Li, D. (1998). "It's always more difficult than you plan or imagine": Teachers' perceived difficulties in introducing the communicative approach in South Korea. *TESOL Quarterly, 32,* 677–703.

Liew, A. (2002). *Witches, wizards and broomsticks: Mapping the journey taken by three learners into the magical world of* Harry Potter. Unpublished course project, University of Malaya, Kuala Lumpur, Malaysia.

Lim, S. G.-L. (2001). Ah mah. In G. R. Bozzini & C. A. Leenerts (Eds.), *Literature without borders: International literature in English for student writers* (pp. 6–7). Upper Saddle River, NJ: Prentice Hall.

Linell, P. (1995). Troubles with mutualities: Towards a dialogical theory of misunderstanding and miscommunication. In I. Markova, C. F. Graumann, & K. Foppa (Eds.), *Mutualities in dialogue* (pp. 176–207). Cambridge: Cambridge University Press.

Liu, J. (1999). Nonnative-English-speaking professionals in TESOL. *TESOL Quarterly, 33,* 85–102.

Longman Corpus Network. (2004). *The Longman learners' corpus.* Retrieved September 16, 2004, from http://www.longman-elt.com/dictionaries/corpus/lclearn.html

Loomer, L. (1998). *The waiting room.* New York: Dramatists Play Service.

Lovejoy, T. (2000). *Biodiversity* (Reith Lectures 2000: Respect for the Earth). Retrieved January 4, 2005, from http://news.bbc.co.uk/hi/english/static/events/reith_2000/lecture2.stm

Lucas, G. (Director). (1977). *Star wars* [Motion picture]. San Rafael, CA: Lucasfilm.

Lustig, R. (2003, August). *Spinning to win* [Radio broadcast]. London: BBC World Service.

Maimon, E. P. (2000). Preface. In S. H. McLeod & M. Soven (Eds.), *Writing across the curriculum: A guide to developing programs* (pp. xii–x). Thousand Oaks, CA: Sage.

Martin, H.-P., & Schumann, H. (1997). *The global trap.* Montreal, Quebec, Canada: Black Rose Books.

Martin, J. (1985). Language, register and genre. In F. Christie (Ed.), *Children's writing study guide* (pp. 21–30). Geelong, Australia: Deakin University Press.

Martin, J. N., & Nakayama, T. K. (2001). *Experiencing intercultural communication.* Mountain View, CA: Mayfield.

Masilamany, G. B. (2001). *Reading in Schools journal.* Unpublished course project, University of Malaya, Kuala Lumpur, Malaysia.

Matsuda, A. (2000). *Japanese attitudes toward English: A case study of high school students.* Unpublished doctoral dissertation, Purdue University, West Lafayette, IN.

Matsuda, A. (2002). Representation of users and uses of English in beginning Japanese EFL textbooks. *JALT Journal, 24,* 80–98.

Matsuda, A. (2003a). Incorporating World Englishes in teaching English as an international language. *TESOL Quarterly, 37,* 719–729.

Matsuda, A. (2003b). The ownership of English: A perspective of Japanese high school students. *World Englishes, 22,* 483–496.

Matsuda, A., & Matsuda, P. K. (2001). Autonomy and collaboration in teacher education:

Journal sharing among native and nonnative English-speaking teachers. *The CATESOL Journal, 13*(1), 109–121.

Matsuura, H., Chiba, R., & Yamamoto, A. (1994). Japanese college students' attitudes towards non-native varieties of English. In D. Graddol & J. Swann (Eds.), *Evaluating language* (pp. 52–61). Clevedon, England: Multilingual Matters.

McKay, S. (1982). Literature in the ESL classroom. *TESOL Quarterly, 16*, 529–536.

McKay, S. (1992). *Teaching English overseas: An introduction.* Oxford: Oxford University Press.

McKay, S. (2000). An investigation of five Japanese English teachers' reflection on their U.S. MATESOL practicum experience. *JALT Journal, 22*, 46–68.

McKay, S. (2002). *Teaching English as an international language.* Oxford: Oxford University Press.

McKay, V. (2000). Understanding the co-culture of the elderly. In L. A. Samovar & R. E. Porter (Eds.), *Intercultural communication: A reader* (9th ed., pp. 180–189). Belmont, CA: Wadsworth.

McLeod, S. H. (2000). Writing across the curriculum: An introduction. In S. H. McLeod & M. Soven (Eds.), *Writing across the curriculum: A guide to developing programs* (pp. 1–8). Thousand Oaks, CA: Sage.

McMurtry, J. (1998). *Unequal freedoms: The global market as an ethical system.* Toronto, Ontario, Canada: Garamond Press.

McPeck, J. (1990). *Teaching critical thinking: Dialogue and dialectic.* New York: Routledge.

Medgyes, P. (1992). *Non-natives in ELT.* London: Macmillan.

Medgyes, P. (1994). *The non-native teacher.* Hong Kong: Macmillan.

Meier, A. J. (2003). Posting the banns: A marriage of pragmatics and culture in foreign and second language pedagogy and beyond. In A. Martínez, E. Usó, & A. Fernández (Eds.), *Pragmatic competence and foreign language teaching* (pp. 185–210). Castelló de la Plana, Spain: Servicio de publicaciones de la Universidad Jaume I.

Mestenhauser, J., & Ellingboe, B. (1998). *Reforming the higher education curriculum: Internationalizing the campus.* Phoenix, AZ: American Council on Education & Oryx Press.

Milambiling, J. (2000). Comments on Vivian Cook's "Going beyond the native speaker in language teaching": How nonnative speakers as teachers fit into the equation. *TESOL Quarterly, 34*, 324–328.

Mohan, B. (1986). *Language and content.* Reading, MA: Addison-Wesley.

Monbukagakusho [Ministry of Education, Culture, Sports, Science, & Technology]. (2001). *Eigo shido houhou tou kaizen no suishin ni kansuru kondankai houkoku shiryou* [Report materials for a meeting on promoting improvements in English teaching methods]. Retrieved August 2, 2002, from http://www.mext.go.jp/b_menu/shingi /chousa/shotou/018/toushin/010110c.htm

Monbusho [Ministry of Education, Science, Sports, & Culture]. (1999a). *Chugakko gakushu shidou youryou kaisetsu: Gaikokugo hen* [A guide for the national curriculum standard for lower secondary school: Foreign languages]. Tokyo: Tokyo Shoseki.

Monbusho [Ministry of Education, Science, Sports, & Culture]. (1999b). *Koutou gakko gakushu shidou youryou kaisetsu: Gaikokugo hen, eigo hen* [A guide for the national curriculum standard for upper secondary school: Foreign languages and English]. Tokyo: Kairyudo.

Morgan, B. (1998). *The ESL classroom: Teaching, critical practice, and community development.* Toronto, Ontario, Canada: University of Toronto Press.

Munro, A. (2001). Friend of my youth. In G. R. Bozzini & C. A. Leenerts (Eds.), *Literature without borders: International literature in English for student writers* (pp. 32–48). Upper Saddle River, NJ: Prentice Hall.

Murphy, B., & Neu, J. (1996). My grades too low: The speech act of complaining. In S. M. Gass & J. Neu (Eds.), *Speech acts across cultures: Challenges to communication in a second language* (pp. 191–216). Berlin: Mouton de Gruyter.

Naysmith, J. (1987). English as imperialism? *Language Issues, 2,* 3–5.

Nelson, G. (1998). Intercultural communication and related courses taught in TESOL masters' degree programs. *International Journal of Intercultural Relations, 22,* 17–33.

New London Group. (1996). A pedagogy of multiliteracies: Designing social futures. *Harvard Educational Review, 66,* 60–92.

Nunan, D. (1988). *The learner centred curriculum: A study in the second language learning.* Cambridge: Cambridge University Press.

Nunan, D. (1992). *Research methods in language learning.* Cambridge: Cambridge University Press.

Nunan, D. (1998). *Second language teaching and learning.* Boston: Heinle & Heinle.

Office of the President. (2001, December). *Presidential initiative: Internationalization.* Retrieved January 28, 2002, from http://www.president.pdx.edu/Initiatives/international/rec&actions01.phtml

Oster, J. (1989). Seeing with different eyes: Another view of literature in the ESL class. *TESOL Quarterly, 23,* 85–103.

Paige, R. M., Jorstad, H., Siaya, L., Klein, F., & Colby, J. (n.d.). *Culture learning in language education: A review of the literature.* Retrieved January 31, 2002, from http://carla.acad.umn.edu/IS-litreview/litreview.html

Paige, R. M., & Martin, J. N. (1996). Ethics in intercultural training. In D. Landis & R. S. Bhagat (Eds.), *Handbook of intercultural training* (2nd ed., pp. 35–60). Thousand Oaks, CA: Sage.

Pakir, A. (1999a). Connecting with English in the context of internationalisation. *TESOL Quarterly, 33,* 103–113.

Pakir, A. (1999b, March). *English as a glocal language: Implications for English language teaching worldwide.* Plenary paper presented at the International Association of Teachers of English as a Foreign Language, Edinburgh, Scotland.

Paulston, R. G. (1976). *Conflicting theories of social and educational change: A typological review.* Pittsburgh, PA: University of Pittsburgh, Center for International Studies. (ERIC Document Reproduction Service No. ED130921)

Paulston, R. (Ed.). (2000). *Social cartography: Mapping ways of seeing social and educational change.* New York: Garland.

Pennycook, A. (1989). The concept of method, interested knowledge, and the politics of language teaching. *TESOL Quarterly, 23,* 589–618.

Pennycook, A. (1995). English in the world/The world in English. In J. W. Tollefson (Ed.), *Power and inequality in language education* (pp. 34–58). Cambridge: Cambridge University Press.

Phillipson, R. (1992). *Linguistic imperialism.* Oxford: Oxford University Press.

Picken, J. (1999). State of the ad: The role of advertisements in EFL teaching. *ELT Journal, 53,* 249–255.

Pomerantz, A. (1984). Pursuing a response. In J. M. Atkinson & J. Heritage (Eds.), *Structures of social action: Studies in conversation analysis* (pp. 152–163). Cambridge: Cambridge University Press.

Prabhu, N. S. (1990). There is no best method—why? *TESOL Quarterly, 24,* 161–176.

Pratt, M. (1996). Arts of the contact zone. In D. Bartholomae & T. Petrosky (Eds.), *Ways of reading* (4th ed., pp. 528–548). Boston: Bedford Books. (Reprinted from *Profession,* 1991, *91,* 33–40)

Precht, K. (1998). A cross-cultural comparison of letters of recommendation. *English for Specific Purposes, 17,* 241–265.

Prince of Wales. (2000). *A royal view* . . . . (Reith Lectures 2000: Respect for the Earth). Retrieved January 4, 2005, from http://www.bbc.co.uk/hi/english/static/events/reith_2000/lecture2.stm

Project completion report on the Secondary Education Development Project (SEDP) Philippines. (n.d.). Unpublished manuscript.

Quirk, R. (1985). The English language in a global context. In R. Quirk & H. Widdowson (Eds.), *English in the world: Teaching and learning the language and literature* (pp. 1–6). Cambridge: Cambridge University Press.

Rampton, M. B. H. (1990). Displacing the "native speaker": Expertise, affiliation and inheritance. *ELT Journal, 44,* 338–343.

Ramsey, S. J. (1998). Interactions between North Americans and Japanese: Considerations of communication style. In M. J. Bennett (Ed.), *Basic concepts of intercultural communication* (pp. 111–130). Yarmouth, ME: Intercultural Press.

Republic of Korea. (1997, May). *The provisional themes for the 2nd APEC Human Resources Development Ministerial Meeting (part 1).* Concept paper presented at the 10th Meeting of the APEC Education Forum, Montreal, Quebec, Canada.

Richard-Amato, P. A., & Snow, M. A. (1992). *The multicultural classroom: Readings for content-area teachers.* London: Longman.

Richards, J., & Luke, K. K. (1981, April). *English in Hong Kong: Functions and status.* Paper presented at the seminar on varieties of English of the Regional English Language Center, Singapore.

Rogers, B. (Producer/Director). (1985). *Rainbow war* [Videotape]. Santa Monica, CA: Pyramid Film & Video.

Ross, R. L. (Ed.). (1991). *International literature in English: Essays on the major writers.* New York: Garland.

Rushdie, S. (1991). "Commonwealth literature" does not exist. In *Imaginary homelands: Essays and criticism, 1981–1991* (pp. 61–70). New York: Viking Penguin.

Sacks, H. (1987). On the preferences for agreement and contiguity in sequences in conversation. In G. Button & J. R. E. Lee (Eds.), *Talk and social organisation* (pp. 54–69). Clevedon, England: Multilingual Matters.

Sage, L. (Ed.). (1999). *The Cambridge guide to women's writing in English.* Cambridge: Cambridge University Press.

Samovar, L. A., & Porter, R. E. (2001). *Communication between cultures.* Belmont, CA: Wadsworth.

Samuel, J. (2001). Grandfather at noon: Lahore, 1957. In G. R. Bozzini & C. A. Leenerts (Eds.), *Literature without borders: International literature in English for student writers* (pp. 9–17). Upper Saddle River, NJ: Prentice Hall.

Samuel, M. (2000). English is an Asian language: Implication for pedagogy. In H. M. Said & N. K. Siew (Eds.), *English is an Asian language* (pp. 26–34). Kuala Lumpur, Malaysia: Macquarie Dictionary & Malaysian Modern Languages Association.

Sasaki, T. (Ed.). (1997). *One world English course 1.* Tokyo: Kyoiku Shuppan.

Savignon, S. (1983). *Communicative competence: Theory and classroom practice; texts and contexts in second language learning.* Reading, MA: Addison-Wesley.

Schegloff, E., & Sacks, H. (1974). Opening up closings. In R. Turner (Ed.), *Ethnomethodology: Selected readings* (pp. 223–264). Harmondsworth, England: Penguin Education.

Schiffrin, D. (1987). *Discourse markers.* Cambridge: Cambridge University Press.

Schön, D. A. (1983). *The reflective practitioner: How professionals think in action.* New York: Basic Books.

Seidlhofer, B. (1999). Double standards: Teacher education in the expanding circle. *World Englishes, 18,* 233–245.

Seidlhofer, B. (2002). Pedagogy and local learner corpora: Working with learning-driven data. In S. Granger, J. Hung, & S. Petch-Tyson (Eds.), *Computer learner corpora, second language acquisition and foreign language teaching* (pp. 213–234). Amsterdam: Benjamins.

Sercu, L. (1989). In-service teacher training and the acquisition of intercultural competence. In M. Byram & M. Fleming (Eds.), *Language learning in intercultural perspectives* (pp. 255–289). Cambridge: Cambridge University Press.

Shamim, F. (1996). Learner resistance to innovation in classroom methodology. In H. Coleman (Ed.), *Society and the language classroom* (pp. 105–122). Cambridge: Cambridge University Press.

Shimaoka, T., Aoki, S. Matsuhata, K., & Wada, M. (Ed.). (1997). *Sunshine English course 1.* Tokyo: Kairyudo.

Shiva, V. (2000). *Poverty and globalisation* (Reith Lectures 2000: Respect for the Earth). Retrieved January 4, 2005, from http://news.bbc.co.uk/hi/english/static/events/reith_2000/lecture5.stm

Shulman, M. (2001). *Cultures in contrast.* Ann Arbor: University of Michigan Press.

Sibayan, B., & Gonzalez, A. (1988). Policy implications and recommendations. In A. Gonzalez & B. Sibayan, *Evaluating bilingual education in the Philippines* (pp. 143–148). Manila: Linguistic Society of the Philippines.

Siegel, M., & Carey, R. (1989). *Critical thinking: A semiotic perspective.* Bloomington, IN: National Council of Teachers of English.

Silko, L. M. (1981). *Storyteller.* New York: Seaver Books.

Silko, L. M. (2001). It was a long time before. In G. R. Bozzini & C. A. Leenerts (Eds.), *Literature without borders: International literature in English for student writers* (pp. 3–4). Upper Saddle River, NJ: Prentice Hall.

Singer, M. (1998). *Perception and identity in intercultural communication.* Yarmouth, ME: Intercultural Press.

Siple, L. A. (2000). Cultural patterns of deaf people. In L. A. Samovar & R. E. Porter (Eds.), *Intercultural communication: A reader* (9th ed., pp. 146–157). Belmont, CA: Wadsworth.

Skow, L. M., & Stephan, L. (2000). Intercultural communication in the university. In L. A. Samovar & R. E. Porter (Eds.), *Intercultural communication: A reader* (9th ed., pp. 355–270). Belmont, CA: Wadsworth.

Smith, F. (1982). *Writing and the writer.* New York: CBS College Publishing.

Smith, F. (1990). *To think.* New York: Teachers College Press.

Smith, L. E. (1983). English as an international language: No room for linguistic chauvinism. In L. Smith (Ed.), *Readings in English as an international language* (pp. 7–11). Oxford: Pergamon Press.

Smith, L. E. (1992). Spread of English and issues of intelligibility. In B. B. Kachru (Ed.), *The other tongue: English across cultures* (pp. 75–90). Urbana: University of Illinois Press.

Snobelen, J. (1995, July 6). [Speech to Ontario Ministry of Education]. Toronto, Ontario, Canada.

Snow, M. (1994, March). *Teaching literature in an intercultural setting.* Paper presented at the 28th Annual TESOL Convention, Baltimore, MD.

Snow, M., & Brinton, D. (Eds.). (1997). *The content-based classroom: Perspectives on integrating language and content.* New York: Longman.

Snyder, I. (Ed.). (2002). *Silicon literacies.* London: Routledge.

Sohier, T. (Director). (1993). *A different place: The intercultural classroom* [Videotape]. Newtonville, MA: Intercultural Resource Corp.

Spack, R. (1985). Literature, reading, writing, and ESL: Bridging the gap. *TESOL Quarterly, 19,* 703–725.

Sridhar, S. N. (1994). A reality check for SLA theories. *TESOL Quarterly, 28,* 800–805.

Stake, R. E. (1995). *The art of case study research.* London: Sage.

Stenhouse, L. (1975). *An introduction to curriculum research and development*. London: Heinemann.

Stephan, W. G., & Abalakina-Papp, M. (1996). Russia and the West. In D. Landis & R. S. Bhagat (Eds.), *Handbook of intercultural training* (2nd ed., pp. 366–382). Thousand Oaks, CA: Sage.

Stern, S. L. (1985). *Teaching literature in ESL/EFL: An integrative approach*. Unpublished doctoral dissertation, University of California at Los Angeles.

Storti, C. (1994). *Cross-cultural dialogues*. Yarmouth, ME; Intercultural Press.

Street, B. (1984). *Literacy in theory and practice*. Cambridge: Cambridge University Press.

Strevens, P. (1983). What is "standard English"? In L. E. Smith (Ed.), *Readings in English as an international language* (pp. 87–93). Oxford: Pergamon Press.

Strevens, P. (1992). English as an international language: Directions in the 1990s. In B. B. Kachru (Ed.), *The other tongue: English across cultures* (pp. 27–47). Urbana: University of Illinois Press.

Summerfield, E. (1993). *Crossing cultures through film*. Yarmouth, ME: Intercultural Press.

Swain, M. (1995). Three functions of output in second language learning. In G. Cook & B. Seidlhofer (Eds.), *Principle and practice in applied linguistics: Studies in honour of H. G. Widdowson* (pp. 125–144). Oxford: Oxford University Press.

Swan, M. (1985). A critical look at the communicative approach (1). *ELT Journal, 39*, 2–12.

Sylvester, P. S. (1997). Elementary school curricula and urban transformation. In I. Hall, C. H. Campbell, & E. J. Miech (Eds.), *Class acts* (pp. 179–202). Cambridge, MA: Harvard Educational Review.

Talib, I. (1992). Why not teach non-native English literature? *ELT Journal, 46*, 51–55.

Tang, C. (1997). On the power and status of nonnative teachers. *TESOL Quarterly, 31*, 577–583.

Tarnopolsky, O. (1999). *Teaching English intensively in a non-English-speaking country: Theory, practice, and results*. (ERIC Document Reproduction Service No. ED428579)

Tarnopolsky, O. (2000). Writing English as a foreign language: A report from Ukraine. *Journal of Second Language Writing, 9*, 209–226.

Tarnopolsky, O. (2003). Sustained content for Business English programs: Structuring, selecting, and implementing learning. *MinneWITESOL Journal, 20*, 39–53.

Thauberger, R. (2001). Goalie. In G. R. Bozzini & C. A. Leenerts (Eds.), *Literature without borders: International literature in English for student writers* (pp. 86–90). Upper Saddle River, NJ: Prentice Hall.

Thiagarajan, S., & Steinwachs, B. (1990). *Barnga: A simulation game on cultural clashes*. Yarmouth, ME: Intercultural Press.

Thomas, J. (1999). Voices from the periphery: Non-native teachers and issues of credibility. In G. Braine (Ed.), *Non-native educators in English language teaching* (pp. 5–14). Mahwah, NJ: Erlbaum.

Ting-Toomey, S. (2000). Managing intercultural conflicts effectively. In L. Samovar & R. E. Porter (Eds.), *Intercultural communication: A reader* (9th ed., pp. 388–400). Belmont, CA: Wadsworth.

Tobin, L. (1993). *Writing relationships: What really happens in the composition class*. Portsmouth, NH: Boynton/Cook.

Tollefson, J. W. (1991). *Planning language, planning inequality*. London: Longman.

Tundel, N. (Producer). (2000). *Postville: When cultures collide* [Videotape]. Johnson: Iowa Public Television.

Twitchin, J. (Producer). (2003). *Crosstalk* [Videotape]. London: BBC Learning Studies.

University of Calgary. (2003). *ARIEL: A review of international English literature*. Retrieved June 30, 2003, from http://www.english.ucalgary.ca/ariel/ariel.htm

Unsworth, L. (2001). *Teaching multiliteracies across the curriculum*. Buckingham, England: Open University Press.

Ury, W. L., Brett, J. M., & Goldberg, S. B. (1988). *Getting disputes resolved: Designing systems to cut the costs of conflict.* San Francisco: Jossey-Bass.

Vuchinich, S. (1990). The sequential organization of closing in verbal family conflict. In A.D. Grimshaw (Ed.), *Conflict talk: Sociolinguistic investigations of arguments in conversations* (pp. 118–138). Cambridge: Cambridge University Press.

Walcott, D. (1987). Tomorrow, tomorrow. In *The Arkansas testament* (p. 79). Boston: Faber & Faber.

Wallraff, B. (2000, November). What global language? *The Atlantic Monthly, 52–66.*

Wang, W. (Director). (1994). *The joy luck club* [Videotape]. Burbank, CA: Hollywood Pictures Home Video.

Waters, A., & Vilches, M. (1998). Foundation-building and potential-realizing: The PELT ELT paradigm (or: the learning cake). *The ACELT Journal, 2*(1), 3–11.

Waters, A., & Vilches, M. (2000). Integrating teacher learning: The school-based follow-up development activity. *ELT Journal, 54,* 126–134.

Waters, A., & Vilches, M. (2001). Implementing ELT innovations: a needs analysis framework. *ELT Journal 55,* 133–141.

Waters, M. (2001). *Globalisation* (2nd ed.). New York: Routledge.

Widdowson, H. G. (1982). The uses of literature. In M. Hines & W. Rutherford (Eds.), *On TESOL '81* (pp. 203–214). Washington, DC: TESOL.

Widdowson, H. (1994). The ownership of English. *TESOL Quarterly, 31,* 377–389.

Widdowson, H. G. (1997). EIL, ESL, EFL: Global issues and local interests. *World Englishes, 16,* 135–146.

Widdowson, H. G. (1998). EIL: Squaring the circles: A reply. *World Englishes, 17,* 397–401.

Wijenaike, P. (2001). Anoma. In G. R. Bozzini & C. A. Leenerts (Eds.), *Literature without borders: International literature in English for student writers* (pp. 79–81). Upper Saddle River, NJ: Prentice Hall.

Willis, J. (1996). *A framework for task-based learning.* Harlow, England: Longman.

Wright, T. (1987). *Roles of teachers and learners.* Oxford: Oxford University Press.

Yamada, H. (1990). Topic management and turn distribution in business meetings: American v. Japanese strategies. *Text, 10,* 271–295.

Yin, R. K. (1994). *Case study research: Design and methods* (2nd ed.). Thousand Oaks, CA: Sage.

Zhang, Y. (Director). (2001). *The shower* [Videotape]. Culver City, CA: Sony Pictures Entertainment.

Zou, J. (1991). *Integrating literature in English language instruction in non-English speaking environments: A theoretical framework for college-level programs.* Unpublished doctoral dissertation, Indiana University, Bloomington.

Index

Page references followed by *t* and *f* refer to tables and figures respectively.

Also Available From TESOL

Academic Writing Programs
Ilona Leki, Editor

Action Research
Julian Edge, Editor

Bilingual Education
Donna Christian and Fred Genesee, Editors

Community Partnerships
Elsa Auerbach, Editor

Content-Based Instruction in Higher Education Settings
JoAnn Crandall and Dorit Kaufman, Editors

Distance-Learning Programs
Lynn Henrichsen, Editor

English for Specific Purposes
Thomas Orr, Editor

Grammar Teaching in Teacher Education
Dilin Liu and Peter Master, Editors

Implementing the ESL Standards for Pre-K–12 Students Through Teacher Education
Marguerite Ann Snow, Editor

Integrating the ESL Standards Into Classroom Practice: Grades Pre-K–2
Betty Ansin Smallwood, Editor

Integrating the ESL Standards Into Classroom Practice: Grades 3–5
Katharine Davies Samway, Editor

Integrating the ESL Standards Into Classroom Practice: Grades 6–8
Suzanne Irujo, Editor

Integrating the ESL Standards Into Classroom Practice: Grades 9–12
Barbara Agor, Editor

Intensive English Programs in Postsecondary Settings
Nicholas Dimmit and Maria Dantas-Whitney, Editors

Interaction and Language Learning
Jill Burton and Charles Clennell, Editors

Internet for English Teaching
Mark Warschauer, Heidi Shetzer, and Christine Meloni

Journal Writing
Jill Burton and Michael Carroll, Editors

Mainstreaming
Effie Cochran, Editor

Teacher Education
Karen E. Johnson, Editor

Technology-Enhanced Learning Environments
Elizabeth Hanson-Smith, Editor

For more information, contact
Teachers of English to Speakers of Other Languages, Inc.
700 South Washington Street, Suite 200
Alexandria, Virginia 22314 USA
Tel 703-836-0774 • Fax 703-836-6447 • publications@tesol.org •
http://www.tesol.org/